MONEY TALK$

MONEY TALK$

The 2500 Greatest
Business Quotes
From Aristotle to DeLorean

EDITED BY

ROBERT W. KENT

PUBLISHED BY POCKET BOOKS NEW YORK

My father taught me to work; he did not teach me to love it.

ABRAHAM LINCOLN

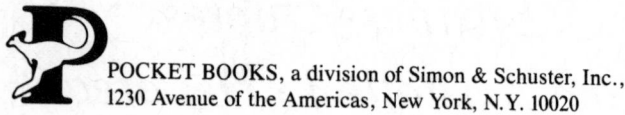

POCKET BOOKS, a division of Simon & Schuster, Inc.,
1230 Avenue of the Americas, New York, N.Y. 10020

Copyright © 1985 by Robert Warren Kent

Published by arrangement with Facts on File

ISBN: 0-671-61963-2

First Pocket Books trade paperback printing June, 1986

10 9 8 7 6 5 4 3 2 1

POCKET and colophon are registered trademarks
of Simon & Schuster, Inc.

Printed in the U.S.A.

CONTENTS

INTRODUCTION

In putting this book together, I have sought quotations that are more than idle talk about business and the profit motive. I have been guided by two criteria: (1) the usefulness of my quotes to people doing business, and (2) the quotability of my selections. I have not attempted to promulgate a social, political, or economic position on the conduct of business through the ages. Critics and advocates of commerce are included without bias.

The quotations in *Money Talks* fall into three broad categories. First, there are the comments of men and women from corporate life—the shrewd, not always temperate statements of the successful manager or entrepreneur. Second, there are statements from authorities on business management, economics, and finance—the professional critics of business. The seminal judgments of Peter F. Drucker, the challenges to corporate enterprise of John Kenneth Galbraith, the traditional strictures of Adam Smith—all are represented here. Third, there are quotations from the poets and outside observers—the novelists and playwrights, humorists and philosophers who have found a stimulus to their imagination in business life. The great classical writers, whose insights into human nature and "the business of life" are often as apt today as they were centuries ago, are here too. I have not been able to avoid a generous sampling of aphorisms and proverbs. They are widely familiar, and yet they represent the wisdom of the ages, eloquently stating principles that we can hear being advocated in our workaday world.

The organization of *Money Talks* stems from my association with the Harvard Business School. For three years I taught a required course in the MBA curriculum called Management Communication. In tutorials with students and in collaborative exercises with faculty, I got to know something about Harvard's well integrated and widely imitated program in business administration. That program served as a model in organizing this book.

The first-year MBA courses at the Harvard Graduate School of

Business Administration are called "Control," "Finance," "Managerial Economics," "Business, Government, and the International Economy," "Marketing," "Production and Operations Management," "Organizational Behavior," "Human Resource Management," "Management Communication," and "Business Policy." I have adopted these course titles for the fourteen sections of *Money Talks,* with 4 modifications: (1) I have dropped the misnomer "Organizational Behavior" and added the headings "Entrepreneurs" and "Managers"; (2) "Managerial Economics" I have retitled "Microeconomics"; (3) I have replaced "Business, Government, and the International Economy" with two sections, "Business and Government" and "Macroeconomics"; (4) I provide an opening section that contains statements about the essence of what business is said to be and do—"Business Is & Business As"—and a closing section of quotes that suggest what it all adds up to—"Bottom Line." Each section title is further explained in an introductory note.

Organization of quotes within each section is historical, by the birthdate of the speaker. Anonymous quotes and proverbs are arranged at the beginning of the section; quotes attributed to figures for whom no birth and death dates were available are arranged alphabetically by the speaker's name at the end. If a date can be assigned to a statement by someone for whom birth and death dates are not provided, the quote is placed in its approximate chronological order.

In adapting the Harvard agenda to *Money Talks,* I have had to make arbitrary decisions about the placement of some quotations. For example, the distinction between quotations in the "Micro-" and "Macroeconomics" sections is narrow, at best, in some instances. Similarly, the "Communications" section embraces many interests, as it does in business—"Marketing," "Human Resources," and "Production & Operations." Such a familiar quotation as "When the sun shineth, make hay" (John Heywood, *Proverbs,* 1546) would fit comfortably in at least four sections—"Policy," "Marketing," "Production & Operations," or "Finance." I have chosen "Policy" for "make hay," and have made it my policy not to repeat entries in different sections.

Sources for quotes are provided whenever possible, unless the source is a standard quote book (borrowed from sparingly) or standard business reference book. These standard references are listed in a bibliography at the end of *Money Talks.*

Finally, I wish to acknowledge the hints, suggestions, and patience of, alphabetically: Kenneth R. Andrews, Robert N. Anthony, Joseph Auerbach, Albert D. Baker, Glenn R. Butterton,

Introduction

Lewis E. Byrd, Roger A. Carolin, Kim Casey, Alfred D. Chandler, Jr., Charles J. Christenson, Douglas P. Conner, Peter H. Dailey, Jr., Lynn Felder, H. Irving Grousbeck, Judy Ingle, C. Susan Kelly, Anna L. Kent, David L. Kent, Margaret H. Lang, Roy K. McCall, David L. McClees, Zachary M. Narrett, Leslie R. Porter, John W. Pratt, John A. Quelch, Floyd Rinker, Andrew Rosenthal, Jan Schreiber, Linda G. Sprague, and Richard E. Stone.

The Banker, *by Honoré Daumier (1808–1879).* ***In*** **Charivari,**
16 October 1835.

BUSINESS IS
&
BUSINESS AS

"Business is business" and "business as usual" are convenient sayings for what business is and does. But they don't explain much except for the busy-ness of business and the regularity and certainty of enterprise. The quotations in this section are various attempts to say more—about the nature of business and the motives of people who engage in it. There are obvious contradictions in such a grouping; there are historical biases and personal obsessions at work. When we reach for words to describe the business of life and the world of business, we tend to invade the Seven Liberal Arts, and sometimes call upon the Seven Deadly Sins.

The Veiled Prophets of St. Louis, *1878*.

What comes by nature costs no money.

Anonymous

When you send a fool to market, the merchants rejoice.

Anonymous

Who buys has need of two eyes
But one's enough to sell the stuff.

Anonymous

Why is the form of money round? Because it is to run from every man.

Anonymous
A Helpe to Discourse, 1619

Of all sorts of callings that in England be,
There is none that liveth so gallant as we;
Our trading maintains us as brave as a knight,
We live at our pleasure, and take our delight;
We heapeth up riches and treasure great store,
Which we get by griping and grinding the poor.
   And this is a way for to fill up our purse,
   Although we do get it with many a curse.

Anonymous (late 17th century)

"The Clothier's Delight; Or, The Rich Men's Joy, and the Poor Men's Sorrow. Wherein is expressed the craftiness and subtility of Many Clothiers in England, by beating down their Workmen's Wages."

Wool workers' song

The cares of gain are threefold: the struggle of getting; the frenzy of increasing; the horror of losing.

Anonymous
Meditations on Wall Street, 1940

I have my clarinet in my sleeve and my breath in my mouth. [I am ready for business.]

Arabic proverb
Collected by J. L. Burckhardt, 1817

3

A man without money is like a wolf without teeth.

French proverb

There are more fools among buyers than among sellers.

French proverb

Business is always business.

German proverb

Money is the man.

German proverb

Money makes everything legitimate, even bastards.

Hebrew proverb

At a good pennyworth pause a little while.

Giovanni Torriano
Italian Proverbs, 1666

Public money is like holy water; everyone helps himself.

Italian proverb

When money is not a servant it is a master.

Italian proverb

When elephants fight it is the grass that suffers.

Kikuyu proverb

The buyer buys for as little as possible; the seller sells for as much as possible.
[Emptor emit quam minimo potest, venditor vendit quam maximo potest.]

Legal maxim

Too much money is the worst of tribulations.

Moroccan proverb

Money is flat and meant to be piled up.

Scottish proverb

Gold and love affairs are difficult to hide.

Spanish proverb

No mountain is so high that an ass loaded with gold cannot climb it.

Spanish proverb

Say what you will against money, it is always a good Catholic.

Spanish proverb

They that go down to the sea in ships, that do business in great waters.
>These see the works of the Lord, and his wonders in the deep.

Bible: Psalms 107:23

False scales are an abomination to the Lord;
But a just weight is his delight.

Bible: Proverbs 11:1

In all labor there is profit; but the talk of the lips tendeth only to penury.

Bible: Proverbs 14:23

The thing that hath been, it is that which shall be; and that which is done is that which shall be done: and there is no new thing under the sun.

Bible: Ecclesiastes 1:9

The sleep of a laboring man is sweet . . . but the abundance of the rich will not suffer him to sleep.

Bible: Ecclesiastes 5:12

Tyre, the crowning city, whose merchants are princes.

Bible: Isaiah 23:8

Gold hath been the ruin of many.

Bible: Ecclesiasticus 21:6

Thy money perish with thee, because thou hast thought that the gift of God may be purchased with money.

Bible: Acts 8:20

The love of money is the root of all evil. *Or, as it is usually shortened to:* Money is the root of all evil.

Bible: 1 Timothy 6:10

Radix malorum est cupiditas.

> Geoffrey Chaucer (c. 1343–1400)
> *Pardoner's Prologue, Canterbury Tales*

In business, everything depends on aid from heaven.

> Talmud

In every trade and pursuit of life both the rich and the poor are to be found.

> Talmud

The pot that belongs to partners is neither hot nor cold.

> Talmud

Money is life to us wretched mortals.

> Hesiod (c. 700 B.C.)
> *Works and Days*

All men's gains are the fruits of venturing.

> Mardonius (died 479 B.C.)
> Said to Xerxes before the expedition against Athens
> In Herodotus, *Histories,* fifth century B.C.

Nothing in the world is worse than money. Money lays waste cities; it sets men to roaming from home; it seduces and corrupts honest men and turns virtue to baseness; it teaches villainy and impiety.

> Sophocles (c. 495–406 B.C.)
> *Antigone,* c. 442 B.C.

Of all employments from which gain is derived, there is none that surpasses agriculture, none more productive, none more delightful, none more worthy of a man of liberal education.

> Cicero (106–43 B.C.)
> *De officiis*

O accurst craving for gold!

> Virgil (70–19 B.C.)
> *Aeneid*

Is this the sort of advice you're looking for?—"Make money. Make it, if you can, fair and square. If not, make it anyway."

> Horace (65–8 B.C.)
> *Epistles,* c. 20 B.C.

When a man's business does not fit him, 'tis as ofttimes with a shoe—if too big for the foot it will trip him, if too small, will chafe.

Horace
Epistles

Men now worship gold to the neglect of the gods. By gold good faith is banished and justice is sold.

Propertius (54 B.C.–A.D. 2)
Elegies

Love yields to business. If you seek a way out of love, be busy; you'll be safe then.

Ovid (43 B.C.–A.D. c. 18)
Remedia amoris

They struggle to gain in order that they may spend, and then to regain what they have spent.

Ovid
Fasti, c. A.D. 8

It is annoying to be honest to no purpose.

Ovid
Ex ponto

Love of money is the disease which makes men most groveling and pitiful.

Longinus (First century)
On the Sublime

Honesty is praised and starves.

Juvenal (c. 50–c. 130)
Satires

He had talents equal to business, and aspired no higher.

Tacitus (c. 55–c. 117)
Annals

The playthings of our elders are called business.

St. Augustine (354–430)
Confessions, 397

Verily man was created avid of gain; when evil befalls him, apt to grieve; when good befalls him, grudging.

Koran 70:19

In their first life, all were so squint-eyed in mind, that they made no expenditure of it with moderation. . . . Ill-giving, and ill-keeping has deprived them of the bright world, and put them into conflict. . . . For all the gold that is beneath the moon, or ever was, could not give rest to a single one of these weary souls.

Dante Alighieri (1265–1321)
The Comedy: Hell, 1472
The Avaricious and the Prodigal

Nowher so bisy a man as he ther nas,
And yet he semed bisier than he was.
[True, there wasn't a busier man than he; and yet he seemed busier than he truly was.]

Geoffrey Chaucer (c. 1343–1400)
General Prologue, Canterbury Tales
Chaucer's Sergeant of the Law, senior member of the bar

An honest man is not accountable for the vice and folly of his trade, and therefore ought not to refuse the exercise of it. It is the custom of his country, and there is profit in it. We must live by the world, and such as we find it, so make use of it.

Michel Eyquem de Montaigne (1533–1592)
Essays, 1588

Corporations cannot commit treason, nor be outlawed nor excommunicate, for they have no souls.

Sir Edward Coke (1552–1634)
Case of Sutton's Hospital, 1612

The first thing we do, let's kill all the lawyers.

William Shakespeare (1564–1616)
Henry VI, Part II, 1591

Every man has business and desire,
Such as it is.

William Shakespeare
Hamlet, 1600–1601

Has this fellow no feeling of his business?

William Shakespeare
Hamlet

O, what a world of vile ill-favor'd faults
Looks handsome in three hundred pounds a year!

William Shakespeare
The Merry Wives of Windsor, 1600–1601

8

Let me have no lying: it becomes none but tradesmen.

> William Shakespeare
> *The Winter's Tale,* 1610–1611

A mere madness, to live like a wretch and die rich.

> Robert Burton (1577–1640)
> *The Anatomy of Melancholy,* 1621–1651

That which is everybody's business is nobody's business.

> Izaak Walton (1593–1683)
> *The Compleat Angler,* 1655

To be at ease is better than to be at business.

> Baltasar Gracián (1601–1658)
> *Oráculo manual y arte de prudencia,* 1647

Mammon led them on,
Mammon, the least erected spirit that fell
From Heaven; for even in Heaven his looks and thoughts
Were always downward bent, admiring more
The riches of Heaven's pavement, trodden gold,
Than aught divine or holy else enjoyed
In vision beatific.

> John Milton (1608–1674)
> *Paradise Lost: Book I,* 1667

A man that cannot sit still in his chamber . . . and that cannot say no . . . is not fit for business.

> Samuel Pepys (1633–1703)
> *Diary,* 8 August 1662

But it is pretty to see what money will do.

> Samuel Pepys
> *Diary,* 21 March 1667

A man is to go about his own business as if he had not a friend in the world to help him in it.

> George Savile, Marquess of Halifax (1633–1695)
> *Political, Moral and Miscellaneous Reflections,* 1750

Go to your business, I say, pleasure, whilst I go to my pleasure, business.

> William Wycherley (c. 1640–1716)
> *The Country Wife,* 1675

He that is busy is tempted by but one devil; he that is idle, by a legion.

Thomas Fuller (1654–1734)
Gnomologia, 1732

Ever busy, ever bare.

James Kelly
Scottish Proverbs, 1721

It is a Question in matters of Commerce, whether the destruction of *Tyre,* by *Nebuchadnezzar,* did good or hurt. If I may give my opinion, I think it was rather good than harm; for tho' it is true, that the Citizens had a very great loss in the demolishing of their Houses, and ruining their public Edifices; yet as it scatter'd a diligent and useful People into divers parts of the World, where they settled immediately to business, some in one place, and some in another: They were as so many Instructors to the Nations whereever they came, to pursue the same Industry, and maintain themselves by Trade, which before, 'tis very likely, they knew little or nothing of.

Daniel Defoe (c. 1660–1731)

The business was to go to Bartholomew Fair, and the end of going to Bartholomew Fair was, in short, to pick pockets.

Daniel Defoe
Colonel Jack, 1722

A man of business may talk of philosophy, a man who has none may practice it.

Jonathan Swift (1667–1745)

What's integrity to an opportunity?

William Congreve (1670–1729)
The Way of the World, 1700

A little house well filled, a little field well tilled, and a little wife well willed, are great riches.

Benjamin Franklin (1706–1790)
Poor Richard's Almanack, 1735

Opportunity is the great bawd.

Benjamin Franklin
Poor Richard's Almanack

There are three faithful friends—an old wife, an old dog, and ready money.

Benjamin Franklin
Poor Richard's Almanack, 1738

He that hath a trade hath an estate, and he that hath a calling hath an office of profit and honor.

Benjamin Franklin
Poor Richard's Almanack, 1757

A merchant may, perhaps, be a man of an enlarged mind, but there is nothing in trade connected with an enlarged mind.

Samuel Johnson (1709–1784)
In Boswell, *Tour to the Hebrides*, 1785
[Said: 18 October 1773]

It very seldom happens to a man that his business is his pleasure.

Samuel Johnson

There are few ways in which a man can be more innocently employed than in getting money.

Samuel Johnson
In Boswell, *Life of Johnson*, 1791
[Said: 27 March 1775]

The business of life is to go forward.

Samuel Johnson
The Idler, No. 72, 1759

Avarice, the spur of industry.

David Hume (1711–1776)
Of Civil Liberty, 1741–1742

I am a bad Englishman, because I think the advantages of commerce are dearly bought for some by the lives of many more.

Horace Walpole (1717–1797)
Letter to Horace Mann, 26 May 1762

The propensity to truck, barter, and exchange . . . is common to all men, and to be found in no other race of animals.

Adam Smith (1723–1790)
Wealth of Nations, 1776

It is not from the benevolence of the butcher, the brewer, or the baker that we expect our dinner, but from their regard of their own self-interest. We address ourselves not to their humanity, but to their self-love, and never talk to them of our own necessities, but of their advantage.

Adam Smith
Wealth of Nations

The busier we are, the more acutely we feel that we live, the more conscious we are of life.

Immanuel Kant (1724–1804)
Lecture at Königsberg, 1775

Did you ever expect a corporation to have a conscience, when it has no soul to be damned, and no body to be kicked?

Attributed to Edward, First Baron Thurlow (1731–1806)

War, traffic, and piracy
Are an indivisible trinity.

Johann Wolfgang von Goethe (1749–1832)

A corporation is an artificial being, invisible, intangible, and existing only in contemplation of the law.

John Marshall (1755–1835)
US Supreme Court, 1819

Business is business.

George Colman the Younger (1762–1836)
The Heir-at-Law, 1797

The power which money gives is that of brute force; it is the power of the bludgeon and the bayonet.

William Cobbett (1763–1835)
Advice to Young Men, 1829

The most sensible people to be met with in society are men of business and of the world, who argue from what they see and know, instead of spinning cobweb distinctions of what things ought to be.

William Hazlitt (1778–1830)
The Ignorance of the Learned, 1821

It is a common observation that any fool can get money; but they are not wise that think so.

Charles Caleb Colton (1780–1832)
Lacon, 1820

Money is human happiness in the abstract: he, then, who is no longer capable of enjoying human happiness in the concrete devotes himself utterly to money.

Arthur Schopenhauer (1788–1860)
In Auden, *A Certain World,* 1970

I have always recognized that the object of business is to make money in an honorable manner. I have endeavored to remember that the object of life is to do good.

Peter Cooper (1791–1883)
Speech, 1874

Money is a good servant but a bad master.

Henry George Bohn (1796–1884)
Handbook of Proverbs, 1855

An institution is the lengthened shadow of one man.

Ralph Waldo Emerson (1803–1882)
Self-Reliance, 1841

It often happens that worthless people are merely people who are worth knowing.

Benjamin Disraeli (1804–1881)

Trade is a social act.

John Stuart Mill (1806–1873)
On Liberty, 1859

The Puritan's idea of Hell is a place where everybody has to mind his own business.

Attributed to Wendell Phillips (1811–1884)

Business first, pleasure afterward, as King Richard said when he stabbed the other king in the Tower, before he smothered the babies.

Charles Dickens (1812–1870)

Here's the rule for bargains: "Do other men, for they would do you." That's the true business precept.

Charles Dickens
Martin Chuzzlewit, 1843–1844

The frontiers are not east or west, north or south, but wherever a man *fronts* a fact.

Henry David Thoreau (1817–1862)
A Week on the Concord and Merrimack Rivers, 1849

What recommends commerce to me is its enterprise and bravery. It does not clasp its hands and pray to Jupiter.

Henry David Thoreau

Take the humbug out of this world; and you haven't much left to do business with.

Josh Billings [Henry Wheeler Shaw] (1818–1885)

There is no better ballast for keeping the mind steady on its keel, and saving it from all risk of crankiness, than business.

James Russell Lowell (1819–1891)
Literary Essays, vol. II, 1870–1890,
"New England Two Centuries Ago" (1865)

There is no wealth but life.

John Ruskin (1819–1900)
Unto This Last, 1862

Value is the life-giving power of anything; cost, the quantity of labor required to produce it; price, the quantity of labor which its possessor will take in exchange for it.

John Ruskin
Munera Pulveris, 1862

The first of all English games is making money.

John Ruskin
The Crown of Wild Olive, 1866

Life without industry is guilt, industry without art is brutality.

John Ruskin
Lectures on Art, 1870

I tells 'ee I means business.

Thomas Hughes (1822–1896)
Tom Brown's Schooldays, 1857

Commerce is the art of exploiting the need or desire someone has for something.

Edmond (1822–1896) and Jules (1830–1870) de Goncourt
Journal, July 1864

Business? It's quite simple. It's other people's money.

Alexandre Dumas the Younger (1824–1895)
La Question d'Argent, 1857

Business is really more agreeable than pleasure; it interests the whole mind, the aggregate nature of man more continuously, and more deeply. But it does not look as if it did.

> Walter Bagehot (1826–1877)
> *The English Constitution,* 1867

All trade is and must be in a sense selfish; trade not being infinite, nay, the trade of a particular place or district being possibly very limited, what one man gains another loses. In the hand-to-hand war of commerce men fight on without much thought of others, except a desire to excel or to defeat them.

> Lord Coleridge
> Mogul vs. McGregor, 1888

Money is a new form of slavery, and distinguishable from the old simply by the fact that it is impersonal—that there is no human relation between master and slave.

> Leo Tolstoi (1828–1910)
> *What Shall We Do?,* 1891

I know that unremitting attention to business is the price of success, but I don't know what success is.

> Charles Dudley Warner (1829–1900)
> *Backlog Studies,* 1873

Business should be like religion and science; it should know neither love nor hate.

> Samuel Butler (1835–1902)

Steel is Prince or Pauper.

> Andrew Carnegie (1835–1919)
> In Hendrick, *Life of Andrew Carnegie,* 1932

That's the definition of business: something goes through, something doesn't. Make use of one, forget the other.

> Henry François Becque (1837–1899)
> *La Parisienne,* 1885

He looked as if he "meant business," and I mean business too.

> William Dean Howells (1837–1920)
> *The Rise of Silas Lapham,* 1885

"But all I did," Schwab said, "was what you have been doing behind locked doors for years."
"That, sir," Morgan replied, "is what doors are for."

J. P. Morgan (1837–1913) and Charles Schwab (1862–1939)

The great business of life is to be, to do, to do without, and to depart.

John Morley, Viscount Morley of Blackburn (1838–1923)
Address on Aphorisms, 1887

The nature of business is swindling.

August Bebel (1840–1913)
Speech in Zürich, December 1892

Achievement, n. The death of endeavor and the birth of disgust.

Ambrose Bierce (1842–c.1914)
The Devil's Dictionary, 1906

Auctioneer, n. The man who proclaims with a hammer that he has picked a pocket with his tongue.

Ambrose Bierce
The Devil's Dictionary

Corporation, n. An ingenious device for obtaining individual profit without individual responsibility.

Ambrose Bierce
The Devil's Dictionary

Future, n. That period of time in which our affairs prosper, our friends are true, and our happiness is assured.

Ambrose Bierce
The Devil's Dictionary

Hand, n. A singular instrument worn at the end of a human arm and commonly thrust into somebody's pocket.

Ambrose Bierce
The Devil's Dictionary

Insurance, n. An ingenious modern game of chance in which the player is permitted to enjoy the comfortable conviction that he is beating the man who keeps the table.

Ambrose Bierce
The Devil's Dictionary

Labor, n. One of the processes by which A acquires property for B.

Ambrose Bierce
The Devil's Dictionary

Lawsuit, n. A machine which you go into as a pig and come out as a sausage.

Ambrose Bierce
The Devil's Dictionary

Philanthropist, n. A rich (and usually bald) old gentleman who has trained himself to grin while his conscience is picking his pocket.

Ambrose Bierce
The Devil's Dictionary

The gambling known as business looks with austere disfavor upon the business known as gambling.

Ambrose Bierce
The Devil's Dictionary

Money entails duties. How shall we get the money and forget the duties? Voilà the great problem!

Edward Carpenter (1844–1929)
England's Ideal, 1887

Mercantile morality is really nothing but a refinement of piratical morality.

Friedrich Wilhelm Nietzsche (1844–1900)
Thus Spake Zarathustra, 1883–1891

Buying and selling is essentially antisocial.

Edward Bellamy (1850–1898)
Looking Backward, 1888

It is not by any means certain that a man's business is the most important thing he has to do.

Robert Louis Stevenson (1850–1894)

Perpetual devotion to what a man calls his business, is only to be sustained by perpetual neglect of many other things.

Robert Louis Stevenson
Virginibus Puerisque, 1881

My own business always bores me to death; I prefer other people's.

Oscar Wilde (1854–1900)
Lady Windermere's Fan, 1892

A great devotee of the Gospel of Getting On.

George Bernard Shaw (1856–1950)
Mrs. Warren's Profession, 1893

Money is indeed the most important thing in the world; and all sound and successful personal and national morality should have this fact for its basis.

George Bernard Shaw
The Irrational Knot, 1905

I am a Millionaire. That is my religion.

George Bernard Shaw
Major Barbara, 1907

The universal regard for money is the one hopeful fact in our civilization, the one sound spot in our social conscience. Money is the most important thing in the world. It represents health, strength, honor, generosity, and beauty as conspicuously as the want of it represents illness, weakness, disgrace, meanness, and ugliness.

George Bernard Shaw
Major Barbara

The Jews generally give value. They make you pay; but they deliver the goods. In my experience the men who want something for nothing are invariably Christians.

George Bernard Shaw
Saint Joan, 1923

Business underlies everything in our national life, including our spiritual life. Witness the fact that in the Lord's Prayer, the first petition is for daily bread. No one can worship God or love his neighbor on an empty stomach.

Woodrow Wilson (1856–1924)
Speech in New York, 23 May 1912

Every great man of business has got somewhere a touch of the idealist in him.

Woodrow Wilson

There is a sense in which the businessmen of America represent America. Because America has devoted herself [to] achievements of peace, and business is the organization of the energies of peace.

Woodrow Wilson

Of all forms of tyranny, the least attractive and the most vulgar is the tyranny of mere wealth, the tyranny of plutocracy.

Theodore Roosevelt (1858–1919)
Autobiography, 1913

One's religion is whatever he is most interested in, and yours is Success.

James M. Barrie (1860–1937)
The Twelve-Pound Look, 1910

A great society is a society in which its men of business think greatly of their functions.

Alfred North Whitehead (1861–1947)

If America is to be civilized, it must be done (at least for the present) by the business class.

Alfred North Whitehead

Idealism rather than dollar-chasing is the motivating force behind big business in the United States.

Charles Schwab (1862–1939)

Those who set out to serve both God and Mammon soon discover that there is no God.

Logan Pearsall Smith (1865–1946)

You can't have money like that and not swell out.

H. G. Wells (1866–1946)
Kipps, 1905

I don't know what a chamber of commerce is unless 'tis a place where business men go to sleep.

Finley Peter Dunne [d.b.a. Mr. Dooley] (1867–1936)

Work is work if you're paid to do it, and it's pleasure if you pay to be allowed to do it.

Finley Peter Dunne

It is difficult but not impossible to conduct strictly honest business. What is true is that honesty is incompatible with the amassing of a large fortune.

Mohandas Karamchand Gandhi (1869–1948)
Non-Violence in Peace and War, 1948

Imperialism is the monopoly stage of capitalism.

Vladimir Ilyich Lenin (1870–1924)
Imperialism, the Highest Stage of Capitalism

The rich are the scum of the earth in every country.

G. K. Chesterton (1874–1936)
The Flying Inn, 1914

The maxim of the British people is "Business as usual."

Winston Churchill (1874–1965)
Speech, Guildhall, 9 November 1914

We have not journeyed all this way across the centuries, across the oceans, across the mountains, across the prairies, because we are made of sugar candy.

Winston Churchill
Speech to Canadian Senate and House of Commons, 1941

A storekeeper might short-measure or short-change his customer. He might even induce his clerk to short-weigh or short-measure. But he could not organize a vast department store on that basis. Either his employees are honest people who would refuse or he would soon have as employees a vast organization of crooks who would beat each other and soon ruin the proprietor himself. Big business does not lend itself readily to dishonesty and crookedness.

Owen D. Young (1874–1962)
General Electric

Working for Warner Bros. is like fucking a porcupine: it's a hundred pricks against one.

Wilson Mizner (1876–1933)
In Niven, *Bring on the Empty Horses,* 1975

He is a rare man of business who draws back from some individual act planned with high motives just because as a type such activities put too much of a strain on human nature, are too often abused and tend to bring the whole profession of business into disrepute.

Wallace B. Donham (1877–?)
"The Emerging Profession of Business,"
Harvard Business Review, July 1927

Business is more exciting than any game.

Lord Beaverbrook (1879–1964)

A holding company is a thing where you hand an accomplice the goods while the policeman searches you.

Will Rogers (1879–1935)

If you can build a business up big enough, it's respectable.

Will Rogers
Autobiography, 1949

All successful newspapers are ceaselessly querulous and bellicose. They never defend anyone or anything if they can help it; if the job is forced upon them, they tackle it by denouncing someone or something else.

H. L. Mencken (1880–1956)
Prejudices, First Series, 1919

He [the businessman] is the only man above the hangman and the scavenger who is forever apologizing for his occupation. He is the only one who always seeks to make it appear, when he attains the object of his labors, *i.e.,* the making of a great deal of money, that it was not the object of his labors.

H. L. Mencken
In the *Smart Set,* February 1921

The easiest job I have ever tackled in this world is that of making money. It is, in fact, almost as easy as losing it. Almost, but not quite.

H. L. Mencken
In *The Baltimore Evening Sun,* 12 June 1922

I go on working for the same reason that a hen goes on laying eggs.

H. L. Mencken

Money Talks

Christmas is over and Business is Business.

Franklin P. Adams [F.P.A.] (1881–1960)

We have always known that heedless self-interest was bad morals; we know now that it is bad economics.

Franklin D. Roosevelt (1882–1945)
Second Inaugural Address, 20 January 1937

Commerce is the most important activity on the face of the earth. It is the foundation on which civilization is built. Religion, society, education—all have their roots in business, and would have to be reorganized in their material aspects should business fail.

James R. Adams
More Power to Advertising, 1937

The organizer of economic enterprise has generally lacked personality of a sort to capture popular imagination. Remarkable individuals may of course be instanced, . . . but as a class, businessmen have been in a sense the victims of their virtues. They have not sacrificed others like tyrants or themselves like saints; through the stormiest ages they were the carriers of morality; the representatives of thrift, temperance, reticence, hard work, domesticity and other qualities which wearied, instead of thrilling readers.

Miriam Beard
A History of the Business Man, 1938

The love of money as a possession—as distinguished from the love of money as a means to the enjoyments and realities of life—will be recognized for what it is, a somewhat disgusting morbidity, one of those semi-criminal, semi-pathological propensities which one hands over with a shudder to the specialists in mental disease.

John Maynard Keynes (1883–1946)
Essay in Persuasion, 1931

In other countries, art and literature are left to a lot of shabby bums living in attics and feeding on booze and spaghetti, but in America the successful writer or picture-painter is indistinguishable from any other decent business man.

Sinclair Lewis (1885–1951)
Babbitt, 1922

Business is a combination of war and sport.

André Maurois (1885–1967)

The man who has a million dollars is as well off as if he were rich.
Attributed to John Jacob Astor III (1886–1971)

Hell is paved with good intentions, but heaven goes in for something more dependable. Solid gold.
Joyce Cary (1888–1957)
The Horse's Mouth, 1944

For us, there is only the trying. The rest is not our business.
T. S. Eliot (1888–1965)
Four Quartets: East Coker, 1940

The hardest job of all is trying to look busy when you're not.
William Feather (1889–   )

Not one tenth of us who are in business are doing as well as we could if we merely followed the principles that were known to our grandfathers.
William Feather

Ethics does not treat of the world. Ethics must be a condition of the world, like logic.
Ludwig Wittgenstein (1889–1951)
In Auden, *A Certain World,* 1970

It is rare for businessmen to look upon their civic duties as important.
Harold Laski (1893–1950)

A conference is a gathering of important people who, singly, can do nothing but together can decide that nothing can be done.
Fred Allen (1894–1956)
Letter to W. M. Martin (president of
New York Stock Exchange), 25 January 1940

The instinct of acquisitiveness has more perverts, I believe, than the instinct of sex. At any rate, people seem to me odder about money than about even their amours.
Aldous Huxley (1894–1963)
Point Counter Point, 1928

This is the business of business; first, to get things ready for use; second, to provide people with purposeful activity; and third, to give people a way to save productively a part of what they earn.

> Beardsley Ruml (1894–?)
> "The Business of Business"
> In *Tomorrow's Business*, 1945

The three great American vices seem to be efficiency, punctuality and the desire for achievement and success.

> Lin Yutang (1895–1976)
> *The Importance of Living*, 1937

Business is a dump for dreams.

> Philip Barry (1896–1949)
> *You and I*, 1923

A living is made, Mr. Kemper, by selling something that everybody needs at least once a year. Yes, sir! And a million is made by producing something that everybody needs every day. You artists produce something that nobody needs at any time.

> Thornton Wilder (1897–1975)
> *The Matchmaker*, 1954

That's not a friend, that's an employer I'm trying out for a few days.

> Thornton Wilder
> *The Matchmaker*

Grub first, then ethics.

> Bertolt Brecht (1898–1956)
> *The Threepenny Opera*, 1928

Crime is a logical extension of the sort of behavior that is often considered perfectly respectable in legitimate business.

> Robert Rice
> *The Business of Crime*, 1956

The pursuit of gain is the only way in which men can serve the needs of others whom they do not know.

> Friedrich August von Hayek (1899–   )
> *Listener*, 1978

24

Big business is basic to the very life of this country; and yet many—perhaps most—Americans have a deep-seated fear and an emotional repugnance to it. Here is monumental contradiction.

David Lilienthal (1899–   )

"The firm"—a proud Victorian word. It evokes the lost sense of Victorian regard for the pride of people in their daily trade.

V. S. Pritchett (1900–   )
Commenting on a poem by John Betjeman
(1906–1984), in *The New Yorker,* 24 June 1985

Capital is past savings accumulated for future production.

Jackson Martindell (1900–   )

We are not in business, we are in politics.

Walter Hallstein (1901–   )
Of the Common Market

American capitalism has been both overpraised and overindicted. . . . It is neither the Plumed Knight nor the monstrous Robber Baron.

Max Lerner (1902–   )
America as a Civilization, 1957

The Bell System is like a damn big dragon. You kick it in the tail, and two years later, it feels it in its head.

Frederick Kappel (1902–   )
AT&T

Whatever he is, the businessman is the product and pilot of the system under which most of us earn our livings.

Crawford H. Greenewalt (1902–   )
Du Pont

Businessmen are notable for a peculiarly stalwart character, which enables them to enjoy without loss of self-reliance the benefits of tariffs, franchises, and even outright government subsidies.

Herbert J. Muller (1905–   )

Business is like riding a bicycle. Either you keep moving or you fall down.

John David Wright (1905–   )

American business is so widely-owned and its benefits so widely-dispersed that when we criticize business, we are, in effect, criticizing ourselves. When business does not do the job expected of it, it is we—all of us—who are both accountable and concerned.

James M. Roche (1906–   )
General Motors

Who on earth invented the silly convention that it is boring or impolite to talk shop? Nothing is more interesting to listen to, especially if the shop is not one's own.

W. H. Auden (1907–1973)
A Certain World, 1970

The urge to consume is fathered by the value system which emphasizes the ability of the society to produce.

John Kenneth Galbraith (1908–   )
The Affluent Society, 1958

Money is a singular thing. It ranks with love as man's greatest source of joy. And with death as his greatest source of anxiety. Money differs from an automobile, a mistress or cancer in being equally important to those who have it and those who do not.

John Kenneth Galbraith
The Age of Uncertainty, 1977

Business has only two functions—marketing and innovation.

Peter F. Drucker (1909–   )

The modern corporation is a political institution; its purpose is the creation of legitimate power in the industrial sphere.

Peter F. Drucker

Today the future occupation of all moppets is to be skilled consumers.

David Riesman (1909–   )
The Lonely Crowd, 1950

Success is that old ABC—ability, breaks and courage.

Charles Luckman (1909–   )
Luckman Management

Primitive society tells us where it's at. Our business is basically sex and hunger.

Henry G. Walter, Jr. (1910–   )
International Flavors & Fragrances

Even for the neurotic executive—as for everyone else—work has great therapeutic value; it is generally his last refuge, and deterioration there marks the final collapse of the man; his marriage, his social life, and the outside interests—all have suffered beforehand.

Richard A. Smith (1911–   )
"The Executive Crack-up," *Fortune,*
May 1955

New York is not the cultural center of America, but the business and administrative center of American culture.

Saul Bellow (1915–   )
Radio interview, *Listener,* 22 May 1969

General Motors is not in the business of making cars. General Motors is in the business of making money.

Thomas A. Murphy (1915–   )
General Motors

Nobody talks more of free enterprise and competition and of the best man winning than the man who inherited his father's store or farm.

C. Wright Mills (1916–1962)

I believe that the social responsibility of the corporation today is fundamentally the same as it has always been: to earn profits for shareholders by serving consumer wants with maximum efficiency. This is not the whole of the matter, but it is the heart of the matter.

Henry Ford II (1917–   )
Ford Motor

Capitalism is based on private property, where normal economic activity consists of commercial transactions between consenting adults.

Irving Kristol (1920–   )

A stake in commercial television is the equivalent of having a license to print money.

Lord Thomson of Fleet (1923–   )
Thomson Newspapers

The good luck that comes to us in our relations with the industrial world is always the good luck of the gambler—not the glory of the warrior or the reward of the cultivator.

Elemire Zolla (1926–   )
The Eclipse of the Intellectual, 1969

The average investor is not a professional. He is not on Wall Street. There is no way that he is going to avoid the occasional drops that will hit the market—even with good advice. The stock market has a history of moving to irrational extremes because, on a short-term basis, stock prices are often more a reflection of fear, greed or other psychological factors than of business and monetary fundamentals.

Joseph L. Oppenheimer (1927–)
Standard & Poor's

There are only two emotions in Wall Street: fear and greed.

William M. LeFevre, Jr. (1927–)
Granger & Company

The whole point of free enterprise—of capitalism—is vigorous, honest competition. Every corner cut, every bribe placed, every little cheating move by a businessman in pursuit of quick plunder instead of honest profit is an outright attack on the real free enterprise system.

William E. Simon (1927–

I sometimes wonder whether there is a relationship, or at least an analogy, between the flight from Wall Street and the rush to legalized gambling. Perhaps the real difference between the track and the market is not in the odds but in the convenience.

Donald E. Weeden (1930–)
Weeden & Company

The business world worships mediocrity. Officially we revere free enterprise, initiative and individuality. Unofficially we fear it.

George Lois (1931–)
The Art of Advertising, 1977

If I had to give a definition of capitalism I would say: the process whereby American girls turn into American women.

Christopher Hampton (1946–)
Savages, 1973

Business without profit is not business any more than a pickle is a candy.

Charles F. Abbott

Business is religion and religion is business.

M. Babcock

What's worth doing is worth doing for money.

> Joseph Donohue
> In Dickson, *The Official Rules,* 1978

The business of our country is small business—at least in numbers. Small business is the real exponent of the free-enterprise system that built this country and will sustain it.

> Thomas S. Kleppe
> U.S. Small Business Administration

Monopoly is business at the end of its journey.

> Henry Demarest Lloyd

Small business is the biggest business of them all.

> J. E. Murray

A criminal is a person with predatory instincts who has not sufficient capital to form a corporation.

> Howard Scott

Business is like fishing. You have to have patience.

> Leopold D. Silberstein
> Penn-Texas

It has been said that this wasn't a business, it was a religion. And during those days, by God, it was a religion. . . . You don't get that out of a General Motors. You don't get that out of an IBM. . . . The product has some kind of strange characteristic. . . . I think it's symbolism. I don't know why, I've spent up to 50 years now trying to figure it out.

> Delony Sledge
> Coca-Cola
> Of the old Coca-Cola spirit

When businessmen call on the clergy to say a prayer for success at the opening of a railroad and airplane route from coast to coast and they also ask the blessing of religion upon a profitable enterprise like the opening of a new dam, the Church pays its homage to a new king. They want a businessman's religion, which means that religion must help them to larger profits.

> C. Everett Wagner

CONTROL

Control is a monitoring function, a fact-finding and interpretive process. In order to "control" costs, one must know what the costs are. But Control is more than counting, and accounting is more than adding up the numbers. "Control" implies responsibility, accountability. What do the numbers mean? Where do they come from and what are they saying? The quantitative facts should lead to a qualitative story: What is the quality of earnings? Where is the business headed? Quotations in the Control section spring from the counting instinct that began at the mouth of the cave.

Syndicated newspaper cartoon by Rollin Kirby, December 1940.

A nearby penny is worth a distant dollar.

Anonymous

Better a steady dime than a rare dollar.

Anonymous

Doesn't matter if it's gold—long as it's silver.

Anonymous
[probably from American vaudeville]

You never lost money by taking a profit.

American saying

Even the blind can see money.

Chinese proverb

If small sums do not go out, large sums will not come in.

Chinese proverb

Profit is better than fame.

Danish proverb

It's a bad bargain where nobody gains.

English proverb

No man ever had enough money.

Gypsy proverb

A heavy purse makes a light heart.

Irish proverb

Where profit is, loss is hidden nearby.

Japanese proverb

Money for which no receipt has been taken is not to be included in the accounts.

The Code of Hammurabi, c. 2000 B.C.

A feast is made for laughter, and wine maketh merry: but money answereth all things.

Bible: Ecclesiastes 10:19

Do not seek dishonest gains: dishonest gains are losses.

> Hesiod (c. 700 B.C.)
> *Works and Days*

On the one hand, loss implies gain; on the other hand, gain implies loss.

> Lao-tze (c. 604–c. 531 B.C.)
> *Tao-te-ching*

Be not allured, my friend, by cunning gains.

> Pindar (c. 518–c. 438 B.C.)
> *Pythian Odes,* 470 B.C.

Gain is pleasant though it be full of lies.

> Attributed to Sophocles (c. 495–406 B.C.)
> In Erasmus (1465–1536), *Adagia*

Where does the bread come in? [What profit is there in this for me?]

> Aristophanes (c. 450–385 B.C.)
> *Clouds,* 423 B.C.

There are times when it is undoubtedly better to incur loss than to make gain.

> Plautus (254–184 B.C.)
> *Captivi,* c. 200 B.C.

Even though work stops, expenses run on.

> Cato the Elder (234–149 B.C.)
> *On Agriculture*

Make moderate use of gains: when all is cost,
What took a long time to get is quickly lost.

> Attributed to Cato the Elder
> *Disticha,* c. 175 B.C.

Why is it that we write down memoranda carelessly, that we make up account books carefully? For what reason? Because the one is to last a month, the other forever; these are immediately expunged, those are religiously preserved; these embrace the recollection of a short time, those pledge the good faith and honesty of a man forever; these are thrown away, those are arranged in order. Therefore, no one ever produced memoranda at a trial; men do produce accounts, and read entries in books.

> Cicero (106–43 B.C.)
> *On Behalf of Roscius*

The public may boo me, but when I go home and think of my money I clap.

> Horace (65–8 B.C.)
> *Epistles*, c. 20 B.C.

Nothing stings more deeply than the loss of money.

> Livy (59 B.C.–A.D. 17)
> *History of Rome*

Whatever you can lose, you should reckon of no account.

> Publilius Syrus (First century B.C.)
> *Sententiae*

The loss which is unknown is no loss at all.

> Publilius Syrus
> *Sententiae*

A great fortune is a great slavery.

> Seneca (c. 4 B.C.–A.D. 65)
> *Moral Essays*

Take my word for it: if you have a penny, you are worth a penny.

> Petronius (First century A.D.)
> *Satyricon*

Let us keep a firm grip upon our money, for without it the whole assembly of virtues are but as blades of grass.

> Bhartrihari (Seventh century)
> *Nita Sataka*

Ther was noon auditour koude on him wynne. [He could beat any audit.]

> Geoffrey Chaucer (c. 1343–1400)
> *General Prologue, Canterbury Tales*
> [The man who could beat any audit was Chaucer's Reeve, or farm superintendent of a large estate]

Better is cost upon something worth than expense upon nothing worth.

> Roger Ascham (1515–1568)
> *Toxophilus*, 1545

Hee that compts all costes, will never put plough in the eard.

> David Ferguson (died 1598)
> *Scottish Proverbs*, 1641

He that forecasts all difficulties that he may meet with in business, will never set about it.

James Kelly
Scottish Proverbs, 1721

What costs little is valued less.

Miguel de Cervantes (1547–1616)
Don Quixote, 1605

In business the keeping close to the matter and not taking of it too much at once, procureth dispatch.

Francis Bacon (1561–1626)
Of Dispatch, 1597

Money never cometh out of season.

Thomas Draxe (?–1618)
Bibliotheca scholastica instructissima, 1616

I am ill at reckoning; it fitteth the spirit of a tapster.

William Shakespeare (1564–1616)
Love's Labour's Lost, 1594–1595

What is aught, but as 'tis valued?

William Shakespeare
Troilus and Cressida, 1601

He that is robbed, not wanting what is stol'n,
Let him not know 't and he's not robbed at all.

William Shakespeare
Othello, 1604–1605

In the state of nature profit is the measure of right.

Thomas Hobbes (1588–1679)
Philosophical Rudiments Concerning Government and Society, 1651

Honor and profit lie not in one sack.

George Herbert (1593–1633)
Outlandish Proverbs, 1640

That is gold which is worth gold.

George Herbert
Outlandish Proverbs

To have money is a fear; not to have it, a grief.

George Herbert
Jacula Prudentum, 1651

The greatest gift is the power to estimate correctly the value of things.

François, Duc de La Rochefoucauld (1613–1680)
Maximes, 1664

Things are only worth what one makes them worth.

Molière (1622–1673)
Les Précieuses Ridicules, 1659

No great loss but some small profit.

John Ray (1627–1705)
English Proverbs, 1670

Money makes up in a measure all other wants in men.

William Wycherley (c. 1640–1716)
The Country Wife, 1675

Is it not as impossible that a *Merchant* should be prosperous in Trade without being a thorough-pac'd Accountant, and having all other Accomplishments suitable to the Nature of his great Employ, as that a Mariner should conduct a Ship to all Parts of the Globe without a Skill in Navigation?

Anonymous merchant of London (c. 1700)

An ass laden with gold overtakes everything.

Thomas Fuller (1654–1734)
Gnomologia, 1732

Business is the salt of life.

Thomas Fuller
Gnomologia

I wot well how the world wags;
He is most loved that hath most bags.

Thomas Fuller
Gnomologia

Money in purse will always be in fashion.

Thomas Fuller
Gnomologia

A tradesman's books are his repeating clock, which upon all occasions are to tell him how he goes on, and how things stand with him in the world; and upon his regular keeping, and fully acquainting himself with his books, depends at least the comfort of his trade, if not the very trade itself.

Daniel Defoe (c. 1660–1731)
The Complete English Tradesman, 1726–1727

Pray do not measure my corn with your bushel.

John Gay (1688–1732)
The Wife of Bath, 1713

Worth is best known by want.

Samuel Richardson (1689–1761)
Clarissa, 1748

The counting-house of an accomplished merchant is a school of method where the great science may be learned of ranging particulars under generals, of bringing the different parts of a transaction together, and of showing at one view a long series of dealing and exchange.

Samuel Johnson (1709–1784)

The real price of everything . . . is the toil and trouble of acquiring it.

Adam Smith (1723–1790)
Wealth of Nations, 1776

SAMUEL JOHNSON: Were I a country gentleman, I should not be very hospitable, I should not have crowds in my house.
JAMES BOSWELL: Sir Alexander Dick tells me, that he remembers having a thousand people in a year to dine at his house: that is, reckoning each person as one, each time that he dines there.
JOHNSON: That, Sir, is about three a day.
BOSWELL: How your statement lessens the idea.
JOHNSON: That, Sir, is the good of counting. It brings every thing to a certainty, which before floated in the mind indefinitely.

James Boswell (1740–1795)
Life of Johnson, 1791
[Said: 18 April 1783]

By Journal Laws—what I receive
Is Debtor made to what I give;
Stock for my Debts must Debtor be,
And Creditor my Property;
Profit and Loss Accounts are plain.
I *debit* Loss, and *credit* Gain.

Patrick Kelly (1756–1842)
The Elements of Book-keeping, 1801
[Verses to help students remember what to credit and what to debit in double-entry bookkeeping]

Control

Nothing is so fallacious as facts, except figures.

George Canning (1770–1827)

There is no way of keeping profits up but by keeping wages down.

David Ricardo (1772–1823)
On Protection to Agriculture, 1820

O money, money, how blindly thou hast been worshiped, and how stupidly abused! Thou art health, and liberty, and strength; and he that has thee may rattle his pockets at the foul fiend.

Charles Lamb (1775–1834)
Letter to Samuel Taylor Coleridge, 1809

DEPARTMENT HEAD: Pray, Mr. Lamb, what are you about?
CHARLES LAMB: Forty, next birthday.
DEPARTMENT HEAD: I don't like your answer.
CHARLES LAMB: Nor I your question.
At another time on being reprimanded for arriving late he calmly replied that he never failed to leave early.

He was neither a neat nor an accurate accountant. He made frequent errors, which he was in the habit of wiping out with his little finger.

CHARLES LAMB: Besides my daylight servitude, I served over again all night in my sleep, and would awake with terrors of imaginary false entries, errors in my accounts, and the like.

CHARLES LAMB: My old desk; the peg where I hung my hat, were appropriated to another. I knew it must be, but I could not take it kindly.

CHARLES LAMB: We have shaken hands with the world's business; we have done with it; we have discharged ourselves of it. Why should we get up? We have neither suit to solicit, nor affairs to manage. The drama has shut in upon us at the fourth act. We have nothing here to expect, but in a short time a sick bed, and a dismissal.

Anecdotes about Charles Lamb (1775–1834)
In L. Fred Boyce, Jr., "Lamb Among the Ledgers,"
The Journal of Accounting, December 1960

He smote the rock of the national resources, and abundant streams of revenue gushed forth. He touched the dead corpse of Public Credit, and it sprung upon its feet.

Daniel Webster (1782–1852)
On Alexander Hamilton, 1831

There's a daily cost, and all of it lost.
> Henry George Bohn (1796–1884)
> *Handbook of Proverbs,* 1855

There are three kinds of lies: lies, damned lies, and statistics.
> Benjamin Disraeli (1804–1881)

With the frenzy of a madman, he drew his broad-brimmed white hat over his eyes, and rushed into the street. The rain and storm were nothing to him. He hurried to the residence of his clerk, in Wall-street, reached the door, and seized the handle of the huge knocker, with which he rapped until the neighborhood was roused with the "loud alarm." The unfortunate clerk poked his night-cap out of an upper window, and demanded, "Wha's there?" "It's *me,* you dom scoundrel!" said the frenzied merchant; *"ye've added up the year of our Laird with the pounds."* Such was the fact. The addition of the year of our Lord among the items had swelled the fortune of the merchant some two thousand pounds beyond its actual amount.
> *Knickerbocker Magazine*
> "The Rich Merchant by Bookkeeping," 1845
> Alleged to be a true story

I don't care a damn for the invention. The dimes are what I'm after.
> Isaac M. Singer (1811–1875)
> On his sewing machine

Annual income twenty pounds, annual expenditure nineteen nineteen six, result happiness. Annual income twenty pounds, annual expenditure twenty pounds ought and six, result misery.
> Charles Dickens (1812–1870)
> *David Copperfield,* 1849–1850

Trifles make the sum of life.
> Charles Dickens
> *David Copperfield*

What I want is Facts. Teach these boys and girls nothing but Facts. Facts alone are wanted in life. Plant nothing else, and root out everything else.
> Charles Dickens
> *Hard Times,* 1854

So soon as we begin to count the cost, the cost begins.
> Henry David Thoreau (1817–1862)
> *Winter,* 18 January 1841

Control

Success, as I see it, is a result, not a goal.

Gustave Flaubert (1821–1880)

The fundamental principles which govern the handling of postage stamps and of millions of dollars are exactly the same. They are the common law of business, and the whole practice of commerce is founded on them. They are so simple that a fool can't learn them; so hard that a lazy man won't.

Philip D. Armour (1832–1901)

If I owe Smith ten dollars, and God forgives me, that doesn't pay Smith.

Robert G. Ingersoll (1833–1899)

Money is always on the brain so long as there is a brain in reasonable order.

Samuel Butler (1835–1902)
Notebooks, 1912

Get your facts first, and then you can distort them as much as you please.

Mark Twain (1835–1910)

At the close of the first day [in 1861] the cash drawer revealed a total intake of $24.67.

Of this sum $24 was spent for advertising and 67 cents saved for making change next morning.

John Wanamaker (1838–1922)
Golden Book of the Wanamaker Stores, 1861–1911,
edited by Joseph H. Appel and Leigh M. Hodges

The value of a thing is the amount of laboring or work that its possession will save the possessor.

Henry George (1839–1897)
The Science of Political Economy, 1898

He uses statistics as a drunken man uses lampposts—for support rather than for illumination.

Andrew Lang (1844–1912)

There must be 500,000,000 rats in the United States; of course, I am speaking only from memory.

Edgar Wilson ("Bill") Nye (1850–1896)

Money Talks

When a man says money can do anything, that settles it: he hasn't any.

Edgar Watson Howe (1853–1937)
Sinner Sermons, 1926

In business the earning of profit is something more than an incident of success. It is an essential condition of success; because the continued absence of profit itself spells failure.

Louis D. Brandeis (1856–1941)
Commencement address, Brown University, 1912

Take it from me—he's got the goods.

O. Henry [William Sydney Porter] (1862–1910)
"The Unprofitable Servant," 1911

What I make on d' peanut I lose on d' damn banan'.

Italian fruit vendor in New York
to Theodore Roosevelt, c. 1890

Statistics are mendacious truths.

Lionel Strachey (1864–1927)

Never ask of money spent
Where the spender thinks it went.
Nobody was ever meant
To remember or invent
What he did with every cent.

Robert Frost (1874–1963)
"The Hardship of Accounting," from
"Ten Mills," in *A Further Range,* 1936

It is very funny about money. The thing that differentiates man from animals is money. All animals have the same emotions and the same ways as men. Anybody who has lots of animals around knows that. But the thing that no animal can do is count, and the thing no animal can know is money.

Men can count, and they do, and that is what makes them have money.

And so, as long as the earth turns around there will be men on it, and as long as there are men on it, they will count, and they will count money.

Gertrude Stein (1874–1946)
"All About Money"

Control

It is better that a man should tyrannize over his bank balance than over his fellow citizens.

> John Maynard Keynes (1883–1946)
> *The General Theory of Employment,*
> *Interest and Money,* 1936

No, I don't know his telephone number. But it was up in the high numbers.

> Attributed to John Maynard Keynes

There are two kinds of statistics, the kind you look up and the kind you make up.

> Rex Stout (1886–1975)
> *Death of a Doxy,* 1966

If you can actually count your money then you are not really a rich man.
    If you can count your money you don't have a billion dollars.

> J. Paul Getty (1892–1976)

Upon this gifted age, in its dark hour,
Rains from the sky a meteoric shower
Of facts . . . they lie unquestioned, uncombined.
Wisdom enough to leech us of our ill
Is daily spun; but there exists no loom
To weave it into fabric; . . .

> Edna St. Vincent Millay (1892–1950)
> *Collected Sonnets,* 1941

The trouble with the profit system has always been that it was highly unprofitable to most people.

> E. B. White (1899–   )
> *One Man's Meat,* 1944

Few have heard of Fra Luca Parioli, the inventor of double-entry book-keeping; but he has probably had much more influence on human life than has Dante or Michelangelo.

> Herbert J. Muller (1905–   )
> *The Uses of the Past,* 1952

Wealth is the product of man's capacity to think.

> Ayn Rand (1905–1982)

The only thing that matters is the bottom line? What a presumptuous thing to say! The bottom line is in heaven.

Edwin Land (1909–   )
Polaroid
To a stockholder

"Absorption of overhead" is one of the most obscene terms I have ever heard.

Peter F. Drucker (1909–   )

Profitability is the sovereign criterion of the enterprise.

Peter F. Drucker

Labor under automation must be considered a capital resource, with wage costs being treated virtually as fixed costs.

Peter F. Drucker
America's Next Twenty Years, 1955

Error is boundless.
Nor hope nor doubt,
Though both be groundless,
Will average out.

J. V. Cunningham (1911–1985)
"Meditation on Statistical Method"
In *The Collected Poems and Epigrams*, 1971

Royalties are nice and all but shaking the beads brings in money quicker.

Gypsy Rose Lee (1914–1970)

"Profit" is today a fighting word. Profits are the lifeblood of the economic system, the magic elixir upon which progress and all good things ultimately depend. But one man's lifeblood is another man's cancer.

Paul A. Samuelson (1915–   )
Massachusetts Institute of Technology

I'm beginning to wonder why they even set up this office. Industry in New York does not advise the legislators—it controls them.

Betty Furness (1916–   )
New York State Consumer Protection Board
Announcing her resignation

Friends may come and go, but enemies accumulate.

Dr. Thomas Jones (1916–1981)
Massachusetts Institute of Technology

If standards are not formulated systematically at the top, they will be formulated haphazardly and impulsively in the field.

John C. Biegler (1921–   )
Price Waterhouse

It is important that I don't get too knowledgeable about the past.

Wallace Booth (1922–   )
United Brands
On taking over as president, 1975

The widespread failure to understand both the function and level, in real terms, of corporate profits and cash flow is blinding many to the fact that business is simply not accumulating and retaining the resources required to meet the challenges facing it.

Harold M. Williams (1928–   )
US Securities and Exchange Commission

I've never been associated with a loss. I don't know what it feels like, and I don't want to find out.

Guy R. Odom (1931–   )
U.S. Home

Establishing Sound Budget Practice: Summary of Eight Principles

Establish your budget system on the highest possible level of motivation.

Anchor your budgeting firmly in a foundation of company planning.

Establish the meaning of control, and then put it into practice.

Insist on a clear-cut organization structure.

Arrange for good, common-sense accounting and complete, simple, and prompt explanations of the content of the items.

In the field of cost control, use your budget as a tool to be placed in your foremen's hands—not as a club to be held over their heads.

Insure the active participation of top management.

See that the controller and his staff express the correct attitude for the responsibility they undertake with respect to budgets.

James L. Pierce
"The Budget Comes of Age," *Harvard Business Review,* 1954

No tool can be used effectively unless the hand that guides it is rightly motivated. Like all other techniques of business, the budget should be a door open to more satisfying and profitable work—not an instrument of torture.

What you can do without a budget you can do better with one.

The entire planning and control procedure, under whatever name, is a device for freeing men to do their best work—not a machine of restriction and condemnation.

Planning is but another word for the vision that sees a creative achievement before it is manifest. Control is but a name for direction.

James L. Pierce
"The Budget Comes of Age," *Harvard Business Review*

Adequate control reports are one of the prime essentials for expansion, diversification, and long-run growth. The better the controls, the greater the degree of decentralization which is possible with safety.

John G. McLean
"Better Reports for Better Control,"
Harvard Business Review, 1957

Net—the biggest word in the language of business.

Herbert Casson

Food profits rise as you come closer to the table.

Claude Fuqua
Anderson, Clayton

When I first knew Elvis he had a million dollars worth of talent. Now he has a million dollars.

Col. Tom Parker
Of Elvis Presley

A man isn't a man until he has to meet a payroll.

Ivan Shaffer

You have to have real values. Money without production and confidence is just paper. Billions of marks—just paper. Dealing at this time on foreign markets, I came to believe in foreign securities. I didn't count any more in marks. I counted only in foreign—what you call hard currencies, hard money.

Leopold D. Silberstein
Penn-Texas

FINANCE

No business can function without cash and
credit; the need for external funding, whatever the source, is basic to enterprise. Insurance, loans, stocks, bonds, the "borrowed
time" in contracts for service—all make
business activity possible. Yet given the demand for cash and credit, and since most
businesses fail or must grow in order to survive, Finance's real interest lies in estimates
of trust and risk, value and change. Money—
worshiped, feared, touched by everyone but
misunderstood—is also a business, competing in a marketplace. The late poet W. H.
Auden touched a live nerve in his commonplace book, *A Certain World* (1970):

> In our modern economy it seems un-
> likely that the middle-class morality
> about money will be able to survive. I,
> for example, was brought up never to
> buy anything until I had the cash to pay
> for it. If everyone did the same, i.e.,
> bought nothing on credit, our economy
> would go smash.

A View from the Royal Exchange.

Nathan Meyer Rothschild (1777–1836), the "young, short, obese Frankforter" who founded the English house of Rothschild. Caricature by Richard Dighton, 1817.

Dictum Meum Pactum: My Word Is My Bond

London Stock Exchange motto, 1773

God made bees, and bees made honey,
God made man, and man made money.

Money is honey, my little sonny,
And a rich man's joke is always funny.

Anonymous

If you invest in a fever, your profit is a disease.

Anonymous

If you invest in a needle, you won't win more than a needle.

Anonymous

Legalized larceny.

Anonymous
Of banking

Wall Street: A thoroughfare that begins in a graveyard and ends in a river.

Anonymous
In Mencken, *New Dictionary of Quotations,* 1942

With money one may command devils; without it, one cannot even summon a man.

Chinese proverb

Money makes the mare go.

English proverb

Money has no ears, but it hears.

Japanese proverb

Money has no legs, but it runs.

Japanese proverb

Money is another kind of blood.

Latin proverb

Ready money, ready medicine.

Latin proverb

If thou lend money to any of my people that is poor by thee, thou shalt not be to him as an usurer, neither shalt thou lay upon him usury.

Bible: Exodus 22:25

He that hath not given forth upon usury, neither hath taken any increase, that hath withdrawn his hand from iniquity, hath executed true judgment between man and man,
Hath walked in my statutes, and hath kept my judgments, to deal truly; he is just, he shall surely live, saith the Lord God.

Bible: Ezekiel 18:8–9

The borrower is servant to the lender.

Bible: Proverbs 22:7

And Jesus went into the temple of God, and cast out all them that sold and bought in the temple, and overthrew the tables of the money-changers, and the seats of them that sold doves,
And said unto them, It is written, My house shall be called the house of prayer; but ye have made it a den of thieves.

Bible: Matthew 21:12–13

Let every man divide his money into three parts, and invest a third in land, a third in business, and a third let him keep in reserve.

Talmud

Money purifies all baseness.

Talmud

If you should put even a little on a little, and should do this often, soon this too would become big.

Hesiod (c. 700 B.C.)
Works and Days

The Law of Debt [a selection]

A creditor shall receive his principal back from his debtor exactly as he had lent it to him.

Property lent bears no further interest after it has been tendered, but refused by the creditor.

On gold the interest shall rise no higher than to make the debt double;

On grain, threefold;

On cloth, fourfold;

On liquids, eightfold;

Of female slaves and cattle, the offspring.

On substances from which spiritous liquor is extracted, on cotton, thread, leather, weapons, bricks, and charcoal, the interest is unlimited.

If he who contracted the debt should die, or become a religious ascetic, or remain abroad for twenty years, that debt shall be discharged by his sons or grandsons;

But not by remoter descendants against their will.

The Institutes of Vishnu, c. 500 B.C.

There is nothing more profitable for a man than to take good counsel with himself; for even if the event turns out contrary to one's hope, still one's decision was right, even though fortune has made it of no effect: whereas if a man acts contrary to good counsel, although by luck he gets what he had no right to expect, his decision was not any the less foolish.

Herodotus (c. 485–c. 425 B.C.)
Histories

Money is the sinews of success.

Bion (c. 325–c. 255 B.C.)
In Diogenes Laertius, *Lives of Eminent Philosophers*
[Also translated: Money is the sinews of business]

To citizens and foreigners this bank gives equal dealing;
Deposit and withdraw, when your account is correctly made up
Let another make excuse: but Caicus even at night
Pays foreign money to those who want it.

Theocritus (c. 310–c. 250 B.C.)
Epigrams
Bank advertisement

You must spend money, if you wish to make money.

Plautus (254–184 B.C.)
Asinaria, c. 200 B.C.

When his questioner asked, "How about money-lending?" Cato replied: "How about murder?"

Cicero (106–43 B.C.)
De Officiis, c. 45 B.C.

Money alone sets the world in motion.

Publilius Syrus (First century B.C.)
Sententiae

For as he who is fallen into the dirt must either rise up and get out of it, or else lie still in the place into which he first fell, for that by tumbling, turning, and rolling about, he does but still more bemire himself; so also those who do but change their creditor, and cause their names to be transcribed from one usurer's book to another's, do by loading and embroiling themselves with new usuries become more and more oppressed.

Plutarch (46–120)
Morals

Investment vs. Usury

A man is forbidden to give his money to another for the purpose of engaging in a joint venture on condition that he share in the profit but not in the loss, this being quasi usury. He who does this is called a wicked man. And if one gave money to another on such a condition, they share the loss, as well as the profit, in accordance with the nature of their venture. He who gives his money on condition that he share in the loss but not in the profit is called a pious man.

The Code of Maimonides
Twelfth Century

If any one hath borrowed anything from the Jews, more or less, and die before the debt be paid, the debt shall pay no interest so long as the heir shall be under age, of whomsoever he may hold, and if that debt shall fall into our hands, we will not take anything except the chattel contained in the bond.

Magna Charta, 1215

If you recall Genesis at the beginning: It behoves man to gain his bread and to prosper. And because the usurer takes another way, he contemns Nature in herself and in her follower, placing elsewhere his hope.

> Dante Alighieri (1265–1321)
> *The Comedy: Hell,* 1472

Manye smale maken a greet.

> Geoffrey Chaucer (c. 1343–1400)
> *Parson's Tale, Canterbury Tales*

God forbid that I should be out of debt, as if, indeed, I could not be trusted.

> François Rabelais (c. 1494–1553)

Nature hath not to any other end created man, but to borrow and lend. . . . Believe me, it is a divine thing to lend, to owe an heroic virtue.

> François Rabelais
> *Pantagruel,* 1545

He who cannot lend, let him take heed of borrowing.

> Michel Eyquem de Montaigne (1533–1592)
> *Essays,* 1580

A little in one's own pocket is better than much in another man's purse. 'Tis good to keep a nest egg. Every little makes a mickle.

> Miguel de Cervantes (1547–1616)
> *Don Quixote,* 1615

Upon a good foundation a good building may be raised, and the best foundation in the world is money.

> Miguel de Cervantes
> *Don Quixote*

When we want money, we want all.

> Thomas Draxe (?–1618)
> *Bibliotheca scholastica instructissima,* 1633

Money is like muck, not good except it be spread.

> Francis Bacon (1561–1626)
> *Of Seditions and Troubles,* 1625

Usury: The Discommodities
   It makes fewer merchants.
   It makes poor merchants.
   It bringeth the treasure of a realm or state into a few hands.
   It beats down the price of land; for the employment of money is chiefly either merchandising or purchasing; and usury waylays both.
   It doth dull and damp all industries, improvements, and new inventions, wherein money would be stirring, if it were not for this slug.
   It is the canker and ruin of many men's estates; which in process of time breeds a public poverty.

Francis Bacon
Of Usury, 1625

How like a fawning publican he looks.
I hate him for he is a Christian;
But more, for that in low simplicity
He lends out money gratis and brings down
The rate of usance here with us in Venice.
If I can catch him once upon the hip,
I will feed fat the ancient grudge I bear him.
He hates our sacred nation, and he rails,
Even there where merchants most do congregate,
On me, my bargains, and my well-worn thrift,
Which he calls interest.

William Shakespeare (1564–1616)
The Merchant of Venice, 1596–1597
[Shylock on Antonio]

Signior Antonio, many a time and oft
In the Rialto you have rated me
About my moneys and my usances.
Still have I borne it with a patient shrug,
For suff'rance is the badge of all our tribe.
You call me misbeliever, cutthroat dog,
And spit upon my Jewish gaberdine,
And all for use of that which is mine own.
Well then, it now appears you need my help.
Go to then. You come to me and you say,
'Shylock, we would have moneys'—you say so,
You that did void your rheum upon my beard
And foot me as you spurn a stranger cur
Over your threshold! Moneys is your suit.

Finance

What should I say to you? Should I not say,
'Hath a dog money? Is it possible
A cur can lend three thousand ducats?' Or
Shall I bend low, and in a bondsman's key,
With bated breath and whisp'ring humbleness,
Say this:
'Fair sir, you spit on me on Wednesday last,
You spurned me such a day, another time
You called me dog; and for these courtesies
I'll lend you thus much moneys'?

William Shakespeare
The Merchant of Venice

Say this:
'Fair sir, you spit on me on Wednesday last,
You spurned me such a day, another time
You called me dog; and for these courtesies
I'll lend you thus much moneys'?

William Shakespeare
The Merchant of Venice

ANTONIO: Let me have judgment and the Jew his will.
BASSANIO: For thy three thousand ducats here is six.
SHYLOCK: If every ducat in six thousand ducats
    Were in six parts and every part a ducat,
    I would not draw them; I would have my bond.
DUKE: How shalt thou hope for mercy, rendering none?

William Shakespeare
The Merchant of Venice

Neither a borrower, nor a lender be;
For loan oft loses both itself and friend,
And borrowing dulls the edge of husbandry.

William Shakespeare
Hamlet, 1600–1601

Money is a good soldier, sir, and will on.

William Shakespeare
The Merry Wives of Windsor, 1600–1601

If money go before, all ways do lie open.

William Shakespeare
The Merry Wives of Windsor

Lend less than thou owest.

> William Shakespeare
> *King Lear*, 1605–1606

She is the sovereign queen of all delights;
For her the lawyer pleads, the soldier fights.

> Richard Barnfield (1574–1627)
> *The Encomium of Lady Pecunia*
> Of money

He that lends, gives.

> George Herbert (1593–1633)
> *Jacula Prudentum*, 1651

Debt is better than death.

> James Howell (c. 1594–1666)
> *Proverbs*, 1659

The creditor hath a better memory than the debtor.

> James Howell
> *Proverbs*

The expectation of an event creates a much deeper impression upon the exchange than the event itself. When large dividends or rich imports are expected, shares will rise in price; but if the expectation becomes a reality, the shares often fall; for the joy over the favorable development and the jubilation over a lucky chance have abated in the meantime.

> Joseph de la Vega
> *Confusion de Confusiones*, 1688
> Of the Amsterdam Stock Exchange

Money, th' only power
That all mankind falls down before.

> Samuel Butler (1612–1680)
> *Hudibras*, 1678

Too great haste in paying off an obligation is a kind of ingratitude.

> François, Duc de La Rochefoucauld (1613–1680)
> *Maximes*, 1665–1678

Money begets money.

> John Ray (1627–1705)
> *English Proverbs*, 1678

Finance

A man without money is no man at all.

Thomas Fuller (1654–1734)
Gnomologia, 1732

A man without money is a bow without an arrow.

Thomas Fuller
Gnomologia

Money, the *Life-Blood* of the Nation,
   Corrupts and stagnates in the Veins,
Unless a proper *Circulation*
   Its Motion and its Heat maintains.

Jonathan Swift (1667–1745)
The Run Upon the Bankers

How sweetly one guinea rhymes to another, and how they dance
to the music of their own clink!

William Congreve (1670–1729)
The Old Bachelor, 1693

Like Heav'n, it hears the orphans' cries,
And wipes the tears from widows' eyes.

John Gay (1688–1732)
Fables, 1727
Of money

Satire's my weapon, but I'm too discreet
To run amuck, and tilt at all I meet;
I only wear it in a land of hectors;
Thieves, supercargoes, sharpers, and directors.

Alexander Pope (1688–1744)
*The First Satire of the Second Book
of Horace Imitated,* 1733

The use of money is all the advantage there is in having money.

Benjamin Franklin (1706–1790)
Poor Richard's Almanack, 1737

Money is of a prolific generating nature. Money can beget money,
and its offspring can beget more.

Benjamin Franklin
Letters: To My Friend, A. B., 1748

'Tis against some Men's Principle to pay Interest, and seems against others' Interest to pay the Principal.

Benjamin Franklin
Poor Richard's Almanack, 1753

If you'd know the value of Money, go and borrow some.

Benjamin Franklin
Poor Richard's Almanack, 1754

Creditors have better memories than debtors.

Benjamin Franklin
Poor Richard's Almanack, 1758

The law against usury is for the protection of creditors as well as of debtors; for if there were no such check, people would be apt, from the temptation of great interest, to lend to desperate persons, by whom they would lose their money.

Samuel Johnson (1709–1784)
In Boswell, *Life of Johnson,* 1791
[Said: 7 April 1776]

Money is none of the wheels of trade; it is the oil which renders the motion of the wheels more smoothe and easy.

David Hume (1711–1776)

It is not a custom with me to keep money to look at.

George Washington (1732–1799)
Letter to J. P. Custis, January 1780

From the Struggle to Establish the First Bank of the United States: 1791

Advantages
1. Capital would be made available for investment.
2. The bank would aid merchants in prompt payment of the customs and other taxes by making short term loans available for such purposes.
3. The bank would be able to loan money to the government.
4. It would diminish usury.
5. It would prevent the hoarding of precious metals by storing them in its vaults and issuing paper money instead.
6. It would facilitate personal remittances from inaccessible places where notes happened to circulate.

Disadvantages
1. Precious metals would be taken out of circulation.
2. The public would be placed at the mercy of possible runs on the bank.
3. The bank would concentrate wealth in a single area.
4. The plan favored a small group of investors who would be able to purchase stock before people far from the capital could subscribe.

James Madison (1751–1836)
In Morgan, "The Origins and Establishment of the First Bank of the United States," *The Business History Review,* December 1956

Andrew Jackson would never recharter that monster of corruption. Sooner than live in a country where such a power prevailed, he would seek an asylum in the wilds of Arabia.

Andrew Jackson (1767–1845)
The President, speaking of himself
and the Second Bank of the United States, 1834

Who borrows easily? He who pays punctually.

Alexander Negris
A Dictionary of Modern Greek Proverbs, 1831

Effects of Ostentation Upon Credit [England]
A retired merchant of enormous fortune, living in great seclusion, is said to have kept his account with a banking firm headed by a baronet. His balance in the bank was generally from thirty to forty thousand pounds, and the baronet deemed it only proper attention to so valuable customer to invite him to dinner at his villa in the country. The splendor of the banquet, to which the old man reluctantly repaired, impelled him on his entrance to apologize to his host for subjecting the latter to so much inconvenience. The baronet replied that, on the contrary, it was incumbent on him to apologize for taking the liberty of asking his guest to partake of a family dinner. Nothing further passed, but the next morning the customer drew his whole balance out of the bank.

Hunt's Merchants' Magazine, November 1843

Speculation is the romance of trade, and casts contempt upon all its sober realities. It renders the stock-jobber a magician, and the exchange a region of enchantment.

Washington Irving (1783–1859)
Wolfert's Roost, 1855

They say that knowledge is power. I used to think so, but I now know that they meant money. . . . Every guinea is a philosopher's stone. . . . Cash is virtue.

> George Gordon, Lord Byron (1788–1824)
> Letter to Douglas Kinnaird, 6 February 1822

Ready money is Aladdin's lamp.

> George Gordon, Lord Byron
> *Don Juan*, 1823

After all, money, as they say, is miraculous.

> Thomas Carlyle (1795–1881)
> *Past and Present*, 1843

Put not your trust in money, but put your money in trust.

> Oliver Wendell Holmes (1809–1894)
> *The Autocrat of the Breakfast Table*, 1858

Interest works night and day, in fair weather and foul. It gnaws at a man's substance with invisible teeth.

> Henry Ward Beecher (1813–1887)
> *Proverbs from Plymouth Pulpit*, 1887

I don't know of anything so remorseless on the face of the earth than seven per cent interest.

> Josh Billings [Henry Wheeler Shaw] (1818–1885)

Live within your income, even if you have to borrow money to do so.

> Josh Billings

Seven per cent has no rest, nor no religion; it works nights, and Sundays, and even wet days.

> Josh Billings

Time is money, and many people pay their debts with it.

> Josh Billings

Borrowers are nearly always ill-spenders, and it is with lent money that all evil is mainly done and all unjust war protracted.

> John Ruskin (1819–1900)
> *The Crown of Wild Olive*, 1866

Pounds are the sons, not of pounds, but of pence.

> Charles Buxton (1822–1871)

A mortgage casts a shadow on the sunniest field.

> Robert G. Ingersoll (1833–1899)
> *Farming in Illinois*, 1877

The holy passion of Friendship is of so sweet and steady and loyal and enduring a nature that it will last through a whole lifetime, if not asked to lend money.

> Mark Twain (1835–1910)
> *Pudd'nhead Wilson*, 1894

There are two times in a man's life when he should not speculate: when he can't afford it, and when he can.

> Mark Twain
> *Following the Equator*, 1897

A banker is a fellow who lends you his umbrella when the sun is shining and wants it back the minute it begins to rain.

> Mark Twain

Dear Sir and Friend:
You seem to be prosperous these days. Could you lend an admirer a dollar and a half to buy a hymn-book with? God will bless you if you do; I feel it, I know it. So will I. If there should be other applications this one not to count.

> Yours, Mark

P.S. Don't send the hymn-book, send the money. I want to Make the selection myself.

> M.
> Mark Twain

The old gentleman said they never engaged in anything that required risk, or trouble, in the management.

> William G. Moorhead
> Report on the Rothschilds, in a letter to his
> brother-in-law and partner, Jay
> Cooke, October 1869

If a man needs beef, he goes to a butcher; if he needs gold, he goes to a banker; if he needs a great deal of beef, he goes to a big butcher; if he requires a great deal of gold, he must go to a big banker and pay his price for it.

> Grover Cleveland (1837–1908)

The first thing is character. . . . Because a man I do not trust could not get money from me on all the bonds in Christendom.

J. P. Morgan (1837–1913)

I am not in Wall Street for my health.

J. P. Morgan

It can hardly be doubted that the pre-existing tendency to encounter risks and "back one's opinion," inborn in the Americans, and fostered by the circumstances of their country, is further stimulated by the existence of so vast a number of joint-stock enterprises, and by the facilities they offer to the smallest capitalists. Similar facilities exist in the Old World; but few of the inhabitants of the Old World have yet learned how to use and abuse them. The Americans, quick at everything, have learned long ago. The habit of speculation is now part of their character, and it increases that constitutional excitability and high nervous tension of which they are proud.

James Bryce, Viscount Bryce (1838–1922)
The American Commonwealth, 1888

Acquaintance, n. A person whom we know well enough to borrow from, but not well enough to lend to.

Ambrose Bierce (1842–c. 1914)
The Devil's Dictionary, 1906

The Lord is my banker; my credit is good.
He maketh me to lie down in the consciousness of omnipresent
    abundance;
He giveth me the key to His strongbox.
He restoreth my faith in His riches;
He guideth me in the paths of prosperity for His name's sake.
Yes, though I walk in the very shadow of debt,
I shall fear no evil, for Thou art with me;
Thy silver and Thy gold, they secure me.
Thou preparest a way for me in the presence of the collector;
Thou fillest my wallet with plenty; my measure runneth over.
Surely goodness and plenty will follow me all the days of my life,
And I shall do business in the name of the Lord forever.

Charles Fillmore (1854–1948)
The Unity School of Christianity

A financier is a pawnbroker with imagination.

Arthur Wing Pinero (1855–1934)
The Second Mrs. Tanqueray, 1893

Finance

A nation is not in danger of financial disaster merely because it owes itself money.

Andrew Mellon (1855–1937)
Quoted in the *Observer*, 31 May 1953
[Said: 1933]

The faults of the burglar are the qualities of the financier.

George Bernard Shaw (1856–1950)
Major Barbara, 1907

A boy does not put his hand into his pocket until every other means of gaining his end has failed.

James M. Barrie (1860–1937)
Sentimental Tommy, 1896

It's a wise child that owes his own father.

Carolyn Wells (1862–1942)

Money is like an arm or a leg—use it or lose it.

Henry Ford (1863–1947)
Interview, *New York Times*, 8 November 1931

Pass the hat for your credit's sake, and pay, pay, pay.

Rudyard Kipling (1865–1936)
The Absent-Minded Beggar, 1899

He had seen the two ends of a great wheat operation—a battle between bear and bull. The stories (subsequently published in the city's press) of Truslow's countermove in selling Hornung his own wheat, supplied the unseen section. The farmer—he who raised the wheat—was ruined upon the one hand; the working man—he who consumed it—was ruined upon the other. But between the two, the great operators, who never saw the wheat they traded in, bought and sold the world's food, gambled in the nourishment of entire nations, practiced their tricks, their chicanery and oblique shifty "deals," were reconciled in their differences, and went on through their appointed way, jovial, contented, enthroned, and unassailable.

Frank Norris (1870–1902)
A Deal in Wheat, 1903

They hired the money, didn't they?

Calvin Coolidge (1872–1933)
Response to question about France and England's war debts, 1925

When you earn it and spend it you do know the difference between three dollars and a million dollars, but when you say it and vote it, it all sounds the same.

Gertrude Stein (1874–1946)
"Money," in *The Saturday Evening Post,* 13 June 1936

It's better to give than to lend, and it costs about the same.

Philip Gibbs (1877–1962)

The chief value of money lies in the fact that one lives in a world in which it is overestimated.

H. L. Mencken (1880–1956)

Our national debt after all is an internal debt owed not only *by* the nation but *to* the nation. If our children have to pay interest on it they will pay that interest to *themselves.*

Franklin D. Roosevelt (1882–1945)
Speech before American Retail Foundation, 22 May 1939

Of the maxims of orthodox finance, none, surely, is more anti-social than the fetish of liquidity. . . . It forgets that there is no such thing as liquidity of investment for the community as a whole.

John Maynard Keynes (1883–1946)
The General Theory of Employment, Interest and Money, 1936

A broker is a man who runs your fortune into a shoestring.

Alexander Woollcott (1887–1943)
Quoted in Drennan, *Wit's End*

The Crash: Stock Prices 1928-1929

	Opening 3 Mar 28	*High 3 Sep 29*	*Adj* 3 Sep 29*	*Low 13 Nov 29*
Amer Can	77	181⅞	181⅞	86
AT&T	179½	304	335⅝	197¼
Anaconda	54½	131½	162	70
GE	128¾	396¼	396¼	168⅛
GM	139¾	72¾	181⅞	36
Mont Ward	132¾	137⅞	466½	49¼
NY Central	160½	256⅜	256⅜	160
Radio	94½	101	505	28
Union Carb	145	137⅞	413⅝	59
US Steel	138⅛	261¾	279⅛	150
Westinghse	91⅝	289⅞	313	102⅝
Woolworth	180¾	100⅜	251	52¼

*Adjusted for splits and exercised rights issues, 3 Mar 28 to 3 Sep 29.

Frederick Lewis Allen (1890–1954)
Only Yesterday, 1931

Finance

Again and again the specialist in a stock would find himself surrounded by brokers fighting to sell—and nobody at all even thinking of buying. To give one single example: during the bull market the common stock of the White Sewing Machine Company had gone as high as 48; on Monday, October 28, [1929,] it had closed at 11⅛. On that black Tuesday, somebody—a clever messenger boy for the Exchange, it was rumored—had the bright idea of putting in an order to buy at 1—and in the temporarily complete absence of other bids he actually got his stock for a dollar a share!

Frederick Lewis Allen
Only Yesterday

What if bright hopes had been wrecked by the sordid disappointments of 1919, the collapse of Wilsonian idealism, the spread of political cynicism, the slow decay of religious certainty, and the debunking of love? In the Big Bull Market there was compensation. Still the American could spin wonderful dreams—of a romantic day when he would sell his Westinghouse common at a fabulous price and live in a great house and have a fleet of shining cars and loll at ease on the sands of Palm Beach. And when he looked toward the future of his country, he could vision an American set free—not from graft, nor from crime, nor from war, nor from control by Wall Street, nor from irreligion, nor from lust, for the utopias of an earlier day left him for the most part skeptical or indifferent; he visioned an America set free from poverty and toil.

Frederick Lewis Allen
Only Yesterday
1929, before The Crash

His unique power in the crisis derived partly from the sense in the back of men's minds that if his leadership failed, the whole financial world would go to ruin, whereas if he succeeded, one would probably prosper much better if Morgan remembered one as an ally in time of need, than if he marked one down as an objector. It derived partly from his organizing ability; partly from the fact that men trusted him to work for the general interest as they would nobody else of remotely comparable authority; partly from the compulsion in his very glance; but mostly from his courage.

Frederick Lewis Allen
The Great Pierpont Morgan, 1949

65

Money is like manure. You have to spread it around or it smells.

J. Paul Getty (1892–1976)

Hollywood money isn't money. It's congealed snow, melts in your hand, and there you are.

Dorothy Parker (1893–1967)
In *Writers at Work: First Series,* 1958

At any rate it all seems a little beyond me now. It is time for younger people to bother about these things. It is time for us to sit by the side of the road to watch the parade go by.

At any rate there is one thing I am certain of. This business will not last, this extravagance of thought and money is abnormal; it is bound to be, with General Electric selling where it is to-day.

John P. Marquand (1893–1960)
The Late George Apley, 1937
Apley writing to his son in 1929

Owing money has never concerned me so long as I know where it could be repaid.

Colonel Henry Crown (1896–   )
Quoted in the *New York Times,* 21 February 1960

J. Pierpont Morgan was a bullnecked irascible man with small black magpie's eyes and a growth on his nose; he let his partners work themselves to death over the detailed routine of banking, and sat in his back office smoking black cigars; when there was something to be decided he said Yes or No or just turned his back and went back to his solitaire.

John Dos Passos (1896–1970)
The House of Morgan: U.S.A., 1938

By 1917 the Allies had borrowed one billion, nine hundred million dollars through the House of Morgan: we went overseas for democracy and the flag;

and by the end of the Peace Conference the phrase *J. P. Morgan suggests* had compulsion over a power of seventyfour billion dollars.

J. P. Morgan is a silent man, not given to public utterances, but during the great steel strike, he wrote Gary: *Heartfelt congratulations on your stand for the open shop, with which I am, as you know, absolutely in accord. I believe American principles of liberty are deeply involved, and must win if we stand firm.*

(Wars and panics on the stock exchange,

machinegunfire and arson,
bankruptcies, warloans,
starvation, lice, cholera and typhus:
good growing weather for the House of Morgan.)

John Dos Passos
U.S.A.

A banker is a person who is willing to make a loan if you present sufficient evidence to show you don't need it.

Herbert V. Prochnow (1897–   )

A monopolist is a fellow who manages to get an elbow on each arm of his theatre chair.

Herbert V. Prochnow

There seems to be, unfortunately, a very human tendency on the part of most people to assume that if a stock's price stands some distance away from its Rating of normal value, there must be something wrong with the Value Line Rating. As soon as this very human assumption takes hold, however, the bars are down. Facts go out the window and the witch of fancy rides off on her broomstick to make sweeping discounts of the future. The devilish thing about her voyaging fancies is that they always have a little truth in them. But it is so little, and so far away. And the lost facts are so big and so near.

Arnold Bernhard (1901–   )
Value Line

Most bankers dwell in marble halls,
which they get to dwell in because they encourage deposits and discourage withdralls.

Ogden Nash (1902–1971)
"Bankers are Just Like Anybody Else, Except Richer," in *I'm a Stranger Here Myself,* 1938

The gold that is put into the vaults at Fort Knox is not *destroyed,* to be sure. But its incarceration virtually amounts to destruction.

J. Philip Wernette (1903–   )
The Future of American Prosperity, 1955

Money Talks

In our modern economy it seems unlikely that the middle-class morality about money will be able to survive. I, for example, was brought up never to buy anything until I had cash to pay for it. If everyone did the same, i.e., bought nothing on credit, our economy would go smash.

W. H. Auden (1907–1973)
A Certain World, 1970

When Karl Marx
Found the phrase 'financial sharks,'
He sang a Te Deum
In the British Museum.

W. H. Auden
Academic Graffiti, 1972

Money is the guiltiest thing in the world. It stinks.

William Saroyan (1908–1981)
The Time of Your Life, 1939

It was hard for me to believe that there were people who didn't give a damn about anything except money—the lawyers, the bankers. The Hanes family spent three generations building this business, and it was taken away from us in 10 days.

Gordon Hanes (1916–   )
Of Consolidated Foods' take-over of Hanes, 1978

We shouldn't knock risk. The market and this country were built on risk.

Donald T. Regan (1918–   )
Merrill Lynch, Pierce, Fenner & Smith

By promoting insurance on the basis of what people think about problems of uncertainty, instead of what they would be correct in thinking about them, i.e., by exploiting the fallacy that one buys insurance to collect for a loss instead of educating them to a realization that the purpose of insurance is to avoid uncertainty, we have invited a plague of problems to distress the industry.

Henry K. Duke (1920–   )
Letter to *Harvard Business Review,* 1959

Credit . . . is the only enduring testimonial to a man's confidence in man.

James Blish (1921–1975)

Banking is a risk industry. Unless bankers take risks, they cannot support their communities nor the industries and businesses making up those communities.

Philip E. Coldwell (1922–   )
Federal Reserve Board

The speculators perform a vital economic function. It is they and they alone who signal to a society that it is engaging in pursuits whose strategic economic consequences are dangerous.

William F. Buckley, Jr. (1925–   )
On The Right, 28 November 1968

Corn doesn't grow in Chicago, and money doesn't grow on the [New York] Stock Exchange.

Martin Mayer (1928–   )
Wall Street: Men and Money, 1955

If a man loses his money in the [stock] market it is almost always [because of] his own greed, stupidity or gullibility. It is certainly never the fault of the exchanges, and it is very rarely the fault of his broker.

Martin Mayer
Wall Street: Men and Money

They used to tell a story about a small businessman, broke and friendless through no fault of his own, who came to Baron Rothschild and told the Baron his . . . tale of circumstance. Rothschild listened and said he would like to help, and then he thought for a moment. "I won't lend you any money," he said. "I'll do something better." He led the trembling businessman from the office and walked with him, arm in arm, across the floor of the London Exchange.

Martin Mayer
Wall Street: Men and Money

The best investment on *earth* is earth.

Louis Glickman (1933–   )
Quoted in the *New York Post,* 3 September 1957

Historically, the bankers have tried to portray themselves as leaders and tribal priests, and the banks have been built on the model of temples. I don't see any reason to believe bankers are any worse or any better than anyone else. But because they operate with a special product—money—there's more temptation.

Edward J. Kane (1935–   )
Ohio State University

Money Talks

Over the past several weeks, my back-group brethren and I have preached to you about the Second Coming of regional bank stock appreciation. Plunged into the depths over recent months . . . regional bank stocks, we suggested, would rise from the market abyss when a sign of the ongoing fundamental strengths of these companies was again reconfirmed to those of wavering faith in these investments. Wait no longer to position in these stocks, O ye of little faith, for the sign is upon us.

Frank J. Barkocy (1944–   )
Merrill Lynch
Quoted in the *New York Times*, 27 October 1985

There is nothing like the ticker tape except a woman—nothing that promises, hour after hour, day after day, such sudden developments; nothing that disappoints so often or occasionally fulfills with such unbelievable, passionate magnificence.

Walter Knowleton Gutman
Quoted in *Coronet*, March 1960

MICRO-ECONOMICS

Economics is a Greek word, *oikonomika,*
which literally means "the management of
household affairs." For a systematic thinker
like Aristotle, the family was the basic economic unit. Man and his property had to be
carefully understood—"First house, then
wife, then oxen for the plough," according to
Hesiod—if household affairs were to be run
efficiently. So would the State, a partnership
of families, have to be businesslike if men
were to live well. And so with modern business, if it is to be profitable. A systematic
approach to problems—how to quantify, to
focus, to evaluate and assess—is indispensable. Decisions have to be made; risks have
to be taken; forecasts have to be arrived at.
Business people do not have the time to re-
treat to Walden Pond, like Thoreau, to understand the "Economy" of life, but they know
daily the economic meaning of Thoreau's
dictum there: "In the long run men hit only
what they aim at."

THE LADDER OF FORTUNE.

The Ladder of Fortune, or Poor Richard *(1875), by Currier (1813–1888) & Ives (1824–1895). Illustration for Ben Franklin's* Poor Richard's Almanack.

Anyone who has to ask the cost can't afford it.

Anonymous

One white foot—try him, Two white feet—buy him, Three white feet—look well about him; Four white feet—go without him.

Anonymous horse-buyer's jingle

What costs nothing is worth nothing.

Anonymous

When you go to buy use your eyes, not your ears.

Czechoslovakian proverb

Small profits and quick returns.

English saying

Buying is cheaper than asking.

German proverb

The buyer needs a hundred eyes; the seller but one.

Italian proverb

The money you refuse will never do you any good.

Italian proverb

Getting money is like digging with a needle; spending it is like water soaking into sand.

Japanese proverb

Let the woman into Paradise: she'll bring her cow along.

Russian proverb

Money is like an eel in the hand.

Welsh proverb

Whatsoever thou takest in hand, remember the end, and thou shalt never do amiss.

Bible: Ecclesiasticus 7:36

If a man take no thought about what is distant, he will find sorrow near at hand.

> Confucius (551–479 B.C.)
> *The Confucian Analects*

He who purposes duly to manage any branch of economy should be well acquainted with the locality in which he undertakes to labor, and should be naturally clever, and by choice industrious and just; for if any one of these qualities be wanting, he will make many mistakes in the business which he intends to take in hand.

> Aristotle (384–322 B.C.)
> *Economics*

Cui bono? [To whose advantage? —profit? —benefit?]

> Cicero (106–43 B.C.)
> *Pro Milone*

Everything is worth what its purchaser will pay for it.

> Publilius Syrus (First century B.C.)
> *Sententiae*

In every enterprise consider where you would come out.

> Publilius Syrus
> *Sententiae*

You cannot put the same shoe on every foot.

> Publilius Syrus
> *Sententiae*

In every affair, consider what precedes and what follows and then undertake it.

> Epictetus (c. 50–120)
> *That Everything Is to Be Undertaken with Circumspection*

Nothing that is God's is obtainable by money.

> Tertullian (c.160–c.230)
> *Apologeticus*

A bargain is a bargain.

> Thomas Wilson (c. 1525–1581)
> *The Arte of Rhetorique*, 1553

Buy cheap, sell dear.

> Thomas Lodge (c. 1558–1625)
> *A Fig for Momus*, 1595

Some bargain's dear bought.

Sir John Davies (1569–1626)
The Scourge of Folly

Penny wise, pound foolish.

Robert Burton (1577–1640)
The Anatomy of Melancholy, 1621–1651

The value or worth of a man is . . . his price—that is to say, so much as would be given for the use of his power.

Thomas Hobbes (1588–1679)
Leviathan, 1651

On a good bargain think twice.

George Herbert (1593–1633)
Outlandish Proverbs, 1640

In everything one must consider the end.

Jean de la Fontaine (1621–1695)
Fables, 1668

Bankrupt of life, yet prodigal of ease.

John Dryden (1631–1700)
Absalom and Achitophel, 1680

The best way to suppose what may come is to remember what is passed.

George Savile, Marquess of Halifax (1633–1695)
Political, Moral and Miscellaneous Reflections, 1750

The first mistake belonging to business is the going into it. [business = public life]

George Savile, Marquess of Halifax
Political, Moral and Miscellaneous Reflections

The first Mistake in public Business, is the going into it.

Benjamin Franklin (1706–1790)
Poor Richard's Almanack, 1758

They who are of opinion that money will do everything may well be suspected to do everything for money.

George Savile, Marquess of Halifax
Political, Moral and Miscellaneous Reflections

He that is of opinion that Money will do every Thing may well be suspected of doing every Thing for Money.

Benjamin Franklin (1706–1790)
Poor Richard's Almanack, 1753

Just enough of a good thing is always too little.

George Savile, Marquess of Halifax
Political, Moral and Miscellaneous Reflections

Money gives an appearance of beauty even to ugliness; but everything becomes frightful with poverty.

Nicolas Boileau-Déspreaux (1636–1711)
Satires

He'll ne'er get a pennyworth that is afraid to ask a price.

Thomas Fuller (1654–1734)
Gnomologia, 1732

He that gets money before he gets wit
Will be but a short while master of it.

Thomas Fuller
Gnomologia

If you buy the cow take the tail into the bargain.

Thomas Fuller
Gnomologia

Money is a merry fellow.

Thomas Fuller
Gnomologia

Money was made for the free-hearted and generous.

John Gay (1688–1732)
The Beggar's Opera, 1728

When the well's dry, we know the worth of water.

Benjamin Franklin (1706–1790)
Poor Richard's Almanack, 1746

Mere parsimony is not economy. . . . Expense, and great expense, may be an essential part of true economy.

Economy is a distributive virtue, and consists not in saving but selection. Parsimony requires no providence, no sagacity, no powers of combination, no comparison, no judgment.

Edmund Burke (1729–1797)
Letter to a Noble Lord, 1796

There are some sensible folks who having great estates have wisdom enough too to spend them properly; there are others who are not less wise, perhaps, as knowing how to shift without 'em. Between these two degrees are they who spend their money dirtily, or get it so.

William Cowper (1731–1800)
Letter to Clotworthy Rowley, 2 September 1762

A business with an income at its heels
Furnishes always oil for its own wheels.

William Cowper
"Retirement," in *Poems,* 1782

She knows nothing of business, and is made to pay for everything through the nose.

Fanny Burney (1752–1840)
Cecilia, 1782

The almighty dollar, that great object of universal devotion throughout our land, seems to have no genuine devotees in these peculiar villages.

Washington Irving (1783–1859)
Wolfert's Roost, 1855

Whoso has sixpence is sovereign (to the length of sixpence) over all men; commands cooks to feed him, philosophers to teach him, kings to mount guard over him—to the length of sixpence.

Thomas Carlyle (1795–1881)
Sartor Resartus, 1833–1834

There are but two ways of paying debt: increase of industry in raising income, increase of thrift in laying out.

Thomas Carlyle
Past and Present, 1843

I am not fond of money, or anxious about it. But, though every day makes me less and less eager for wealth, every day shows me more and more strongly how necessary a competence is to a man who desires to be either great or useful.

Thomas Babington Macaulay (1800–1859)
Letter to Hannah M. Macaulay, 1833

Money Talks

Money, which represents the prose of life, and which is hardly spoken of in parlors without an apology, is, in its effects and laws, as beautiful as roses.

> Ralph Waldo Emerson (1803–1882)
> *Nominalist and Realist,* 1844

Money often costs too much.

> Ralph Waldo Emerson

Shallow men believe in luck.

> Ralph Waldo Emerson
> *Worship,* 1860

We often buy money very much too dear.

> William Makepeace Thackeray (1811–1863)
> *Barry Lyndon,* 1852

A man is rich in proportion to the number of things which he can afford to let alone.

> Henry David Thoreau (1817–1862)
> *Walden,* 1854

Our horizon is never quite at our elbows.

> Henry David Thoreau
> *Walden*

Our life is frittered away by detail. . . . Simplify, simplify.

> Henry David Thoreau
> *Walden*

The force of the guinea you have in your pocket depends wholly on the default of a guinea in your neighbor's pocket. If he did not want it, it would be of no use to you.

> John Ruskin (1819–1900)
> *Unto This Last,* 1862

Many priceless things can be bought.

> Marie Freifrau von Ebner-Eschenbach (1830–1916)

All business proceeds on beliefs, on judgments of probabilities, and not on certainties.

> Charles W. Eliot (1834–1926)

Life is the art of drawing sufficient conclusions from insufficient premises.

Samuel Butler (1835–1902)
Notebooks, 1912

Put all your eggs in the one basket and—WATCH THAT BAS-KET.

Mark Twain (1835–1910)
Pudd'nhead Wilson, 1894

Any man who has to ask about the annual upkeep of a yacht can't afford one.

Attributed to J. P. Morgan (1837–1913)

Certainty generally is illusion, and repose is not the destiny of man. [*The Path of the Law,* 1897]

Certitude is not the test of certainty. [*Natural Law,* 1918]
Oliver Wendell Holmes, Jr. (1841–1935)

What? You have voted a war with such rapidity and such indif-ference?
—Oh, it is a war of no importance. It will cost only eight million dollars.
And men?
—The men are included in the eight million.

Anatole France (1844–1924)

One of the difficult tasks in this world is to convince a woman that even a bargain costs money.

Edgar Watson Howe (1853–1937)

It is only by not paying one's bills that one can hope to live in the memory of the commercial classes.

Oscar Wilde (1854–1900)

What is a cynic? A man who knows the price of everything, and the value of nothing.

Oscar Wilde
Lady Windermere's Fan, 1892

Except during the nine months before he draws his first breath, no man manages his affairs as well as a tree does.

George Bernard Shaw (1856–1950)

Science is always wrong: it never solves a problem without creating ten more.

George Bernard Shaw

We have no more right to consume happiness without producing it than to consume wealth without producing it.

George Bernard Shaw
Candida, 1898

Form ever follows function.

Louis Henri Sullivan (1856–1924)
"The Tall Office Building Artistically Considered,"
Lippincott's Magazine, March 1896

When I think of all the sorrow and all the barrenness that has been wrought in my life by want of a few more pounds per annum than I was able to earn, I stand aghast at money's significance.

George Gissing (1857–1903)
The Private Papers of Henry Ryecroft, 1903

A good folly is worth whatever you pay for it.

George Ade (1866–1944)
Fables in Slang, 1899

Draw your salary before spending it.

George Ade
Forty Modern Fables, 1901

So far I haven't heard of anybody who wants to stop living on account of the cost.

Frank McKinney ("Kin") Hubbard (1868–1930)

When you pay high for the priceless, you're getting it cheap.

Joseph Duveen (1869–1939)

The engine which drives Enterprise is not Thrift, but Profit.

John Maynard Keynes (1883–1946)
A Treatise on Money, 1930

Practical men, who believe themselves to be quite exempt from any intellectual influences, are usually the slaves of some defunct economist. . . . It is ideas, not vested interests, which are dangerous for good or evil.

John Maynard Keynes
The General Theory of Employment, Interest and Money, 1936

Entrepreneurial profit . . . is the expression of the value of what the entrepreneur contributes to production in exactly the same sense that wages are the value expression of what the worker "produces." It is not a profit of exploitation any more than are wages.

Joseph Alois Schumpeter (1883–1950)
The Theory of Economic Development, 1934

We all know how the size of sums of money appears to vary in a remarkable way according as they are being paid in or paid out.

Julian Huxley (1887–1975)
Essays of a Biologist, 1923

Economy: cutting down other people's wages.

J. B. Morton ["Beachcomber"] (1893–1979)

It is better to know some of the questions than all of the answers.

James Thurber (1894–1961)

Armaments, universal debt and planned obsolescence—those are the three pillars of Western prosperity.

Aldous Huxley (1894–1963)
Island

Every young man should have a hobby. Learning how to handle money is the best one.

Jack Hurley (1897–1972)

Business more than any other occupation is a continual dealing with the future; it is a continual calculation, an instinctive exercise in foresight.

Henry R. Luce (1898–1967)
Speech quoted in *Fortune* promotional material, October 1960

A fool and his money are soon parted. What I want to know is how they got together in the first place.

Cyril Fletcher (1904–   )
BBC radio program, 28 May 1969

America's best buy for a nickel is a telephone call to the right man.

Ilka Chase (1905–1978)

My problem lies in reconciling my gross habits with my net income.

Errol Flynn (1909–1959)
Quoted in Mercer, *Great Lovers of the Movies*

Automation is not gadgeteering, it is not even engineering; it is a concept of the structure and order of economic life, the design of its basic patterns integrated into a harmonious, balanced, organic whole.

Peter F. Drucker (1909–)
America's Next Twenty Years, 1955

If a business is to be considered a continuous process, instead of a series of disjointed stop-and-go events, then the economic universe in which a business operates—and all the major events within it—must have rhyme, rhythm, or reason.

Peter F. Drucker
America's Next Twenty Years

Economics as a positive science is a body of tentatively accepted generalizations about economic phenomena that can be used to predict the consequences of changes in circumstances.

Milton Friedman (1912–)
Essays in Positive Economics, 1953

Fundamentally, there are only two ways of coordinating the economic activities of millions. One is central direction involving the use of coercion—the technique of the army and of the modern totalitarian state. The other is voluntary cooperation of individuals—the technique of the marketplace.

Milton Friedman
Capitalism and Freedom, 1962

What then is the present status of the classical theory of the firm? There can no longer be any doubt that the microassumptions of the theory, the assumptions of perfect rationality, are contrary to fact. It is not a question of approximations; they do not even remotely describe the processes that human beings use for making decisions in complex situations.

Herbert A. Simon (1916–)
Speech accepting the Nobel Prize in Economic Science, 1978

A large number of the ills of our business system come about as a result of the Detroit psychology. You lay off people when business falls, you add people madly as volume increases, and you strike them from the rolls as volume goes down again, rather than trying to strike an average that would restrain growth to something that could be sustainable.

Kenneth R. Andrews (1916–)
Harvard Business Review
Quoted in *Boston Magazine,* April 1983

Clearly money has something to do with life
—In fact, they've a lot in common, if you enquire:
You can't put off being young until you retire.

Philip Larkin (1922–)
"Money"

People who use stocks in a consistent and thoughtful way can't help but prosper over the long pull because they are betting on the future growth of the country—and that is as sound a bet as I know how to make.

Thomas R. Reeves (1923–)
Investors Diversified Services

A cult of equity has arisen: Buy because there's not enough to go around—the most dangerous and capricious reason to buy stock.

Carl E. Hathaway (1933–)
Morgan Guaranty

There is no harm in wanting to accomplish; the harm is in having to accomplish.

Hugh Prather (1938–)

BUSINESS
AND
GOVERNMENT

Today, government *is* business—big business—and the old claim that it is best when it governs least seems useless. All businesses, big and small, are in one way or another tied to government's power to tax and regulate, to print money and produce services, to conserve goods and exploit resources. Capital formation has become as much a goal of government as of business. The history of this rivalry is stormy. "History suggests," according to Milton Friedman, "that capitalism is a necessary condition for political freedom." "Clearly," he adds, "it is not a sufficient condition" (*Capitalism and Freedom,* 1962). In that insufficiency hangs a tale—the subject of the quotes in this section.

The Bosses of the Senate, *by J. Keppler. In* Puck, *23 January 1889.*

I'm glad Sears is taking on someone its own size.

Anonymous
Sears
[On Sears' suing the US Government, 1979]

Peace makes money and money makes war.

French proverb

Under capitalism man exploits man; under socialism the reverse is true.

Polish proverb

Put not your trust in princes.

Bible: Psalms 146:3

Endless money forms the sinews of war.

Cicero (106–43 B.C.)
Philippics

And I say that Your Highnesses ought not to consent that any foreigner does business or sets foot here, except Christian Catholics, since this was the end and the beginning of the enterprise, that it should be for the enhancement and glory of the Christian religion, nor should anyone who is not a good Christian come to these parts.

Christopher Columbus (1451–1506)
Journal of the First Voyage, 27 November 1492

War seldom enters but where wealth allures.

John Dryden (1631–1700)
The Hind and the Panther, 1687

He who findeth fault meaneth to buy.

Thomas Fuller (1654–1734)
Gnomologia, 1732

No nation was ever ruined by trade.

Benjamin Franklin (1706–1790)
Thoughts on Commercial Subjects

Excise—A hateful tax levied upon commodities, and adjudged not by the common judges of property, but wretches hired by those to whom excise is paid.

Samuel Johnson (1709–1784)
Dictionary, 1755

A monopoly granted either to an individual or to a trading company has the same effect as a secret in trade or manufactures. The monopolists, by keeping the market constantly understocked, by never fully supplying the effectual demand, sell their commodities much above the natural price, and raise their emoluments, whether they consist in wages or profit, greatly above their natural rate.

Adam Smith (1723–1790)
Wealth of Nations, 1776

People of the same trade seldom meet together, even for merriment and diversion, but the conversation ends in a conspiracy against the public, or in some contrivance to raise prices. It is impossible indeed to prevent such meetings by any law which either could be executed, or would be consistent with liberty and justice.

Adam Smith
Wealth of Nations

To found a great empire for the sole purpose of raising up a people of customers, may at first sight appear a project fit only for a nation of shopkeepers. It is, however, a project altogether unfit for a nation of shopkeepers; but extremely fit for a nation whose government is influenced by shopkeepers.

Adam Smith
Wealth of Nations

To prohibit a great people, however, from making all that they can of every part of their own produce, or from employing their stock and industry in the way that they judge most advantageous to themselves, is a manifest violation of the most sacred rights of mankind.

Adam Smith
Wealth of Nations

Let your discourse with men of business be short and comprehensive.

George Washington (1732–1799)
Early copy-book, before 1748

It accorded well with two favorite ideas of mine, of leaving commerce free, and never keeping an unnecessary soldier.

Thomas Jefferson (1743–1826)

It is better to abolish monopolies in all cases than not to do it in any.

Thomas Jefferson
Letter to James Madison, 1788

The merchants will manage commerce the better, the more they are left free to manage for themselves.

Thomas Jefferson
Letter to Gideon Granger, 1800

Still one thing more, fellow citizens—a wise and frugal government, which shall restrain men from injuring one another, which shall leave them otherwise free to regulate their own pursuits of industry and improvement, and shall not take from the mouth of labor the bread it has earned. This is the sum of good government, and this is necessary to close the circle of our felicities.

Thomas Jefferson
First Inaugural Address, 4 March 1801

A national debt, if it is not excessive, will be to us a national blessing. It will be a powerful cement of our Union. It will also create a necessity for keeping up taxation to a degree which, without being oppressive, will be a spur to industry, remote as we are from Europe, and shall be from danger. It were otherwise to be feared our popular maxim would incline us to too great parsimony and indulgence. We labor less now than any civilized nation of Europe; and a habit of labor is as essential to the health and vigor of . . . minds and bodies, as it is conducive to the welfare of the state.

Alexander Hamilton (1755–1804)
Letter to Robert Morris, 1781

The power to tax involves the power to destroy.

John Marshall (1755–1835)
US Supreme Court, 1819

The power to tax is not the power to destroy while this Court sits.

Oliver Wendell Holmes, Jr. (1841–1935)
US Supreme Court, 1928

The Bank is trying to kill me, but I will kill it.
Andrew Jackson (1767–1845)
To his vice president and successor Van Buren

There are persons who constantly clamor. They complain of oppression, speculation, and pernicious influence of wealth. They cry out loudly against all banks and corporations, and a means by which small capitalists become united in order to produce important and beneficial results. They carry on mad hostility against all established institutions. They would choke the fountain of industry and dry all streams.
Daniel Webster (1782–1852)
Speech, US Senate, 1838

Commerce is entitled to a complete and efficient protection in all its legal rights, but the moment it presumes to control a country, or to substitute its fluctuating expedients for the high principles of natural justice that ought to lie at the root of every political system, it should be frowned on, and rebuked.
James Fenimore Cooper (1789–1851)
In *The American Democrat,* 1838

The philosopher and lover of man have much harm to say of trade: but the historian will see that trade was the principle of liberty; that trade planted America and destroyed Feudalism; that it makes peace and keeps peace.

Trade is a plant which grows wherever there is peace, as soon as there is peace, and as long as there is peace.
Ralph Waldo Emerson (1803–1882)
The Young American, 1844

To secure to each laborer the whole product of his labor, or as nearly as possible, is a worthy object of any good government.
Abraham Lincoln (1809–1865)
Speech, 1 December 1847

No matter who reigns, the merchant reigns.
Henry Ward Beecher (1813–1887)
Proverbs from Plymouth Pulpit, 1887

We don't want to fight, but, by jingo, if we do,
We've got the ships, we've got the men, we've got the money, too.
G. W. Hunt (c. 1829–1904)
Song, 1878

It was from America that the plain ideas that men ought to mind their business, and that the nation is responsible to Heaven for the acts of the State—ideas long locked in the breast of solitary thinkers, and hidden among Latin folios—burst forth like a conqueror upon the world they were destined to transform, under the title of the Rights of Man . . . and the principle gained ground, that a nation can never abandon its fate to an authority it cannot control.

> Lord Acton (1834–1902)
> *The History of Freedom and Other Essays*, 1907

Great cases like hard cases make bad law.
> Oliver Wendell Holmes, Jr. (1841–1935)
> US Supreme Court, 1904

Taxes are what we pay for a civilized society.
> Oliver Wendell Holmes, Jr.
> US Supreme Court 1904

Subject to compensation when compensation is due, the legislature may forbid or restrict any business when it has sufficient force of public opinion behind it.
> Oliver Wendell Holmes, Jr.
> US Supreme Court, 1926

Big business is not dangerous because it is big, but because its bigness is an unwholesome inflation created by privileges and exemptions which it ought not to enjoy.
> Woodrow Wilson (1856–1924)
> Acceptance speech, Democratic National Convention, 7 July 1912

The real fight today is against inhuman, relentless exercise of capitalistic power. . . . The present struggle in which we are engaged is for social and industrial justice.
> Louis D. Brandeis (1856–1941)
> US Supreme Court

Progress needs the brakeman, but the brakeman should not spend all his time putting on the brakes.
> Elbert Hubbard (1856–1915)

The very word "panic" denotes a fear so great as to make those who experience it to become for the time being crazy; and when crazy with fear men both say and do foolish things, and, moreover, always seek for someone to hold responsible for their sufferings. . . . Surely, you can hardly believe that all this is due to my action in enforcing the law against wealthy wrong-doers.

Theodore Roosevelt (1858–1919)

Where a trust becomes a monopoly the state has an immediate right to interfere.

Theodore Roosevelt
Message to New York Legislature, 3 January 1900

It is difficult for me to understand why there should be this belief in Wall Street that I am a wild-eyed revolutionist. . . . I wish to do everything in my power to aid every honest business man, and the dishonest business man I wish to punish simply as I would punish the dishonest man of any type.

Theodore Roosevelt
Letter to Jacob Schiff, head of Kuhn, Loeb, 28 March 1907

I hold it to be our duty to see that the wage-worker, the small producer, the ordinary consumer, shall get their fair share of the benefit of business prosperity. But it either is or ought to be evident to everyone that business has to prosper before anybody can get any benefit from it.

Theodore Roosevelt
Address to Ohio Constitutional Convention, 1 February 1912

We demand that big business give the people a square deal; in return we must insist that when any one engaged in big business honestly endeavors to do right he shall himself be given a square deal.

Theodore Roosevelt
Autobiography, 1913

You shall not press down upon the brow of labor this crown of thorns. You shall not crucify mankind upon a cross of gold.

William Jennings Bryan (1860–1925)
Speech at National Democratic Convention, 1896

Why shouldn't the American people take half my money from me? I took all of it from them.

Edward A. Filene (1860–1937)
Quoted in Schlesinger, *The Coming of The New Deal*, 1959

Do you want to know the cause of war? It is capitalism, greed, the dirty hunger for dollars. Take away the capitalist and you will sweep war from the earth.

Henry Ford (1863–1947)
Interview, *Detroit News*

I niver knew a pollytician to go wrong ontil he's been contaminated by contact with a business man.

Finley Peter Dunne (1867–1936)

"Th' American nation in th' Sixth Ward is a fine people," he says. "They love th' eagle," he says, "on th' back iv a dollar."

Finley Peter Dunne
Mr. Dooley in Peace and in War, 1898

When the corruption of American politics was laid on the threshold of business—like a bastard on the doorstep of his father—a tremendous disturbance resulted.

Vernon Louis Parrington (1871–1929)

America recognizes no aristocracy save those who work.

Calvin Coolidge (1872–1933)

This country would not be a land of opportunity, America would not be America, if the people were shackled with government monopolies.

Calvin Coolidge
Acceptance speech, 14 August 1924

Corporations have at different times been so far unable to distinguish freedom of speech from freedom of lying that their freedom has to be curbed.

Carl Becker (1873–1945)

The primary aim of all government regulation of the economic life of the community should be, not to supplant the system of private economic enterprise, but to make it work.

Carl Becker

The inherent vice of capitalism is the unequal sharing of blessings; the inherent virtue of socialism is the equal sharing of miseries.

Winston Churchill (1874–1965)

Lobbyists are the touts of protected industries.

Winston Churchill

Some see private enterprise as a predatory target to be shot, others as a cow to be milked, but few are those who see it as a sturdy horse pulling the wagon.

Winston Churchill

The business of government is to keep the government out of business—that is, unless business needs government aid.

Will Rogers (1879–1935)

England elects a Labor Government. When a man goes in for politics over here, he has no time to labor, and any man that labors has no time to fool with politics. Over there politics is an obligation; over here it's a business.

Will Rogers
Autobiography, 1949

Let Wall Street have a nightmare and the whole country has to help get them back in bed again.

Will Rogers
Autobiography

Every day I have matutinal indisposition that emanates from the nauseous effluvia of that oppressive slave statute.

John L. Lewis (1880–1969)
On the Taft-Hartley Act, 1954

All forms of government fall when it comes up to the question of bread—bread for the family, something to eat. Bread to a man with a hungry family comes first—before his union, before his citizenship, before his church affiliation. Bread!

John L. Lewis
In the *Saturday Evening Post,* 12 October 1963

In the first months of N.R.A. [National Recovery Administration] it seemed as though a great part of the business world had "got religion."

Donald Richberg (1881–1960)
Quoted in Schlesinger, *The Coming of The New Deal,* 1959

No business is above Government; and Government must be empowered to deal adequately with any business that tries to rise above Government.

Franklin D. Roosevelt (1882–1945)

Out of this modern civilization economic royalists carved new dynasties. . . . The royalists of the economic order have conceded that political freedom was the business of the Government, but they have maintained that economic slavery was nobody's business.

> Franklin D. Roosevelt
> Speech, accepting renomination for President, 27 June 1936

Private enterprise is ceasing to be free enterprise.

Private enterprise, indeed, became too private. It became privileged enterprise, not free enterprise.

> Franklin D. Roosevelt

Beware of that profound enemy of the free enterprise system who pays lip-service to free competition—but also labels every anti-trust prosecution as a "persecution."

> Franklin D. Roosevelt
> Speech, Chicago, 28 October 1944

Capitalism inevitably and by virtue of the very logic of its civilization creates, educates and subsidizes a vested interest in social unrest.

> Joseph Alois Schumpeter (1883–1950)
> *Capitalism, Socialism and Democracy,* 1942

Businessmen don't elect Presidents anyway. The common people elect them. I proved that back in 1948.

> Harry S. Truman (1884–1972)
> Statement at press conference, New York, 9 January 1964

For many years I thought that what was good for our country was good for General Motors, and vice versa.

> Harry S. Truman
> Statement at press conference, New York

The fear of capitalism has compelled socialism to widen freedom, and the fear of socialism has compelled capitalism to increase equality.

> Will (1885–1981) and Ariel (1898–1981) Durant

Conflicting economic interest is relatively unimportant as a cause of war.

> Frank Hyneman Knight (1885–1974)
> *Freedom and Reform,* 1947

In the councils of government, we must guard against the acquisition of unwarranted influence, whether sought or unsought, by the military-industrial complex. The potential for the disastrous rise of misplaced power exists and will persist.

Dwight D. Eisenhower (1890–1969)
Farewell address, 17 January 1961

What is good for the country is good for General Motors, and what's good for General Motors is good for the country.

Charles E. Wilson (1890–1961)
Before a congressional committee, 1952

It would be madness to let the purposes or the methods of private enterprise set the habits of the age of atomic energy.

Harold Laski (1893–1950)
Plan or Perish, 1945

If small business goes, big business does not have any future except to become the economic arm of a totalitarian state.

Philip D. Reed (1899–   )

Only in time of peace can the wastes of capitalism be tolerated.

F. R. Scott (1899–   )

When the men in Russia foul up, they are dismissed, sometimes losing their necks. But we protect those who fail and press them to the government bosom.

Hyman G. Rickover (1900–   )
US Navy

If it is not in the interest of the public it is not in the interest of business.

Joseph H. Defrees (1905–   )

What's good for the United States is good for the New York Stock Exchange. But what's good for the New York Stock Exchange might not be good for the United States.

William McChesney Martin, Jr. (1906–   )
Federal Reserve Board

We haven't done anything for business this week—but it is only Monday morning.

Lyndon B. Johnson (1908–1973)
Speech to US Chamber of Commerce, 27 April 1964

When the government talks about "raising capital" it means printing it. That's not very creative, but it's what we're going to do.

Peter F. Drucker (1909–   )

There is nothing mutually exclusive about making a profit and serving the needs of society. Personally, I have no doubt that the companies that will be the most profitable in the long run will be those that serve society best. . . . Society will reward those that help unclog our highways, rebuild and vitalize our cities, cleanse our streams and conquer poverty and disease—not those whose pursuit of the dollar blinds them to such needs.

Charles B. McCoy (1909–   )
Du Pont

Business is a workhorse, a mule—and do you ask a mule to be a Pegasus? Business should not be a government or a church. Its main responsibility is to be politically responsible. Businessmen should advocate and support the right kind of public policies. But I'm suspicious of organizations taking over the functions of government.

Kenneth E. Boulding (1910–   )
University of Colorado

Some 25 years ago, you could make a long distance call on a privately owned telephone system from San Francisco to New York for $28. For that same amount of money, you could send 1,376 letters. Today, you could make the same telephone call for two dollars and a half and for that amount you can only send 41 letters. So the government is investigating the Bell System!

Ronald Reagan (1911–   )
When Governor of California

Capitalism in the United States has undergone profound modification, not just under the New Deal but through a consensus that continued to grow after the New Deal. . . . Government in the U.S. today is a senior partner in every business in the country.

Norman Cousins (1912–   )

Inflation is one form of taxation that can be imposed without legislation.

Milton Friedman (1912–   )

What kind of society isn't structured on greed? The problem of social organization is how to set up an arrangement under which greed will do the least harm; capitalism is that kind of a system.

Milton Friedman
In *Playboy*, 1973

Free enterprise is dead in some segments of our economy and seemingly on its death bed in others. It, however, is not beyond cure. The medicine I propose is a large dose of antitrust.

Philip A. Hart (1912–1976)
US Senate

A necessary condition to a healthy economy is freedom from the petty tyranny of massive government regulation.

Gerald R. Ford (1913–   )

The system that has delivered more self-respect to more human beings than any other system devised by man deserves to be treated with more respect itself.

Richard M. Nixon (1913–   )
Before US Chamber of Commerce

It seems to me that our responsible public officials should be doing more important things than writing Federal specifications for panty-hose or the size of lettering on a can of sardines.

Max E. Brunk (1914–   )
Cornell University

If we in business cannot put the brakes on this creeping socialism, the free enterprise system will become a thing of the past.

Barton A. Cummings (1914–   )

Goverment today sits as an invisible partner of every company, every family and every individual in the country.

William L. Wearly (1915–   )
Ingersoll-Rand

It should be made clear to the American people that business cannot and should not attempt to solve all of our present social ills. . . . It is no more reasonable to expect business to do everything than it is to expect government to do everything.

Arjay Miller (1916–   )
Ford Motor

If a businessman wants to have an impact, he better get his facts organized, go to Washington to present them and be prepared to take the heat if he's wrong. We are not always right. But, by God, if we pull our facts together and tell our story we'll come out okay because the facts of business are pretty good.

Irving S. Shapiro (1916–   )
Du Pont

I think there is a great deal to be said for the Ralph Nader approach—stand outside and holler at everybody.

Betty Furness (1916–   )
New York State Consumer Protection Board

American business today is rated as low as lawyers. And when you reach that low you don't have much further to go—unless you are a member of Congress.

John B. Connally, Jr. (1917–   )

Like so many in American life, businessmen have made their share of mistakes, and often the decisions they made were not popular with those who feared change. But . . . it is worth remembering that 200 years ago the American Revolution itself started as a businessmen's revolution. That is, after all, what the Boston Tea Party and the Stamp Act protests were all about. And it is also worth remembering that *one* hundred years ago it was the businessman who began translating the "heroic age of invention" into a better life for Americans, and the world. In our own day, it has been the businessman, with his practical development of medical technology, the computer, the jet, the Xerox machine, new sources of energy, anti-pollution devices, and much else, who has continued to enhance the quality of life not only for the select and the wealthy but for all of us. This is what the American Revolution, with its dedication to free enterprise, promised. And it would be tragic if America were to allow progress to be blunted.

Francis J. Dunleavy (1917–   )
International Telephone and Telegraph

At times, the demands of government are so contradictory or idiotic as to give you a feeling of schizophrenia, since every pull of every bureaucratic demand may be accompanied by the shove of being denounced for the very ability to meet the demand. On Monday, you are exhorted, as a major multinational, to marshal your resources abroad to help close the growing balance-ofpayments gap; but—on Tuesday—you, along with every other multinational, are denounced as imperialists threatening to undermine democracy. On Wednesday, you are importuned, as the provider of 80 per cent of all jobs, to bend every effort to provide still more; but—on Thursday—you confront a corporate income tax that impairs your ability to increase employment or modernize your plants. On Friday, you are urged, as a company engaged in oil production, to stretch every muscle to increase supplies and thus help meet the energy shortage; but—on Saturday—you are prevented from doing anything about it because the regulators refuse to believe anything the oil and gas companies say. On the seventh day you rest—if you can.

J. Paul Sticht (1917–   )
R. J. Reynolds

It is appalling that there are now so few business leaders within the Carter administration. In fact, we often find that key elements of our overgrown, unresponsive Federal bureaucracy are headed by yesterday's hard-shell antibusiness activists. Business leaders have the skill and experience to help contribute to our society's progress. Perhaps they can be encouraged now to regain the determination to serve in and with government. We need a new era of business statesmanship to enable the United States to reach beyond yesterday's achievements.

J. Paul Sticht
R. J. Reynolds

The costs of government regulation fall ultimately on the same people who are benefited by regulation. The problem is not to abolish sin at any cost, but to find the best balance between benefits to people as citizens and costs to people as consumers.

Henry Ford II (1917–   )

Henry Ford, in his day, was looked upon as an industrial hero. Today, he would be regarded as a monopolizing fiend upon whom the antitrust prosecutors should be unleashed. The 1921 Ford Company, with its more than 60 percent share of the market, would today be called a dominant firm and charged with violating the antitrust laws.

Yale Brozen (1917–   )
University of Chicago

Too many politicians are running on the platform of more taxation of big corporations—claiming, in effect, that if they can raise corporate taxes they will then have enough money to buy ointment for every social ill. This may appear to us to be seminal lunacy.

> Donald T. Regan (1918–   )
> Merrill Lynch, Pierce, Fenner & Smith

The bureaucracies that constitute governments determinedly and too often successfully murder free enterprise and the ability of a person or a business to profit. Yet the profitable life of both of them is essential to keep these vampires fed. A familiar mystery plot—how to keep the vampires alive without killing their food source!

> Malcolm S. Forbes (1919–   )

Wages and price controls are a military solution to an economic problem.

> Irving Kristol (1920–   )

The business and financial community of this country is the soft underbelly of freedom. Whenever there's been a choice between their own purse and the national interest, the business and financial community in this country has always voted for their own purse.

> Lane Kirkland (1922–   )
> AFL-CIO

When the Republicans are in, business wins because it owns the Party. When the Democrats are in, business wins because it extracts the price of "business confidence."

> Lane Kirkland
> AFL-CIO

Frankly, I'd like to see the government get out of war altogether and leave the whole field to private industry.

> Joseph Heller (1923–   )
> *Catch-22*, 1961

The problem of the paralyzing labor union is essentially the problem of government. It is government that immunized labor unions from the anti-monopoly laws.

> William F. Buckley, Jr. (1925–   )
> *National Review*, 5 May 1964

If the government assaults a citizen, puts him through grand jury meetings and public trials—and fails to make its case, leaving the intended victim exonerated but exhausted, why shouldn't the government assume at least the financial burden of the exonerated defendant?

William F. Buckley, Jr.
On The Right, 3 December 1968

Wealth is not the fruit of labor but the result of organized protected robbery. Rich people are no longer respectable people, they are nothing more than flesh-eating animals, jackals and vultures which wallow in the people's blood.

Frantz Fanon (1925–1961)

Defensive research, what companies call defending themselves against government, is a rising share of corporate research and development. In many ways, regulations are creating a subtle bureaucratization of industry. You don't take risks; you think like a bureaucrat.

Murray L. Weidenbaum (1927–   )
Center for the Study of American Business,
Washington University

Capitalism . . . is outrageously unjust; it requires a continuing maldistribution of wealth in order to exist. . . . We live in the twilight of an epoch. . . . I am absolutely convinced that we are moving toward some kind of planned economy.

Michael Harrington (1928–   )

Surely we should be as concerned about the erosion of capitalism as we may be impatient about the slowness of our moral advancement.

Frankly, I am far more concerned about the ability of our corporations to raise equity capital than I am about whether we can raise the level of management conduct.

Roderick M. Hills (1931–   )
US Securities and Exchange Commission

Nothing is illegal if 100 businessmen decide to do it.

Andrew Young (1932–   )

They tend to a heavy, authoritarian style of management: oppressive and bullying to those who work for them; servile and sycophantic to those under whose direction they serve.

They are casual with the truth. They are preoccupied with control: controlling information, controlling dissent, controlling their media images, controlling leaks, controlling emotions. Order becomes a higher value than creativity, innovation, resourcefulness, commitment.

> Michael Pertschuk (1933–   )
> *The Performance of the Federal*
> *Trade Commission,* 1977–1984

We surveyed our members as to what's troubling them. Number 1 is government. Number 2 is government. Number 3 is government. And number 4 is government.

> Richard L. Lesher (1933–   )
> US Chamber of Commerce

The government is basically controlled by the industries which it purports to regulate.

> Ralph Nader (1934–   )

I have a consistent rule: The American people should know as much about the Pentagon as the Soviet Union and China do, as much about General Motors as Ford does, and as much about City Bank as Chase Manhattan does.

> Ralph Nader

Nothing short of a Federal investigation can begin to disclose the abuses which have woven a fine web of mutually implicating relationships between businessmen and government officials.

> Ralph Nader

The truth is that on many issues, consumerists are firing popguns compared to some of the big howitzers that business rolls into Washington.

> Elizabeth Hanford Dole (1936–   )
> Federal Trade Commission

Business in America should not be the captive handmaiden of government. It should be an institution responding efficiently to consumers in a free market.

> James C. Miller III (1942–   )
> Federal Trade Commission

A completely planned economy ensures that when no bacon is delivered, no eggs are delivered at the same time.

> Leo Frain
> Quoted in the London *Sunday Telegraph,* January 1965

Money Talks

Why is it legitimate to invite a member of Congress to make a speech before a trade association and pay him $5,000 when everyone knows he has nothing to say? Isn't that a subtle form of corruption?

Peter Nehemkis
UCLA School of Management

MACRO-
ECONOMICS

It is a commonplace that today's economies are global and interdependent and, on a smaller scale, that a nation's economy results from a compromise of mutual interests—capital, labor, natural resources, government. For the organization of this book, Macroeconomics is a section of quotations that concern the function of business in a national or world economy, including world trade. Another section, Business and Government, has quotations that deal with the challenges and threats of government intervention. Yet another section, Microeconomics, has to do with the internal economics of business and the business of life. Quotations about conflicting ideologies, major economic events such as The Crash of 1929, and world market competition all inform Macroeconomics.

Antitrust cartoon, by Dalrymple. In Puck, *7 May 1890.*

Business will be fine in 1929.

Anonymous

Japan   Just in time.
USA   Just in case.
China   All at once.

Anonymous

Trade should be free, even in Hell.

Dutch saying

What is the difference between Capitalism and Communism?
Capitalism is the exploitation of man by man; communism is the
reverse.

Polish joke

Money is a guarantee that we may have what we want in the
future. Though we need nothing at the moment, it insures the
possibility of satisfying a new desire when it arises.

Aristotle (384–322 B.C.)
Nichomachean Ethics

Not Philip, but Philip's gold, took the cities of Greece.

Plutarch (46–120)
Lives

A man who is furnished with arguments from the mint will
convince his antagonist much sooner than one who draws them
from reason and philosophy.

Joseph Addison (1672–1719)
The Spectator, 4 December 1711

Gold is a wonderful clearer of the understanding; it dissipates
every doubt and scruple in an instant, accommodates itself to the
meanest capacities, silences the loud and clamorous, and brings
over the most obstinate and inflexible.

Joseph Addison
The Spectator

The round of nations in a golden chain.

> James Thomson (1700–1748)
> *The Seasons: Summer,* 1727

The iron law of wages.

> Anne Robert Jacques Turgot (1727–1781)
> *Réflexions sur la formation et la distribution des richesses,* 1766

Honor sinks where commerce long prevails.

> Oliver Goldsmith (1728–1774)
> *The Traveller,* 1765

No nation ought to be without a debt. A national debt is a national bond; and when it bears no interest, is in no case a grievance.

> Thomas Paine (1737–1809)
> *Common Sense,* 1776

I am for free commerce with all nations.

> Thomas Jefferson (1743–1826)
> Letter to Elbridge Gerry, 1799

The selfish spirit of commerce knows no country, and feels no passion or principle but that of gain.

> Thomas Jefferson
> Letter to Larkin Smith, 1809

Merchants have no country. The mere spot they stand on does not constitute so strong an attachment as that from which they draw their gains.

> Thomas Jefferson
> Letter to Horatio G. Spafford, 1814

On the stimulation of the economy by a national bank
This, I regard, in some shape or other, as an expedient essential to our safety and success. . . . There is no other that can give to government that extensive and systematic credit which the defect of our revenues makes indispensably necessary to its operations. . . . The tendency of a national bank is to increase public and private credit. The former [public credit] gives power to the State, for the protection of its rights and interests; and the latter [private credit] facilitates and extends the operations of commerce among individuals. Industry is increased, commodities are multi-

plied, agriculture and manufactures flourish, and herein consists the true wealth and prosperity of a state.

Alexander Hamilton (1755–1804)
Letter to Robert Morris, 1781

On the purpose of a national bank

Public utility is more truly the object of public banks than private profit. And it is the business of government to constitute them on such principles that, while the latter will result in a sufficient degree to afford competent motives to engage in them, the former be not made subservient to it.

Alexander Hamilton
Report on a National Bank, 1790

When nations grow old the Arts grow cold
And Commerce settles on every tree.

William Blake (1757–1827)

In matters of commerce the fault of the Dutch
Is offering too little and asking too much.
The French are with equal advantage content,
So we clap on Dutch bottoms just 20%.

George Canning (1770–1827)
Dispatch to Sir Charles Bagot,
British minister at The Hague, 31 January 1826

Labor, like all other things which are purchased and sold, and which may be increased or diminished in quantity, has its natural and its market price. The natural price of labor is that price which is necessary to enable the laborers, one with another, to subsist and perpetuate their race, without either increase or diminution.

David Ricardo (1772–1823)
On the Principles of Political Economy and Taxation, 1817

Wages should be left to the fair and free competition of the market, and should never be controlled by the interference of the legislature.

David Ricardo
On the Principles of Political Economy and Taxation

Nothing contributes so much to the prosperity and happiness of a country as high profits.

David Ricardo
On Protection to Agriculture, 1820

The call for free trade is as unavailing as the cry of a spoiled child for the moon. It never has existed; it never will exist.

Henry Clay (1777–1852)
Speech in the US Senate, 2 February 1832

Can anybody remember when the times were not hard and money not scarce?

Ralph Waldo Emerson (1803–1882)
Works and Days, 1870

Trade, that pride and darling of our ocean, that educator of nations, that benefactor in spite of itself, ends in shameful defaulting, bubble, and bankruptcy, all over the world.

Ralph Waldo Emerson
Works and Days

Free trade is not a principle; it is an expedient.

Benjamin Disraeli (1804–1881)
Speech in the House of Commons, 25 April 1843

The commerce of the world is conducted by the strong, and usually it operates against the weak.

Henry Ward Beecher (1813–1887)
Proverbs from Plymouth Pulpit, 1887

Through want of enterprise and faith men are where they are, buying and selling, and spending their lives like serfs.

Henry David Thoreau (1817–1862)
Walden, 1854

In the pre-capitalist stages of society, commerce rules industry. The reverse is true of modern society.

Karl Marx (1818–1883)
Das Kapital, 1867–1883

Whenever money is the principal object of life with either man or nation, it is both got ill, and spent ill; and does harm both in the getting and spending.

John Ruskin (1819–1900)
The Crown of Wild Olive, 1866

Isn't this a billion dollar country?

Charles Foster (1828–1904)
Retorting to a gibe about "a million dollar Congress"

All progress is based upon a universal innate desire on the part of every organism to live beyond its income.

Samuel Butler (1835–1902)
Notebooks, 1912

So long as all the increased wealth which modern progress brings goes but to build up great fortunes, to increase luxury and make sharper the contrast between the House of Have and the House of Want, progress is not real and cannot be permanent.

Henry George (1839–1897)
Progress and Poverty, 1879

Large consumption is at the basis of saving in manufacture, and hence high wages contribute their share to progress.

Thomas B. Reed (1839–1902)
US House, 1894

America, the land of unlimited possibilities.

Ludwig Max Goldberger (1848–1913)
*Land of Unlimited Possibilities: Observations on
Economic Life in the United States of America*, 1903

No man knows where his business ends and his neighbor's begins.

Edgar Watson Howe (1853–1937)

What this country needs is a good five-cent cigar.

Thomas Riley Marshall (1854–1925)
US Vice President
Remark to John Crockett, chief Senate clerk, 1917

For four wicked centuries the world has dreamed this foolish dream of efficiency; and the end is not yet.

George Bernard Shaw (1856–1950)
John Bull's Other Island, 1907

If all economists were laid end to end, they would not reach a conclusion.

Attributed to George Bernard Shaw

Depressions may bring people closer to the church, but so do funerals.

Clarence Darrow (1857–1938)

There is much more hope for humanity from manufacturers who enjoy their work than from those who continue in irksome business with the object of founding hospitals.

Alfred North Whitehead (1861–1947)

The United States is like a gigantic boiler. Once the fire is lighted under it there is no limit to the power it can generate.

Edward, Viscount Grey of Fallodon (1862–1933)
Quoted in Churchill, *Their Finest Hour,* 1949

I think some folks are foolish to pay what it costs to live.

Frank McKinney ("Kin") Hubbard (1868–1930)

Only one fellow in ten thousand understands the currency question, and we meet him every day.

Frank McKinney ("Kin") Hubbard

Who recalls when folks got along without something if it cost too much?

Frank McKinney ("Kin") Hubbard

It's called political economy because it has nothing to do with either politics or economy.

Stephen Leacock (1869–1944)

Economic distress will teach men, if anything can, that realities are less dangerous than fancies, that fact-finding is more effective than fault-finding.

Carl Becker (1873–1945)
Progress and Power, 1935

The growth of a large business is merely the survival of the fittest. . . . The American Beauty rose can be produced in the splendor and fragrance which bring cheer to the beholder only by sacrificing the early buds which grow up around it.

John D. Rockefeller, Jr. (1874–1960)

If you would know what the Lord God thinks of money, you have only to look at those to whom He gives it.

Maurice Baring (1874–1945)
Quoted by Dorothy Parker
In *Writers at Work: First Series,* 1958

In an English ship, they say, it is poor grub, poor pay, and easy work; in an American ship, good grub, good pay, and hard work. And this is applicable to the working populations of both countries.

Jack London (1876–1916)
The People of the Abyss, 1903

A theory can be proved by experiment; but no path leads from experiment to the birth of a theory.

Albert Einstein (1879–1955)
Quoted in the London *Sunday Times,* 18 July 1976

Invest in inflation. It's the only thing going up.

Will Rogers (1879–1935)

What this country needs is a good five-cent nickel.

Franklin P. Adams [F.P.A.] (1881–1960)
Quoted in *Liberty,* 2 January 1943
[Said in 1932]

It is Enterprise which builds and improves the world's possessions. . . . If Enterprise is afoot, wealth accumulates, whatever may be happening to Thrift; and if Enterprise is asleep, Wealth decays, whatever Thrift may be doing.

John Maynard Keynes (1883–1946)
A Treatise on Money, 1930

Lenin is said to have declared that the best way to destroy the capitalist system was to debauch the currency. By a continuing process of inflation, governments can confiscate, secretly and unobserved, an important part of the wealth of their citizens. . . . Lenin was certainly right.

John Maynard Keynes
Essay in Persuasion, 1931

There are no intrinsic reasons for the scarcity of capital.

John Maynard Keynes
The General Theory of Employment, Interest and Money, 1936

Without development there is no profit, without profit no development. For the capitalist system it must be added further that without profit there would be no accumulation of wealth.

Joseph Alois Schumpeter (1883–1950)
The Theory of Economic Development, 1934

There is inherent in the capitalist system a tendency toward self-destruction.

Joseph Alois Schumpeter
Capitalism, Socialism and Democracy, 1942

Space beckons us to the three brass balls of the pawnbroker.

Lord Brabazon (1884–1964)
Speech, House of Lords, November 1962

It's a recession when your neighbor loses his job; it's a depression when you lose your own.

Harry S. Truman (1884–1972)
Quoted in the *Observer*, 6 April 1958

We have before us the fiendishness of business competition and the world war, passion and wrongdoing, antagonism between classes and moral depravity within them, economic tyranny above and the slave spirit below.

Karl Barth (1886–1968)
The Word of God and the Word of Man, 1957

Inflation is like sin; every government denounces it and every government practices it.

Sir Frederick Leith-Ross (1887–1968)
Quoted in the *Observer*, 30 June 1957

The instability of the economy is equaled only by the instability of economists.

John Henry Williams (1887–1980)
Harvard University
Quoted in the *New York Times*, 2 June 1956

Unemployed purchasing power means unemployed labor and unemployed labor means human want in the midst of plenty. This is the most challenging paradox of modern times.

Henry A. Wallace (1888–1965)
Address, 1934

At its present cost, life is worth about thirty cents on the dollar.

Don Herold (1889–1966)

The forces of a capitalist society, if left unchecked, tend to make the rich richer and the poor poorer.

Jawaharlal Nehru (1889–1964)
Credo, in the *New York Times*, 7 September 1958

There's nothing surer,
The rich get rich and the poor get poorer,
In the meantime, in between time,
Ain't we got fun.

Gus Kahn (1886–1941) and Raymond B. Egan (1890–1952)
Ain't We Got Fun, 1921

Capitalism did not arise because capitalists stole the land . . . but because it was more efficient than feudalism. It will perish because it is not merely less efficient than socialism, but actually self-destructive.

J. B. S. Haldane (1892–1964)

A little inflation is like a little pregnancy—it keeps on growing.

Leon Henderson (1895–   )

The Swiss who are not a people so much as a neat clean quite solvent business.

William Faulkner (1897–1962)
Intruder in the Dust, 1948

The ascending spiral of greatness in America has risen because industry has produced wealth, which in turn has supported educational institutions, which in turn have supplied leadership to industry in order that with each succeeding generation it might produce more wealth.

Wallace F. Bennett (1898–   )
Bennett's

There are compelling reasons for the proposition that the actual importance of business monopolies for inflation is quite small compared with that of labor unions.

Gottfried Haberler (1900–   )
Economic Growth and Stability, 1974

If all the rich men in the world divided up their money amongst themselves, there wouldn't be enough to go round.

Christina Stead (1902–1983)
House of All Nations, 1938

We have learned the lesson that when opportunities for profit diminish, opportunities for jobs likewise disappear.

Executive Council, American Federation of Labor, 1940

If you mean by capitalism the God-given right of a few big corporations to make all the decisions that will affect millions of workers and consumers and to exclude everyone else from discussing and examining those decisions, then the unions are threatening capitalism.

Max Lerner (1902–   )
Actions and Passions, 1949

Lenin was the first to discover that capitalism "inevitably" caused war; and he discovered this only when the first World War was already being fought. Of course he was right. Since every great state was capitalist in 1914, capitalism obviously "caused" the First World War; but just as obviously it had "caused" the previous generation of Peace.

A. J. P. Taylor (1906–   )
The Origins of the Second World War, 1961

At General Motors, we realize we are an important influence in the scheme of things. . . . Maybe that's why some people regard us as a menace.

James M. Roche (1906–   )
General Motors

I'm sure a crash like 1929 will happen again. The only thing is that one doesn't know when. All it takes for another collapse is for the memories of the last insanity to dull.

John Kenneth Galbraith (1908–   )
Harvard University

I am a devout support of more contacts, contacts, contacts which would bring more contracts, contracts, contracts.

Nikolai S. Patolichev (1908–   )
Minister of Foreign Trade, USSR
Advocating Soviet-US Trade

Free enterprise: A huge area of the American economy is still noticeable to observers with peripheral vision after they subtract the public sector, conglomerates, federally supported agriculture, monopolies, duopolies, and oligopolies.

Bernard Rosenberg (1908–   )

After all, for mankind as a whole there are no exports. We did not start developing by obtaining foreign exchange from Mars or the moon. Mankind is a closed society.

E. F. Schumacher (1911–1977)
Small Is Beautiful, 1973

There is no way profits can be too high. Profits are the fuel cells that energize our economy. . . . Profits are the barometer of our economic climate, the standard by which we measure our economic well-being and the sole source of funding all civic, social, cultural and educational activities. To understand this is to recognize that the higher the profits, the more financial support for the better life.

Allen P. Stults (1913–)
American Bankers Association

Profits are part of the mechanism by which society decides what it wants to see produced.

Henry C. Wallich (1914–)
Quoted in *Newsweek,* 1967)

When Tokyo went into the bicycle business, first came repair work cannibalizing imported bicycles, then manufacture of some of the parts most in demand for repair, then manufacture of still more parts, finally assembly of whole, Tokyo-made bicycles.

Jane Jacobs (1916–)
Cities and the Wealth of Nations:
Principles of Economic Life, 1984

Backward cities must trade most heavily with other backward cities. Any crude city-made goods that Venice might have produced—imitations of Constantinople's least sophisticated products—would have been of no interest in Constantinople.

Jane Jacobs
Cities and the Wealth of Nations:
Principles of Economic Life

National or imperial currencies give faulty and destructive feedback to city economies.

Jane Jacobs
Cities and the Wealth of Nations:
Principles of Economic Life

We live in a world of trade.

John B. Connally, Jr. (1917–)

"The millionaires in all countries," wrote Lenin, "are behaving on an international scale in a way that deserves our heartiest thanks." No one should be surprised that the Communists continue to get their most effective co-operation from the frightened, ignorant and despairing rich, driven by dark impulses beyond their own control to conspire in their own destruction.

Arthur M. Schlesinger, Jr. (1917–   )
The Vital Center, 1949

Those who invented the law of supply and demand have no right to complain when this law works against their interest.

Anwar el-Sadat (1918–1981)
On the West's oil crisis, 1978

American companies put 25 cents of every dollar they invested last year into foreign operations, and goddammit, that's not free trade.

William Winpisinger (1924–   )
International Association of Machinists

Every day, in every way, things are getting worse and worse.

William F. Buckley, Jr. (1925–   )
National Review, 2 July 1963

Inflation in the Sixties was a nuisance to be endured, like varicose veins or French foreign policy.

Bernard Levin (1928–   )
The Pendulum Years, 1971

A fair price for oil is whatever you can get plus ten per cent.

Ali Ahmed Attiga (1931–   )
OPEC, 1974

Remember this, Griffin. The revolution eats its own. Capitalism recreates itself.

Mordecai Richler (1931–   )
Cocksure, 1968

One problem one-bank holding companies have is the misunderstanding that if it's big, it's bad. In our economy you need large companies and their large capital to progress. After all, you can't build an L-1011 in your garage.

Robert H. Volk (1932–   )
Unionamerica

Macroeconomics

Our lost momentum in the world's marketplaces is largely our own fault. Back when we were basking in the dreams of an economic never-never land, Numbers 2 and 3 and on down the line were gearing up for just what we've always said American society thrived on—competition. We thought they could never catch up, but they tried harder, and here we are—to paraphrase an old American slogan, a Sony in every house and two Toyotas in every garage.

George A. Keyworth III (1939–)
US Office of Science and Technology Policy

A study of economics usually reveals that the best time to buy anything is last year.

Marty Allen

We've got imports from Belgium, Japan, Italy, Taiwan, West Germany, France, South Africa, Korea and Romania—all of them selling lower than Kaiser. Now, you tell me how the West Coast is a natural market for Romania, and I'll eat everything they sell.

Mark Anthony
Kaiser Steel

PRODUCTION
&
OPERATIONS

If, as Peter F. Drucker says, "Business has two functions—marketing and innovation," then the innovative half, production, has to be responsive to new technology and to political, social and economic reality. If someone can make a better mousetrap, if somehow, somewhere, he can produce it cheaply and deliver it profitably, then all producers of mousetraps have to become more productive, or cease making mousetraps. But the production of goods and services isn't limited to necessities, and without effective marketing no amount of capacity planning and quality control is worth the cost and trouble. To quote Mr. Drucker again, "Profitability is the sovereign criterion of the enterprise." Between people who make products and people who sell them there is tension—creative tension, in successful business operations. When there's trouble, as W. Edwards Deming once observed, "management is 85% of the problem." The quotes included in this section offer observations on how to operate effectively and produce abundantly.

Samuel Slater's textile mill (1790s), on the Blackstone River, Pawtucket, Rhode Island.

Eight Rules for Office Workers in 1872

1. Office employees each day will fill lamps, clean chimneys and trim wicks. Wash windows once a week.
2. Each clerk will bring in a bucket of water and a scuttle of coal for the day's business.
3. Make your pens carefully. You may whittle nibs to your individual taste.
4. Men employees will be given an evening off each week for courting purposes, or two evenings a week if they go regularly to church.
5. After thirteen hours of labor in the office, the employee should spend the remaining time reading the Bible and other good books.
6. Every employee should lay aside from each pay day a goodly sum of his earnings for his benefit during his declining years so that he will not become a burden on society.
7. Any employee who smokes Spanish cigars, uses liquor in any form, or frequents pool and public halls or gets shaved in a barber shop, will give good reason to suspect his worth, intentions, integrity and honesty.
8. The employee who has performed his labor faithfully and without fault for five years, will be given an increase of five cents per day in his pay, providing profits from business permit it.

Anonymous
Boston *Sunday Herald*, 5 October 1958

Entrances are wide; exits are narrow.

Anonymous

Even the best plan degenerates into work.

Anonymous

Everything but the squeal.

Anonymous

FIFO: First In, First Out.

Anonymous

FISH: First In, Still Here.

Anonymous

GIGO: Garbage in, garbage out.

Anonymous computer jargon

Get a bigger hammer.

Anonymous

I seen my duty and I done it.
  You seen your duty and you done it noble.

Anonymous

In Japan the award for quality and productivity is the Deming Prize. In the United States it's an antitrust suit.

Anonymous

It's easier to get into something than to get out of it.

Anonymous

KISS: Keep It Simple, Stupid.

Anonymous

LIFO: Last In, First Out.

Anonymous

Make it right the first time.

Anonymous

Project Planning Meeting: The activity which brings all work and progress to a standstill.

Anonymous

Spartan simplicity must be observed. Nothing will be done merely because it contributes to beauty, convenience, comfort, or prestige.

Anonymous US Army directive

The difficult we do immediately. The impossible takes a little longer.

Anonymous US Army slogan

The first 90% of the project takes the first 90% of the time. The last 10% of the project takes the last 90% of the time.

Anonymous

There is no crisis to which academics will not respond with a seminar.

Anonymous

Time is of the essence.

Anonymous

Use it up, wear it out;
Make it do, or do without.

Anonymous New England maxim

We try to operate with the heart and sensitivity of a small company and the brains of a big one.

Anonymous
Whirlpool

When in doubt, stock it out.

Anonymous

You can't inspect quality into the product.

Anonymous

Hold back some goods for a thousand days and you will be sure to sell at a profit.

Chinese proverb

You can't make an omelet without breaking eggs.

French proverb

Non multa sed multum. [Not many but much: Not quantity but quality.]

Latin proverb

Luck is infatuated with the efficient.

Persian proverb

The eggs do not teach the hen.

Russian proverb

Where there is no vision, the people perish.

Bible: Proverbs 29:18

Observe due measure, for right timing is in all things the most important factor.

Hesiod (c. 700 B.C.)
Works and Days

The dawn speeds a man on his journey, and speeds him too in his work.

> Hesiod
> *Works and Days*

The beginning is the most important part of the work.

> Plato (c. 428–348 B.C.)
> *Republic*

He who has begun has half done. Dare to be wise; begin!

> Horace (65–8 B.C.)
> *Epistles*

More haste, less speed.

> [In Suetonius, *Augustus.* Greek proverb; in Latin, *Festina lente*.]
> Caesar Augustus (63 B.C.–A.D. 14)

Do not turn back when you are just at the goal.

> Publilius Syrus (First century B.C.)
> *Sententiae*

Fortune is not satisfied with inflicting one calamity.

> Publilius Syrus
> *Sententiae*

It is a very hard undertaking to seek to please everybody.

> Publilius Syrus
> *Sententiae*

It takes a long time to bring excellence to maturity.

> Publilius Syrus
> *Sententiae*

Nothing can be done at once hastily and prudently.

> Publilius Syrus
> *Sententiae*

Ther nys no werkman, whatsoevere he be,
That may bothe werke wel and hastily.

> Geoffrey Chaucer (c. 1343–1400)
> *Merchant's Tale, Canterbury Tales*

Practice is the best of all instructors.

> Publilius Syrus
> *Sententiae*

It is quality rather than quantity that matters.

Seneca (c. 4 B.C.–A.D. 65)
Epistles

No great thing is created suddenly, anymore than a bunch of grapes or a fig. If you tell me that you desire a fig, I answer you that there must be time. Let it first blossom, then bear fruit, then ripen.

Epictetus (c. 50–120)
Discourses

Practice yourself, for heaven's sake, in little things; and thence proceed to greater.

Epictetus
Discourses

The materials are indifferent, but the use we make of them is not a matter of indifference.

Epictetus
Discourses

Everything has two handles—by one of which it ought to be carried and by the other not.

Epictetus
Encheiridion

A hard beginning maketh a good ending.

John Heywood (c. 1497–c. 1580)
Proverbs, 1546

Haste maketh waste.

John Heywood
Proverbs

Hold their noses to the grindstone.

John Heywood
Proverbs

Many hands make light work.

John Heywood
Proverbs

Of a good beginning cometh a good end.

John Heywood
Proverbs

Rome was not built in one day.

John Heywood
Proverbs

Deal closely and secretly in all your affairs and business, and before you enterprise anything, do you after courteous and gentle manner ask counsel.

Be most faithful and just in all your accounts with every man, and defraud no man willingly not the value of one farthing.

John Browne (early 16th century)
The Merchants Avizo [The Merchant's Guide], 1589

He that will not apply new remedies must expect new evils; for time is the greatest innovator.

Francis Bacon (1561–1626)
Of Innovations, 1612

To choose time is to save time.

Francis Bacon
Of Dispatch, 1625

You take my life
When you do take the means whereby I live.

William Shakespeare (1564–1616)
The Merchant of Venice, 1596–1597

For want of a nail the shoe is lost, for want of a shoe the horse is lost, for want of a horse the rider is lost.

George Herbert (1593–1633)
Jacula Prudentum, 1651

The mill cannot grind with the water that's past.

George Herbert
Jacula Prudentum

Thursday come, and the week is gone.

George Herbert
Jacula Prudentum

The first thing that apprentices should have in mind is love and fear of God.

Second . . . faithfulness to their masters.

Third . . . blind obedience to their masters.

Fourth . . . great respect toward their masters; speaking only with cap in hand.

Fifth . . . to keep their masters' affairs secret.

Sixth . . . to keep up a good understanding with their comrades and other servants of the house, not quarreling or fighting.

Seventh and last is to dress modestly, but properly.

> Jacques Savary (17th century)
> *Le Parfait Négociant [The Perfect Merchant]*, 1675

By the work one knows the workman.

> Jean de la Fontaine (1621–1695)
> *Fables*, 1668

Busy till night, pleasing myself mightily to see what a deal of business goes off a man's hands when he stays by it.

> Samuel Pepys (1633–1703)
> *Diary*, 14 January 1667

I find that two days' neglect of business do give more discontent in mind than ten times the pleasure thereof can repair again, be it what it will.

> Samuel Pepys
> *Diary*

Misspending a man's time is a kind of self-homicide.

> George Savile, Marquess of Halifax (1633–1695)
> *Political, Moral and Miscellaneous Reflections*, 1750

Cheat me in the price but not in the goods.

> Thomas Fuller (1654–1734)
> *Gnomologia*, 1732

The less one has to do, the less time one finds to do it in.

> Lord Chesterfield (1694–1773)

Whatever is worth doing at all, is worth doing well.

> Lord Chesterfield
> *Letters*, 10 March 1746

Money Talks

He that riseth late must trot all day, and shall scarce overtake his business at night.

Benjamin Franklin (1706–1790)
Poor Richard's Almanack, 1742

Dost thou love life? Then do not squander Time; for that's the stuff Life is made of.

Benjamin Franklin
Poor Richard's Almanack, 1746

Lost time is never found again.

Benjamin Franklin
Poor Richard's Almanack, 1748

Remember that time is money.

Benjamin Franklin
Advice to a Young Tradesman, 1748

Consumption is the sole end and purpose of production; and the interest of the producer ought to be attended to only so far as it may be necessary for promoting that of the consumer.

Adam Smith (1723–1790)
Wealth of Nations, 1776

While we have hand to labor, then, let us never wish to see our citizens occupied at a work-bench or twirling a distaff. . . . For the general operations of manufacture let our workshops remain in Europe. It is better to carry provisions and materials to work-men there than bring them to the provisions and materials and with them their manners and principles.

Thomas Jefferson (1743–1826)
In Churchill, *The Age of Revolution,* 1957

Without haste, but without rest.

Johann Wolfgang von Goethe (1749–1832)
Motto

Gentlemen, tell your troubles to Mr. Whitney. He can make anything. [*Or:* He can do anything. The widow of the Revolutionary War general, Nathanael Greene, speaking of her guest at Mulberry Grove, Eli Whitney (1765–1825), inventor of the cotton gin.]

Catherine Greene (?–1812)
Quoted in Whitridge, "Eli Whitney—Nemesis of the South,"
American Heritage, April 1955

Men reluctantly quit one course of occupation and livelihood for another, unless invited to it by very apparent and proximate advantages.

Alexander Hamilton (1755–1804)
Report on the Subject of Manufactures, 1790

And did those feet in ancient time
Walk upon England's mountains green?
And was the holy Lamb of God
On England's pleasant pastures seen?

And did the Countenance Divine
Shine forth upon our clouded hills?
And was Jerusalem builded here
Among these dark Satanic Mills?

William Blake (1757–1827)
Milton, c. 1809

My invention was new and distinct. . . . I should have had no difficulty in causing my rights to be respected if it had been less valuable and used only by a small portion of the community. [Of the worthlessness of the cotton gin to the inventor]

Eli Whitney (1765–1825)
Letter to Robert Fulton, quoted in Whitridge, "Eli Whitney—Nemesis of the South," *American Heritage,* April 1955

PRESIDENT JACKSON: I understand you taught us how to spin, so as to rival Great Britain in her manufactures; you set all these thousands of spindles to work, which I have been delighted in viewing, and which have made so many happy, by a lucrative employment.

SAMUEL SLATER: Yes, sir, I suppose that I gave out the psalm, and they have been singing to the tune ever since.

Samuel Slater (1768–1835)
Quoted in Welles, "Father of Our Factory System,"
American Heritage, April 1958

Since the introduction of inanimate mechanism into British man-
ufactories, man, with few exceptions, has been treated as a sec-
ondary and inferior machine; and far more attention has been
given to perfect the raw materials of wood and metals than those
of body and mind. Give but due reflection to the subject, and you
will find that man, even as an instrument for the creation of
wealth, may be still greatly improved.

Robert Owen (1771–1858)
*A New View of Society or Essays on the Principle of the Formation of the
Human Character and the Application of the Principle of Practice,* 1813

I am no longer . . . clerk of the Firm of &c. I am Retired Leisure.
I am to be met with in trim gardens. I am already come to be
known by my vacant face and careless gesture, perambulating at
no fixed pace, nor with any settled purpose. I walk about; not to
and from. They tell me, a certain *cum dignitate* air, that has been
buried so long with my other good parts, has begun to shoot forth
in my person. I grow into gentility perceptibly. When I take up a
newspaper, it is to read the state of the operat. *Opus operandum
est.* I have done all that I came into this world to do. I have
worked task work, and have the rest of the day to myself.

Charles Lamb (1775–1834)
"The Superannuated Man," *Essays of Elia,* 1835

But what most astonishes me in the United States, is not so much
the marvelous grandeur of some undertakings, as the innumerable
multitude of small ones.

Alexis de Tocqueville (1805–1859)
Democracy in America, 1835

Soon shall thy power, unconquered Steam! afar
Drag the swift barge and drive the rapid car.

Charles Robert Darwin (1809–1882)

For I dipped into the future, far as human eye could see,
Saw the Vision of the world, and all the wonder that would be;
Saw the heavens fill with commerce, argosies of magic sails,
Pilots of the purple twilight, dropping down with costly bales.

Alfred, Lord Tennyson (1809–1892)
Locksley Hall, 1842

Skewered through and through with office pens and bound hand
and foot with red tape.

Charles Dickens (1812–1870)
David Copperfield, 1849–1850

132

Those who have most to do, and are willing to work, will find the most time.

Samuel Smiles (1812–1904)
Self-Help, 1859
Quoted by Smiles as a saying

The eye may see for the hand, but not for the mind.

Henry David Thoreau (1817–1862)
A Week on the Concord and Merrimack Rivers, 1849

As for doing good, that is one of the professions which are full.

Henry David Thoreau
Walden, 1854

To him whose elastic and vigorous thought keeps pace with the sun, the day is a perpetual morning.

Henry David Thoreau
Walden

Through gale or calm, now swift, now slack, yet steadily
    careering;
Type of the modern—emblem of motion and power—pulse of the
    continent,
For once come serve the Muse and merge in verse, even as here
    I see thee,
With storm and buffeting gusts of wind and falling snow.

Walt Whitman (1819–1892)
"To a Locomotive in Winter," *Leaves of Grass,* 1891

Reflect upon the extraordinary advance which machines have made during the last few hundred years, and note how slowly the animal and vegetable kingdoms are advancing. The more highly organized machines are creatures not so much of yesterday, as of the last five minutes, so to speak, in comparison with past time.

Samuel Butler (1835–1902)
Erewhon, 1872

There is but one rule among Americans—the tools to those who can use them.

Andrew Carnegie (1835–1919)
Autobiography, 1920

The causes which most disturbed or accelerated the normal progress of society in antiquity were the appearance of great men; in modern times they have been the appearance of great inventions.

William Edward Hartpole Lecky (1838–1903)
History of European Morals, 1869

The riders in a race do not stop short when they reach the goal. There is a little finishing canter before coming to a standstill. There is time to hear the kind voice of friends and to say to one's self: "The work is done." But just as one says that, the answer comes: "The race is over, but the work never is done while the power to work remains." The canter that brings you to a standstill need not be only coming to rest. It cannot be, while you still live. For to live is to function. That is all there is to living.

Oliver Wendell Holmes, Jr. (1841–1935)
Radio address on his ninetieth birthday, 1931

Everything comes to him who hustles while he waits.

Thomas A. Edison (1847–1931)
Golden Book, April 1931

I am long on ideas, but short on time. I expect to live to be only about a hundred.

Thomas A. Edison
Golden Book

There is no expedient to which a man will not go to avoid the real labor of thinking.

Thomas A. Edison
Posted on signs in the Edison laboratories

The fact is, that civilization requires slaves. The Greeks were quite right there. Unless there are slaves to do the ugly, horrible, uninteresting work, culture and contemplation become almost impossible. Human slavery is wrong, insecure, and demoralizing. On mechanical slavery, on the slavery of the machine, the future of the world depends.

Oscar Wilde (1854–1900)
The Soul of Man Under Socialism, 1895

One machine can do the work of fifty ordinary men. No machine can do the work of one extraordinary man.

Elbert Hubbard (1856–1915)

A high-priced man. [I.e., ready to work for more money. I.e., willing "to do exactly as he's told from morning till night." I.e., able to work, with "the aid of a man better educated than he is," in accordance with the principles of scientific management. I.e., "first, the careful selection of the workman, and, second and third, the method of first inducing and then training and helping the workman to work according to the scientific method." I.e., "the science of laboring through time study." I.e., *not* "a manner which is usual under the management of 'initiative and incentive.'"]

Frederick W. Taylor (1856–1915)
The Principles of Scientific Management, 1911

In almost all of the mechanic arts the science which underlies each workman's act is so great and amounts to so much that the workman who is best suited actually to do the work is incapable (either through lack of education or through insufficient mental capacity) of understanding this science.

Frederick W. Taylor
The Principles of Scientific Management

Nothing is ever done in this world until men are prepared to kill one another if it is not done.

George Bernard Shaw (1856–1950)
Major Barbara, 1907

The outcome of any serious research can only be to make two questions grow where only one grew before.

Thorstein Veblen (1857–1929)
The Place of Science in Modern Civilization, 1919

Give them quality. That's the best kind of advertising.

Milton S. Hershey (1857–1945)
Hershey

The greatest task before civilization at present is to make machines what they ought to be, the slaves, instead of the masters of men.

Havelock Ellis (1859–1939)
Little Essays of Love and Virtue, 1922

Civilization advances by extending the number of important operations which we can perform without thinking about them.

Alfred North Whitehead (1861–1947)
An Introduction to Mathematics, 1911

Mass production is not merely quantity production; for this may be had with none of the prerequisites of mass production. Nor is it merely machine production, which may also exist without any resemblance to mass production. Mass production is the focusing upon a manufacturing project of the principles of power, accuracy, economy, system, continuity, and speed. And the normal result is a productive organization that delivers in quantities a useful commodity of standard material, workmanship, and design at minimum cost.

> Henry Ford (1863–1947)

Everybody wants to be someplace he ain't. As soon as he gets there he wants to go right back.

> Henry Ford

Everybody wants to go from A to B sitting down.

> William S. Knudsen (1879–1948)
> Ford Motor
> In Livesay, *American Made,* 1979

I can find methods of manufacturing that will make high wages. If you cut wages, you just cut the number of your customers.

> Henry Ford

If you think of "standardization" as the best that you know today, but which is to be improved tomorrow—you get somewhere.

> Henry Ford

It is not the employer who pays wages—he only handles the money. It is the product that pays wages.

> Henry Ford

Any color, so long as it's black.

> Attributed to Henry Ford
> Of the colors available on the Model T Ford car

The working of great institutions is mainly the result of a vast mass of routine, petty malice, self interest, carelessness, and sheer mistake. Only a residual fraction is thought.

> George Santayana (1863–1952)
> *The Crime of Galileo*

From the savings made by greater efficiency in production—that is, in the time we have saved from other occupations—we have added the automobile and the good road, the movies, the radio and the phonograph directly to the standard of living. We have increased the diffusion of electric light, power, telephone, plumbing, better housing, and a dozen other things. Some feel that in all this we are deadening the soul of man by machine production and standardization. . . . I may observe that the man who has a standard telephone, a standard bathtub, a standard electric light, a standard radio, and one and a half hours' more daily leisure is more of a man and has a fuller life and more individuality than he has without the tools for varying his life.

Herbert Hoover (1874–1964)

The factory was very fine;
He wished it all the modern speed.
Yet, after all, 'twas not divine,
That is to say, 'twas not a church.
He never would assume that he'd
Be any institution's need.
But he said then and still would say
If there should ever come a day
When industry seemed like to die
Because he left it in the lurch,
Or even merely seemed to pine
For want of his approval, why,
Come get him—they knew where to search.

Robert Frost (1874–1963)
"A Lone Striker, or, Without Prejudice to Industry"

How many times it thundered before Franklin took the hint! How many apples fell on Newton's head before he took the hint! Nature is always hinting at us. It hints over and over again. And suddenly we take the hint.

Robert Frost

There may be enough poetry in the whirr of our machines so that our machine age will become immortal.

Owen D. Young (1874–1962)
General Electric

The machine threatens all achievement.

Rainer Maria Rilke (1875–1926)
Sonnets to Orpheus, 1923

Money Talks

We tore the iron from the mountain's hold,
  By blasting fires we smithied it to steel;
Out of the shapeless stone we learned to mold
  The sweeping bow, the rectilinear keel;
We hewed the pine to plank, we split the fir,
We pulled the myriad flax to fashion her.

Out of a million lives our knowledge came,
  A million subtle craftsmen forged the means;
Steam was our handmaid and our servant flame,
  Water our strength—all bowed to our machines.
Out of the rock, the tree, the springing herb
We built this wandering beauty so superb.

John Masefield (1878–1967)
The Ship and Her Makers: "The Workers," 1914

Work smarter, not harder.

Allan Mogensen and Lillian Gilbreth (1878–1972)

Hog butcher for the World,
Tool Maker, Stacker of Wheat,
Player with Railroads and the Nation's Freight Handler;
Stormy, husky, brawling,
City of the Big Shoulders.

Carl Sandburg (1878–1967)
Chicago, 1916

Worst of any, however, were the fertilizer men, and those who served in the cooking rooms. These people could not be shown to the visitor—for the odor of a fertilizer man would scare any ordinary visitor at a hundred yards, and as for the other men, who worked in tank rooms full of steam, and in some of which there were open vats near the level of the floor, their peculiar trouble was that they fell into the vats; and when they were fished out, there was never enough of them left to be worth exhibiting— sometimes they would be overlooked for days, till all but the bones of them had gone out to the world as Durham's Pure Leaf Lard!

Upton Sinclair (1878–1968)
The Jungle, 1906

Who is responsible for this work of development [in the Aircraft Ministry] on which so much depends? To whom must the praise be given? To the boys in the back rooms. They do not sit in the limelight. But they are the men who do the work.

Lord Beaverbrook (1879–1964)
Broadcast, 1941

We must put a stop to paper "management" and switch to genuine, businesslike, Bolshevik work. Let one chairman and several vice-chairmen remain at the head of a combine. That will be quite enough for its management. The other members of the board should be sent to the factories and mills. That will be far more useful, both for the work and for themselves.

Joseph Stalin (1879–1953)
New Methods of Work, New Methods of Management, 1931

All democratic theories, whether socialistic or bourgeois, necessarily take in some concept of the dignity of labor. If the have-not were deprived of this delusion that his sufferings on the assembly line are somehow laudable and agreeable to God, there would be little left in his ego save a bellyache. Nevertheless, a delusion is a delusion, and this is one of the worst. It arises out of confusing the pride of workmanship of the artist with the dogged, painful docility of the machine. The difference is important and enormous. If he got no reward whatever, the artist would go on working just the same; his actual reward, in fact, is often so little that he almost starves. But suppose a garment worker got nothing for his labor: would he go on working just the same? Can one imagine his submitting voluntarily to hardship and sore want that he might express his soul in 200 more pairs of ladies' pants?

H. L. Mencken (1880–1956)
Prejudices, Third series, 1922

Up, to the office . . . and so to bed.

Franklin P. Adams [F. P. A.] (1881–1960)

Why only twelve?
—That's the original number.
Well, go out and get thousands.

Attributed to Samuel Goldwyn (1882–1974)
When filming *The Last Supper*

A good composer does not imitate; he steals.

Igor Stravinsky (1882–1971)

Supercapitalism would like all babies to be born the same length so that cradles could be standardized, all children to like the same toys, all men to dress in the same uniform, to read the same book, to have the same tastes at the cinema, and all to desire a so-called labor-saving machine.

Benito Mussolini (1883–1945)
Fascism—Doctrine and Institutions, 1935

Money Talks

The number one book of the ages was written by a committee, and it was called The Bible.

Louis B. Mayer (1885–1957)
Said to writers who complained
about changes made in their work

It is altogether possible that we may wear the earth out even before we blow it up.

Lyman Bryson (1888–1959)
An Outline of Man's Knowledge of the Modern World, ed. Bryson, 1960

Work is a form of nervousness.

Don Herold (1889–1966)

Work is the greatest thing in the world, so we should always save some of it for tomorrow.

Don Herold

DOMIN: What sort of worker do you think is the best from a practical point of view?

HELENA: Perhaps the one who is most honest and hard-working.

DOMIN: No; the one that is the cheapest. The one whose requirements are the smallest. Young Rossum invented a worker with the minimum amount of requirements. He had to simplify him. He rejected everything that did not contribute directly to the progress of work—everything that makes man more expensive. In fact, he rejected man and made the Robot. My dear Miss Glory, the Robots are not people. Mechanically they are more perfect than we are, they have an enormously developed intelligence; but they have no soul.

Karel Čapek (1890–1938)
R.U.R. (Rossum's Universal Robots), 1923

The Oriental civilization is built primarily on human labor as the source of power whereas the modern civilization of the West is built on the basis of the power of machinery. . . . It is a difference in degree which in the course of time has almost amounted to a difference in kind.

Hu Shih (1891–1962)
"The Civilizations of the East and the West,"
in *Whither Mankind,* edited by
Charles A. Beard, 1928

Every person in the United States has thirty-five invisible slaves working for him. . . . The American workman is not a wage slave, but a boss of a considerable force, whether he realizes it or not.

Thomas T. Read (1893–   )
"The American Secret," *Atlantic,* March 1927

Discovery consists of seeing what everybody has seen and thinking what nobody has thought.

> Albert Szent-Györgyi von Nagyrapolt (1893–   )
> In Good, *The Scientist Speculates*

A squat gray building of only thirty-four stories. Over the main entrance the words, CENTRAL LONDON HATCHERY AND CONDITIONING CENTER, and, in a shield, the World State's motto, COMMUNITY, IDENTITY, STABILITY.

> Aldous Huxley (1894–1963)
> *Brave New World*, 1932 [opening paragraph]

Wintriness responded to wintriness. The overalls of the workers were white, their hands gloved with a pale corpse-colored rubber.

> Aldous Huxley
> *Brave New World*

Any labor that accepts the conditions of competition with slave labor, accepts the conditions of slave labor, and is essentially slave labor.

> Norbert Wiener (1894–1964)
> *Cybernetics*, 1948

There is no rate of pay at which a United States pick-and-shovel laborer can live which is low enough to compete with the work of a steam shovel as an excavator.

> Norbert Wiener
> *Cybernetics*

The man doesn't merely give orders to the machine while the machine blindly obeys. There must be a dialogue in which the machine acquaints the machine-tender with the difficulties of the task to be accomplished and reinterprets the machine-tender's orders so as to perform these tasks in the best possible way. The best possible way is capable of a sharp mathematical definition.

> Norbert Wiener
> *The Tempter*, 1959

The future offers very little hope for those who expect that our new mechanical slaves will offer us a world in which we may rest from thinking. Help us they may, but at the cost of supreme demands upon our honesty and our intelligence. The world of the future will be an ever more demanding struggle against the limitations of our intelligence, not a comfortable hammock in which we can lie down to be waited upon by our robot slaves.

> Norbert Wiener
> *God and Golem, Inc.*, 1964

Synergy means behavior of whole systems unpredicted by the behavior of their parts.

R. Buckminster Fuller (1895–1983)
What I Have Learned, 1966

However far modern science and technics have fallen short of their inherent possibilities, they have taught mankind at least one lesson: Nothing is impossible.

Lewis Mumford (1895–   )
Technics and Civilization, 1934

As the flights got longer
the Wright brothers got backers,
engaged in lawsuits,
lay in their beds at night sleepless with the whine of phantom
millions, worse than the mosquitoes at Kitty Hawk.
. . . .
Aeronautics became the sport of the day
The Wrights don't seem to have been very much impressed by
the upholstery and the braid and the gold medals and the parades
of plush horses,
they remained practical mechanics
and insisted on doing all their own work themselves,
even to filling the gasolinetank.

John Dos Passos (1896–1970)
U.S.A., 1937

They were home for Christmas in Dayton, Ohio, where they'd
been born in the seventies of a family who had been settled west
of the Alleghenies since eighteen fourteen, in Dayton, Ohio, where
they'd been to grammarschool and highschool and joined their
father's church and played baseball and hockey and worked out on
the parallel bars and the flying swing and sold newspapers and
built themselves a printingpress out of odds and ends from the
junkheap and flown kites and tinkered with mechanical con-
traptions and gone around town as boys doing odd jobs to turn an
honest penny. [Wilbur and Orville Wright]

John Dos Passos
U.S.A.

This island is almost made of coal and surrounded by fish. Only
an organizing genius could produce a shortage of coal and fish in
Great Britain at the same time.

Aneurin Bevan (1897–1960)
Speech at Blackpool, 18 May 1945

The dogma of the Ghost is the Machine.

> Gilbert Ryle (1900–1976)
> *The Concept of Mind*, 1949

Cynicism is cheap—you can buy it at any Monoprix store—it's built into all poor-quality goods.

> Graham Greene (1904–   )
> *The Comedians*, 1966

I remember the rage I used to feel when a prediction went awry. I could have shouted at the subjects of my experiments, "Behave, damn you, behave as you ought!" Eventually I realized that the subjects were always right. It was I who was wrong. I had made a bad prediction.

> B. F. Skinner (1904–   )
> *Walden Two*, 1948

The real problem is not whether machines think but whether men do.

> B. F. Skinner
> *Contingencies of Reinforcement*, 1969

What General Brass can
  Do, A.T.&T. can.
Detroit can, Milan can,
  And Steel can and Silk can,
American Can can
  And Carnation Milk can.

> Phyllis McGinley (1905–1977)
> "Love Letter to a Factory"
> *The Love Letters of Phyllis McGinley*, 1954

We continue to overlook the fact that work has become a leisure activity.

> Mark Abrams (1906–   )
> Quoted in the *Observer*, 3 June 1962

I don't ship shit.

> Charles Revson (1906–1975)
> Revlon

Though "music while you work" is now our wont
It's not so nice as "music while you don't."

> John Betjeman (1906–1984)
> Quoted by V. S. Pritchett in *The New Yorker*, 24 June 1985

One cannot walk through a mass-production factory and not feel that one is in Hell.

W. H. Auden (1907–1973)

It is easy to overlook the absence of appreciable advance in an industry. Inventions that are not made, like babies that are not born, are rarely missed.

John Kenneth Galbraith (1908–   )
The Affluent Society, 1958

We are becoming the servants in thought, as in action, of the machine we have created to serve us.

John Kenneth Galbraith
The New Industrial State, 1967

The enemy of the market is not ideology but the engineer.

John Kenneth Galbraith
The New Industrial State

And we take a step (for mankind?) into the last third of the twentieth century, having walked on and dumped our technological junk upon the face of the once mysterious moon.

Mark Schorer (1908–1977)
"General Introduction,"
The Literature of America: Twentieth Century, 1970

The only thing that keeps us alive is our brilliance. The only thing protecting our brilliance is our patents.

Edwin Land (1909–   )
Polaroid

Work expands so as to fill the time available for its completion. General recognition of this fact is shown in the proverbial phrase "It is the busiest man who has time to spare."

C. Northcote Parkinson (1909–   )
Parkinson's Law, 1957

Perfection of planning is a symptom of decay. During a period of exciting discovery or progress, there is no time to plan the perfect headquarters. The time for that comes later, when all the important work has been done.

C. Northcote Parkinson
Parkinson's Law

It might be termed the Law of Triviality. Briefly stated, it means that the time spent on any item of the agenda will be in inverse proportion to the sum involved.

C. Northcote Parkinson
Parkinson's Law

The man who is denied the opportunity of taking decisions of importance begins to regard as important the decisions he is allowed to take. He becomes fussy about filing, keen on seeing that pencils are sharpened, eager to ensure that the windows are open (or shut) and apt to use two or three different-colored inks.

C. Northcote Parkinson
Parkinson's Law

The automatic factory is the end product rather than the beginning of automation. Automation properly does not start with production at all, but with an analysis of the business and its redesign on automation principles. The form that automatic production takes in the plant is determined by that analysis and redesign; and mechanization, the replacement of human labor by machines, is a detail of automation and not always the essential one. The reason for this, the reason why automation has to be business-focused rather than production-focused, is that it radically shifts the area of *business risk.*

Peter F. Drucker (1909–)
America's Next Twenty Years, 1955

In early industry, as typified by the job shop, the integrating principle of work was skill. In Henry Ford's concept of mass production the organizing principle was the product. In automation, however, the entire activity of the business is a whole entity which must be harmoniously integrated to perform at all.

Peter F. Drucker
America's Next Twenty Years

If there is one thing certain under automation it is that the job— even the bottom job—will change radically and often.

Peter F. Drucker
America's Next Twenty Years

145

McLuhan's most important insight is not that "the medium is the message." It is that technology is an extension of man rather than "just a tool." It is not "man's master." But it changes man and his personality and what man is—or perceives himself to be—just as it changes what he can do.

Peter F. Drucker
Adventures of a Bystander, 1978

Business has become more a system of conglomerates that will make anything, any item and any different variety of items, with the sole idea being to make some money. Nobody has pride in what they're doing; they just want to show a little profit. Now, there's nothing wrong with making money. But I think there's something to be said for a manufacturer learning how to make what he started out to make and doing it well.

Barry M. Goldwater (1909–   )
US Senate

Technology . . . the knack of so arranging the world that we don't have to experience it.

Max Frisch (1911–   )
Homo Faber, 1957

Small Is Beautiful: Economics As If People Mattered.

E. F. Schumacher (1911–1977)
Title of book, 1973

Any intelligent fool can make things bigger, more complex, and more violent. It takes a touch of genius—and a lot of courage—to move in the opposite direction.

E. F. Schumacher
Quoted in Obituary, the *Guardian,* 6 September 1977

For tribal man space was the uncontrollable mystery. For technological man it is time that occupies the same role.

Marshall McLuhan (1911–1980)
The Mechanical Bride, 1951

Work . . . does not exist in a non-literate world. . . . Where the whole man is involved there is no work. Work begins with the division of labor.

Marshall McLuhan
Understanding Media, 1964

The Swiss managed to build a lovely country around their hotels.

George Mikes (1912–)
Down With Everybody!, 1951

A brief written presentation that winnows fact from opinion is the basis for decision making around here.

Edward G. Harness (1918–)
Procter & Gamble

Efficiency has this double edge—by its very success, it can crush competition.

Miles W. Kirkpatrick (1918–)

The Laws of Robotics

(1) A robot may not injure a human being, or through inaction allow a human being to come to harm.
(2) A robot must obey the orders given it by human beings, except where such orders would conflict with the First Law.
(3) A robot must protect its own existence as long as such protection does not conflict with the First and Second Laws.

Isaac Asimov (1920–)
I, Robot, 1950

Don't forecast. Derive.

Joseph A. Orlicky (1922–)
IBM

Don't lie to the master schedule.

Joseph A. Orlicky
IBM

Everything the cow makes can be made from vegetable oil and vegetable protein, and that's what we want to do.

Thomas J. Barlow (1922–)
Anderson, Clayton

In the spage age the most important space is between the ears.

Ann Armstrong (1924–)
Quoted in the *Guardian*, 30 January 1974

This fantastic conception that a large industry could be run like a soup kitchen; like a welfare comfort station. I know what the old-timers think of me. I've grown up getting stared at by a lot of tongue-clucking old fogies who think I'm ruthless. People whose, whose thinking might have kept this business from growing to anything like its present size. This preoccupation with morality: this fantastic stupid black-and-white idea that honesty and profit are incompatible. I just happen to feel that the atmosphere of a large corporation *can't* be constantly churchlike.

Rod Serling (1924–1975)
Mr. Ramsie in *Patterns,* a television play, 1955

Most of the time innovations do not take place within the industry in which one would have expected them to take place.

Peter G. Peterson (1926–   )
Bell & Howell

Filing is concerned with the past; anything you actually need to see again has to do with the future.

Katharine Whitehorn (1928–   )
Sunday Best, 1976

The way to do research is to attack the facts at the point of greatest astonishment.

Celia Green (1935–   )
The Decline and Fall of Science, 1976

Replicate, don't innovate. . . . Someone else has gone and done your homework for you. They have taken the risk, the time, and spent the dollars.

Steven W. Lapham
Sterling Drug

I never spent a nickel on laboratories or chemists.

Charles Manville
Johns Manville

If I make a machine anyone can make, my competition hounds me, but if I am highly specialized, then I have no competition.

Leopold D. Silberstein
Penn-Texas

You must know your materials. Study them. Know everything about them—what they can do, their history, what they can do in the future. And you must have the ability to make the right decisions.

Leopold D. Silberstein
Penn-Texas

OSWO: Oh Shit! We're Out!

Oliver W. Wight

MARKETING

The drama of two people striking a deal—directly or indirectly, retail or wholesale—is pervasive and unending. As Robert Louis Stevenson put it, "Every one lives by selling something." The quotations of this section tell many stories, big and small. There are many markets. The so-called marketplace of ideas is as much an exchange for profit as any: the power to convince someone of the value of an idea is also a sales effort—to civilize. "It is a great art," says Gracián, "to know how to sell wind."

Chaucer's fourteenth-century Merchant, "with a forked berd," as represented in an early eighteenth century edition of Chaucer.

The codfish lays ten thousand eggs,
The homely hen lays one.
The codfish never cackles
To tell you what she's done.
And so we scorn the codfish,
While the humble hen we prize,
Which only goes to show you
That it pays to advertise.

Anonymous
It Pays to Advertise

The halls of fame are open wide
And they are always full;
Some go in by the door called "push,"
And some by the door called "pull."

Anonymous
Quoted by Stanley Baldwin (1867–1947) in a speech in the House of Commons

I see a strange connection between your slogan, "The pause that
refreshes," and Christ's own words, "Come unto me, all ye that
travail, and I will refresh you."

Anonymous
A minister, to Coca-Cola bottler

Whole eviscerated turkeys are good business for Land O'Lakes
turkey growers. But they're even better business after they've been
further processed into turkey parts, roasts, slabs, slices, rolls,
cubes, patties and other products.

Anonymous
Land O' Lakes

The market of debauch is always open.

Arabic proverb
Collected by J. L. Burckhardt, 1817

Money gives a man thirty years more of dignity.

Chinese proverb

Shear the sheep, but don't flay them.

Dutch proverb

Caveat emptor. [Buyer, beware. *Literally,* Let the buyer beware.]

Latin proverb

It is naught, it is naught, saith the buyer: but when he is gone his way, then he boasteth.

Bible: Proverbs 20:14

The market-place is a place set apart where men may deceive and overreach each other.

Anacharsis (c. 600 B.C.)
Sententiae

You know how to make your market, or avail yourself of the market. [Scisti uti foro.]

Terence (c. 190–159 B.C.)
Phormio, 161 B.C.

Nothing is stronger than habit.

Ovid (43 B.C.–A.D. c. 18)
Ars Amatoria

The merchant must be no more pessimist than optimist, since pessimism induces him to hold back his capital, but optimism induces him to take such risks that he has more to fear than to hope.

Abu al-Fadl Ja'far ibn 'Ali al-Dimishqi (late 9th century)
The Beauties of Commerce

All merchants shall have safety and security in coming into England, and going out of England, and in staying and in travelling through England, as well by land as by water, to buy and sell, without any unjust exactions, according to ancient and right customs, excepting in the time of war, and if they be of a country at war against us: and if such are found in our land at the beginning of a war, they shall be apprehended without injury of their bodies and goods, until it be known to us, or to our Chief Judiciary, how the Merchants of our country are treated who are found in the country at war against us; and if ours be in safety there, the others shall be in safety in our land.

Magna Charta, 1215

Marketing

Chaucer's Merchant: Portrait of a Well-Heeled Entrepreneur

A Marchant was ther with a forked berd,
In mottelee, and hye on horse he sat;
Upon his heed a Flaundryssh bevere hat,
His bootes clasped faire and fetisly.
His resons he spak ful solempnely,
Sownynge alway th'encrees of his wynnyng.
He wolde the see were kept for any thing
Betwixen Middelburgh and Orewelle.
Wel koude he in eschaunge sheeldes selle.
This worthy man ful wel his wit besette:
Ther wiste no wight that he was in dette,
So estatly was he of his governaunce,
With his bargaynes, and with his chevyssaunce.
For sothe he was a worthy man with alle,
But, sooth to seyn, I noot how men hym calle.

There was a *Merchant* with a forking beard
And motley dress; high on his horse he sat,
Upon his head a Flemish beaver hat
And on his feet daintily buckled boots.
He told of his opinions and pursuits
In solemn tones, and how he never lost.
The sea should be kept free at any cost
(He thought) upon the Harwich-Holland range,
He was expert at currency exchange.
This estimable Merchant so had set
His wits to work, none knew he was in debt,
He was so stately in negotiation,
Loan, bargain and commercial obligation.
He was an excellent fellow all the same;
To tell the truth I do not know his name.

Geoffrey Chaucer (c. 1343–1400)
Prologue, Canterbury Tales
Translation by Nevill Coghill

Scarcity raises the price of everything.

François Rabelais (c. 1494–1553)
Pantagruel, 1552

Well, sir, if your market may be made no where els, home again.

Thomas Lodge (c. 1558–1625)
Rosalynde, 1590

Fortune is like the market, where many times, if you can stay a little, the price will fall.

Francis Bacon (1561–1626)
Of Delays, 1625

But in the way of bargain, mark you me,
I'll cavil on the ninth part of a hair.

Shakespeare (1564–1616)
Henry IV, Part I, 1597–1598

As in other things, so in men, not the seller but the buyer determines the price.

Thomas Hobbes (1588–1679)
Leviathan, 1651

A good bargain is a pick-purse.

George Herbert (1593–1633)
Outlandish Proverbs, 1640

He that blames would buy.

George Herbert
Outlandish Proverbs

Ill ware is never cheap. Pleasing ware is half sold.

George Herbert
Jacula Prudentum, 1651

The buyer needs a hundred eyes, the seller not one.

George Herbert
Jacula Prudentum

It is a great art to know how to sell wind.

Baltasar Gracián (1601–1658)
Oráculo manual y arte de prudencia, 1647

The sign brings customers.

Jean de La Fontaine (1621–1695)
Fables, 1678–1679

He that cannot abide a bad market, deserves not a good one.

John Ray (1627–1705)
English Proverbs, 1678

Then I saw in my Dream, that when they were got out of the wilderness, they presently saw a town before them, and the name of that Town is Vanity, and at the town there is a Fair kept, called Vanity Fair. It is kept all the year long, it beareth the name of Vanity Fair because the town where 'tis kept is lighter than Vanity; and also because all that is there sold, or that cometh thither, is Vanity.

John Bunyan (1628–1688)
The Pilgrim's Progress, 1678

Nature abhors a vacuum.

Baruch Spinoza (1632–1677)
Ethics, 1677

You must sell, as Markets go.

Thomas Fuller (1654–1734)
Gnomologia, 1732

It is no sin to sell dear, but a sin to give ill measure.

James Kelly
Scottish Proverbs, 1721

He that speaks ill of the Mare will buy her.

Benjamin Franklin (1706–1790)
Poor Richard's Almanack, 1742

Few men have virtue to withstand the highest bidder.

George Washington (1732–1799)
Letter to Robert Howe, 17 August 1779

There is not a more mean, stupid, dastardly, pitiful, selfish, spiteful, envious, ungrateful animal than the Public. It is the greatest of cowards, for it is afraid of itself.

William Hazlitt (1778–1830)
Table Talk, 1821–1822

I do not regard a broker as a member of the human race.

Honoré de Balzac (1790–1859)

No grass grows in the market-place.

Henry George Bohn (1796–1884)
Handbook of Proverbs, 1855

The craft of the merchant is this bringing a thing from where it abounds, to where it is costly.

> Ralph Waldo Emerson (1803–1882)
> *The Conduct of Life*, 1860

It is well known what a middleman is: he is a man who bamboozles one party and plunders the other.

> Benjamin Disraeli (1804–1881)
> Speech, 11 April 1845

It is true that you may fool all the people some of the time; you can even fool some of the people all the time; but you can't fool all of the people all the time.

> Abraham Lincoln (1809–1865)
> To a caller at the White House

You can fool too many of the people too much of the time.

> James Thurber (1894–1961)
> *Fables for Our Time*, 1940

There is hardly anything in the world that some man can't make a little worse and sell a little cheaper, and the people who consider price only are this man's lawful prey.

> John Ruskin (1819–1900)

Any fool can paint a picture, but it takes a wise man to be able to sell it.

> Samuel Butler (1835–1902)

The Ancient Mariner would not have taken so well if it had been called *The Old Sailor*.

> Samuel Butler
> *Notebooks*, 1912

The public buys its opinions as it buys its meat, or takes its milk, on the principle that it is cheaper to do this than to keep a cow. So it is, but the milk is more likely to be watered.

> Samuel Butler
> *Notebooks*

Many a small thing has been made large by the right kind of advertising.

> Mark Twain (1835–1910)
> *A Connecticut Yankee at King Arthur's Court*, 1889

Half the money I spend on advertising is wasted, and the trouble is I don't know which half.

John Wanamaker (1838–1922)
Quoted in Ogilvy, *Confessions of an Advertising Man,* 1963

There are very honest people who do not think that they have had a bargain unless they have cheated a merchant.

Anatole France (1844–1924)

Every one lives by selling something.

Robert Louis Stevenson (1850–1894)
Across the Plains, 1892

Sirs, I have tested your machine. It adds a new terror to life and makes death a long felt want.

Sir Herbert Beerbohm Tree (1853–1917)
To a gramophone company that asked for a testimonial

[Oscar Wilde claimed that he once saw in a French journal, under a drawing of a bonnet, the words:] With this style the mouth is worn slightly open.

Oscar Wilde (1854–1900)

With an evening coat and a white tie, anybody, even a stockbroker, can gain a reputation for being civilized.

Oscar Wilde

Never give a sucker an even break.

Edward F. Albee (1857–1930)
[W. C. Fields made this remark famous.]

Conspicuous consumption of valuable goods is a means of reputability to the gentleman of leisure.

Thorstein Veblen (1857–1929)
The Theory of the Leisure Class, 1899

The customer is always right.

H. Gordon Selfridge (?1864–1947)
Slogan

You can tell the ideals of a nation by its advertisements.

Norman Douglas (1868–1952)
South Wind, 1917

Money Talks

It makes no difference what it is, a woman will buy anything she thinks a store is losing money on.

Frank McKinney ("Kin") Hubbard (1868–1930)

Advertising may be described as the science of arresting the human intelligence long enough to get money from it.

Stephen Leacock (1869–1944)

Do you know,
considering the market, there are more
Poems produced than any other thing?
No wonder poets sometimes have to *seem*
So much more businesslike than businessmen.
Their wares are so much harder to get rid of.

Robert Frost (1874–1963)
New Hampshire, 1923

The middle-class woman of England, as of America . . . think of her in bulk . . . is potentially the greatest money-spending machine in the world.

Harley Granville-Barker (1877–1946)
The Madras House, 1910

The booboisie.

H. L. Mencken (1880–1956)
Passim

In the United States, doing good has come to be, like patriotism, a favorite device of persons with something to sell.

H. L. Mencken

No one ever went broke underestimating the intelligence of the American people.

Attributed to H. L. Mencken
[Also quoted as: . . . underestimating the taste . . .]

Why should people go out and pay money to see bad films when they can stay at home and see bad television for nothing?

Samuel Goldwyn (1882–1974)
Quoted in the Observer, 9 September 1956

His name was George F. Babbitt, and . . . he was nimble in the calling of selling houses for more than people could afford to pay.

A thing called Ethics, whose nature was confusing, but if you had it you were a High-class Realtor, and if you hadn't you were a shyster, a piker, and a fly-by-night.

Sinclair Lewis (1885–1951)
Babbitt, 1922

People will buy anything that's one to a customer.

Sinclair Lewis

The crossroads of trade are the meeting place of ideas, the attrition ground of rival customs and beliefs; diversities beget conflict, comparison, thought; superstitions cancel one another, and reason begins.

Will Durant (1885–1981)
The Life of Greece, 1939

Advertising did not invent the products or services which called forth jobs, nor inspire the pioneering courage that built factories and machinery to produce them. What advertising did was to stimulate ambition and desire—the craving to possess, which is the strongest incentive to produce. To satisfy this craving the factory was impelled to turn itself into a growing factory; and then, by the pressure of mass demand, into many factories. Mass production made possible mass economies, reflected in declining prices, until the product that began as the luxury of the rich became the possession of every family that was willing to work.

Bruce Barton (1886–1967)
In first issue of *Reader's Digest* to carry advertisements, April 1955

Advertising is of the very essence of democracy. An election goes on every minute of the business day across the counters of hundreds of thousands of stores and shops where the customers state their preferences and determine which manufacturer and which product shall be the leader today, and which shall lead tomorrow.

Bruce Barton
In first issue of *Reader's Digest* to carry advertisements, April 1955

The best books about advertising are not about advertising.

James W. Young (1886–1973)

The philosophy behind much advertising is based on the old observation that every man is really two men—the man he is and the man he wants to be.

William Feather (1889–   )
The Business of Life, 1949

The mendaciousness of American advertising is absolutely vomitorious—the gullibility of the American public, which opens its ears like mouths as if they could stretch the whole ear tunnel to listen to more guff.

Janet Flanner (1892–1978)

Virtue has its own reward, but no sale at the box office.

Mae West (1892–1980)
Quoted in Weintraub, *Peel Me a Grape*

Advertising agency: eighty-five per cent confusion and fifteen per cent commission.

Fred Allen (1894–1956)

You're peddling your fish in the wrong market.

Dashiell Hammett (1894–1961)
The Thin Man, 1934

A city where wise guys peddle gold bricks to each other and Truth, crushed down to earth, rises again as phoney as a glass eye.

Ben Hecht (1894–1964)
Of New York, in the film, *Nothing Sacred*

When you are skinning your customers, you should leave some skin on to grow so that you can skin them again.

Nikita Sergeyevich Krushchev (1894–1971)
To British businessmen, 1961

Production goes up and up because high pressure advertising and salesmanship constantly create new needs that must be satisfied: this is *Admass*—a consumer's race with donkeys chasing an electric carrot.

J. B. Priestley (1894–1984)
Thoughts in the Wilderness, 1957

It is far easier to write ten passably effective sonnets, good enough to take in the not too enquiring critic, than to write one effective advertisement that will take in a few thousand of the uncritical buying public.

Aldous Huxley (1894–1963)
Quoted in Tunstall, *The Advertising Man,* 1964

I believe that advertising is an investment where risk taking is inordinately rewarded and where the penalty for failure is not correspondingly severe.

Chester A. Posey (1896–1971)
McCann-Erickson

We must look at the price system as . . . a mechanism for communicating information if we want to understand its real function.

Friedrich August von Hayek (1899–)
Individualism and Economic Order, 1948

There is no such thing as "soft sell" and "hard sell." There is only "smart sell" and "stupid sell."

Charles Brower (1901–)
News reports, 20 May 1958

There is nothing as universal in this world as human thirst. . . . Our market is as big as the world and the people in it.

Lee Talley (1901–1976)
Coca-Cola
Quoted in *Newsweek,* 19 May 1958

I cannot imagine a housewife not being glad to come by a dish-washing machine. But for some couples the electric dish-washer eliminated the one thing they did together every day; one of them washed while the other dried. As one woman put it, she now enjoys not only less fatigue but a pure gift of time. Yet she added wistfully, "But it *was* cozy, just the two of us together for that little while every night after we got the kids to bed. . . ."

Bruno Bettelheim (1903–)

Advertising is what you do when you can't go see somebody. That's all it is.

Fairfax M. Cone (1903–1977)
Foote, Cone & Belding
Quoted in the *Christian Science Monitor,* 20 March 1963

Pink is the navy blue of India.

Attributed to Diana Vreeland (1903–   )

Ours is not so much an age of vulgarity as of vulgarization; everything is tampered with or touched up, or adulterated or watered down, in an effort to make it palatable, in an effort to make it pay.

Louis Kronenberger (1904–1980)
Company Manners, 1954

Merchandising reached its apogee in the Lux advertisements which portrayed two articles of lingerie discussing their wearers' effluvia, for all the world like rival stamp collectors.

S. J. Perelman (1904–1979)

One of the first declarations of business philosophy I heard from my father, soon after I came to work at Neiman-Marcus in 1926, was, "There is never a good sale for Neiman-Marcus unless it's a good buy for the customer."

Stanley Marcus (1905–   )
Neiman-Marcus

In the factory we make cosmetics. In the store we sell hope.

Charles Revson (1906–1975)
Revlon

What we are selling are hopes and dreams, not frozen peas.

Michel C. Bergerac (1932–   )
Revlon

John Milton
Never stayed in a Hilton
Hotel,
Which was just as well.

W. H. Auden (1907–1973)
Academic Graffiti, 1972

Doing business without advertising is like winking at a girl in the dark. You know what you are doing, but nobody else does.

Steuart Henderson Britt (1907–1979)
Quoted in the *New York Herald Tribune,* 30 October 1956

The individual serves the industrial system not by supplying it with savings and the resulting capital; he serves it by consuming its products.

John Kenneth Galbraith (1908–   )
The New Industrial State, 1967

Advertising, after all, is the mirror of man, and man has never been in serious danger of becoming bogged down in grace.

Advertising is the whip which hustles humanity up the road to the Better Mousetrap. It is the vision which reproaches man for the paucity of his desires.

E. S. Turner (1909–   )
The Shocking History of Advertising, 1952

The world in which Advertisement dwells is a one-day world. . . . The average man is invited to slice his life into a series of one-day lives, regulated by the clock of fashion. The human being is no longer the unit. He becomes the containing frame for a generation or sequence of ephemerids, roughly organized into what he calls his personality.

Marshall McLuhan (1911–1980)
The Mechanical Bride, 1951

When producers want to know what the public wants, they graph it in curves. When they want to tell the public what to get, they say it in curves.

Marshall McLuhan
The Mechanical Bride

Ads push the principle of noise all the way to the plateau of persuasion. They are quite in accord with the procedures of brain-washing.

Marshall McLuhan
Understanding Media, 1964

The car has become the carapace, the protective and aggressive shell, of urban and suburban man.

Marshall McLuhan
Understanding Media

Advertising is the greatest art form of the twentieth century.

Marshall McLuhan
In *Advertising Age,* 1968

Gutenberg made everybody a reader. Xerox makes everybody a publisher.

Marshall McLuhan
Interview in the *Washington Post,* 1977

The advertiser who thinks he has to choose between the straight-forward and dull or the beautiful but dumb is mistaken. The trick is to be relevant as well as bright.

> William Bernbach (1911–1982)
> Doyle Dane Bernbach

The big thing is recognizing that honesty sells. There is no reason why honesty cannot be combined with the skills of persuasion. People are shouted at by so many manufacturers today that they don't know what to believe.

> William Bernbach

Advertising is the place where the selfish interests of the man-ufacturer coincide with the interests of society.

> David Ogilvy (1911–   )
> Ogilvy & Mather
> Quoted in Mayer, *Madison Avenue, USA,* 1958

Try to make working at Ogilvy & Mather *fun.* When people aren't having any fun, they seldom produce good advertising. Kill grim-ness with laughter. Maintain an atmosphere of informality. En-courage exuberance. Get rid of sad dogs that spread gloom.

> David Ogilvy
> *Principles of Management,* 1968

The new breed has no regard for how well an ad sells the product. These pseudo-intellectuals who are now flocking to advertising, these callow, half-baked, overpaid young men and women haven't the slightest interest in how the consuming public reacts to stimuli any more than abstract painters have. They are departing from tested formulae and going to things that are very doubtful.

> David Ogilvy

There's a big difference between American and European ads. In America a commercial may be crass but it's been tested, whereas here [in France] there's very little testing. French advertising is much more sophisticated because it's not researched.

> David Ogilvy

Consumers with dollars in their pockets are not, by any stretch of the imagination, weak. To the contrary, they are the most mer-ciless, meanest, toughest market disciplinarians I know.

> Edwin S. Bingham (1912–   )

Stepping into his new Buick convertible he [the American] knows that he would gladly do without it, but imagines that to his neighbor, who is just backing *his* out of the driveway, this car is the motor of life.

Mary McCarthy (1912–   )
On the Contrary, 1961

Who are these advertising men kidding, besides the European tourist? Between the tired, sad, gentle faces of the subway riders and the grinning Holy Families of the Ad-Mass, there exists no possibility of even a wishful identification.

Mary McCarthy
On the Contrary

The consumer today is the victim of the manufacturer who launches on him a regiment of products for which he must make room in his soul.

Mary McCarthy
On the Contrary

In the twentieth century our highest praise is to call the Bible "the World's Best-Seller." And it has come to be more and more difficult to say whether we think it is a best-seller because it is great, or vice versa.

A best-seller was a book which somehow sold well simply because it was selling well.

Daniel J. Boorstin (1914–   )
The Image, 1961

The Hidden Persuaders.

Vance Packard (1914–   )
Title of book, 1957

Willy was a salesman. And for a salesman, there is no rock bottom to the life. He don't put a bolt to a nut, he don't tell you the law or give you medicine. He's a man way out there in the blue, riding on a smile and a shoeshine. And when they start not smiling back—that's an earthquake. And then you get yourself a couple of spots on your hat, and you're finished. Nobody dast blame this man. A salesman is got to dream, boy. It comes with the territory.

Arthur Miller (1915–   )
Death of a Salesman, Requiem, 1949

If American industry continues to sow contempt for the consumer, it will reap contempt from the consumer. And from Congress, it will reap statutes. It could be the most spectacular case of statutory reap in history.

Betty Furness (1916–)
New York State Consumer Protection Board

Advertising is found in societies which have passed the point of satisfying the basic animal needs.

Marion Harper, Jr. (1916–)
Quoted in the *New York Herald Tribune,* 1960

Germany. The Year, 1550 Odd.

Andreas Ryff, a merchant, bearded and fur-coated, is coming back to his home in Baden; he has visited thirty markets and is troubled with saddle-burn. As he travels he is stopped approximately once every six miles to pay a customs toll; between Basle and Cologne he pays thirty-one levies.

And that is not all. Each community he visits has its own money, its own rules and regulations, its own law and order. In the area around Baden alone there are 112 different measures of length, 92 different square measures, 65 different dry measures, 163 different measures for cereals and 123 for liquids, 63 special measures for liquor, and 80 different pound weights.

Robert L. Heilbroner (1919–)
The Worldly Philosophers, 1953

Banks do not raise or lower interest rates depending upon how they feel about it. A bank buys money like a grocer buys bananas—and then adds on salaries and rent and sells the product.

Llewellyn Jenkins (1919–)
Manufacturers Hanover
American Bankers Association

If we can get the Soviet people to enjoy good consumer goods, they'll never be able to do without them again.

Donald M. Kendall (1921–)
Pepsico

My commitment is to give the consumer what she wants; and if her "wants" have an emotional component to them, it behooves me to recognize that fact.

Donald M. Kendall

I don't believe that advertising ever gets you a quality reputation. If you don't have it, advertising won't help you a bit. And if you do have it, word of mouth is enough.

F. James McDonald (1922–   )
General Motors

Kodak sells film, but they don't advertise film. They advertise memories.

Theodore Levitt (1925–   )
Harvard Business School

Truth in advertising, and in business, is neither likely nor entirely possible.

Neal W. O'Connor (1925–   )
American Association of Advertising Agencies

A consumer is a shopper who is sore about something.

Harold Coffin (1926–   )

Advertising is not spending; it's an investment to get a piece of the mind of millions of Americans.

Alph B. Peterson (1926–   )
Benrus

Youth is an easy sale and a safe bet. . . . Perhaps advertising people have come to the conclusion that middle age is obscene.

Charles F. Adams (1927–   )
MacManus, John & Adams

There is very little glory in advertising. If you sell the product, you get the rewards. It was childish a few years ago; now it is very adult, very complex; it requires a good deal of work. . . . I don't think it's fun.

Mary Wells Lawrence (1928–   )
Wells, Rich, Greene

The most important thing is to seize a trend, and when we come in with our might it won't matter that we weren't the first. Everyone will think we were.

Michel C. Bergerac (1932–   )
Revlon

Money Talks

Sears Catalogue

Our Acme Queen Parlor Organ, $27.45. 25 Years' Guarantee. Free
. . . With this organ we present you FREE and ship with it, a fine
Organ Stool and a very complete and valuable Instruction Book.
For the benefit of our customers in the west and northwest, we
will ship this organ from our factory at St. Paul, Minn., thus
making a big saving in freight charges, but where we can secure
cheaper freight rates from Chicago, we will ship direct from our
Chicago house.

1902

Vin Vitae. Wine of Life. Retail Price, per bottle, $1.25. Our Price,
69 Cents. A new and perfect tonic stimulant for the tired, weak
and sick of all classes. A renewer of energy, a stimulant for the
fatigued, a strengthener for the weak, an effective and agreeable
food for the blood, brain and nerves. Not a medicine, because it is
delightful to the taste and to the stomach. Not merely a stimulant,
but a genuine toner and strengthener. A Tonic which we find is as
yet Unequaled. [Page is illustrated with a drawing of a very young
and very naked, fin de siècle Herakles gently tearing apart the
Nemean lion's jaws. Caption: Vin Vitae gives health and strength]

1902

$21.75 Buys This Black China Dogskin Fur Coat, Specially Con-
structed for Automobilists and Driving Purposes.

c.1909

Sears Motor Buggy. Speedy, Economical, Noiseless, Durable and
Safe. A Child Can Run It. All Speeds from 1 to 25 Miles Per Hour.
$395.00 for Car Complete with Rubber Tires, Timken Roll-
Bearing Axles, Top, Storm Front, Three Oil-Burning Lamps,
Horn and One Gallon Lubricating Oil. Nothing to Buy but Gas-
oline. [Shown with woman driver]

1909

A good ad should be like a good sermon; it must not only comfort
the afflicted, it also must afflict the comfortable.

Bernice FitzGibbon
Macy's, Gimbels & Me, 1967

Successful firms pay more attention to the market than do failures. Successful innovators innovate in response to market needs,
involve potential users in the development of the innovation, and
understand user needs better.

Christopher Freeman et al.
Quoted in Peters and Waterman, *In Search of Excellence,* 1982

Marketing

To be Catholic or Jewish isn't chic. Chic is Episcopalian.
Elizabeth Arden [Florence Nightingale Graham]

Be everywhere, do everything, and never fail to astonish the customer.
Margaret Getchell
Macy's
Motto

Honesty in advertising is a matter of pragmatics as well as morality. You can use advertising to get people to buy a product once, but if it doesn't live up to expectation or its advertising claims, who's going to buy it a second time? I can't think of a faster way to ruin a product than with advertising that's not truthful.
Joan Seidman
Batten, Barton, Durstine & Osborn

ENTREPRENEURS

In his *American Made: Men Who Shaped the American Economy* (1979), Harold C. Livesay reports an exchange between Henry Ford and his lieutenant, Charles Sorenson. About 1915, as Model T production was rising and as unit costs were falling, Sorenson did calculations to show economies of scale. "That's enough, Charlie," said Ford. "Don't show me any more figures; I've got the smell of the thing now." The ability to "smell" a thing is a business concept: the quick, instinctive sense of what's what and how to do it well, however partial, prejudiced, even wrong; and the nerve and will and capacity to act—these are qualities that make the entrepreneur. Entrepreneurs adapt to changing conditions, quickly; they take risks; they're informal, independent. And, when the times are "right," they reap the rewards. The quotes in this section are about the businessmen who have smelled opportunity and acted. They represent the best and the worst of entrepreneurial know-how.

Jim Fisk (1834–1872) by Thomas Nast (1840–1902).

I was figuring on starting some kind of business, but most every business is already engaged in more than's necessary; and then I ain't got no business ability. What I want is something that don't call for no kind of ability whatsoever and no kind of exertion to speak of, and ain't out of town, and pays good, and has a future.

Anonymous

Sow a thought, and you reap an act;
Sow an act, and you reap a habit;
Sow a habit, and you reap a character;
Sow a character, and you reap a destiny.

Anonymous
Quoted by Samuel Smiles (1812–1904) in *Life and Labor*

Trade may make you a king but it robs you of leisure.

Anonymous

The money-getter is never tired.

Chinese proverb

Money is a defense.

Bible: Ecclesiastes 7:12

Not greedy of filthy lucre.

Bible: 1 Timothy 3:8

He has not acquired a fortune; the fortune has acquired him.

Bion (c.325–c.255 B.C.)
In Diogenes Laertius, *Lives of Eminent Philosophers*

Nothing is a greater proof of a narrow and groveling disposition than to be fond of money, while nothing is more noble and exalted than to despise it, if thou hast it not; and if thou hast it, to employ it in beneficence and liberality.

Cicero (106–43 B.C.)
De officiis

While we stop to think, we often miss our opportunity.

Publilius Syrus (First century B.C.)
Sententiae

Love of bustle is not industry.

> Seneca (c.4 B.C.–A.D. 65)
> *Epistles*

It is a rough road that leads to the heights of greatness.

> Seneca
> *Epistles*

He who wishes to be rich in a day will be hanged in a year.

> Leonardo da Vinci (1452–1519)
> *Notebooks*, c.1500

My money doth make me full merry to be,
And without my money none careth for me.

> Thomas Deloney (c.1543–c.1600)
> *Jack of Newbury*, 1619

Keep thy shop, and thy shop will keep thee.
Light gains make heavy purses.

> George Chapman (c.1559–1634)
> *Eastward Ho* (1605), written by Chapman, Ben Jonson
> (c.1573–1637), and John Marston (c.1575–c.1634)

Chiefly the mold of a man's fortune is in his own hands.

> Francis Bacon (1561–1626)
> *Of Fortune*, 1625

Eagerness is apt to overlook consequences, it is loth to be stopped in its career; for when men are in great haste they see only in a straight line.

> George Savile, Marquess of Halifax (1633–1695)
> *Political, Moral and Miscellaneous Reflections*, 1750

Money makes not so many true friends as real enemies.

> Thomas Fuller (1654–1734)
> *Gnomologia*, 1732

No modest man ever did or ever will make a fortune.

> Lady Mary Wortley Montagu (1689–1762)
> Letter to Wortley Montagu, 1714

The busy man has few idle visitors; to the boiling pot the flies come not.

> Benjamin Franklin (1706–1790)
> *Poor Richard's Almanack*, 1752

Entrepreneurs

He may well win the race that runs by himself.

Benjamin Franklin
Poor Richard's Almanack, 1757

Work as if you were to live a hundred years, Pray as if you were to die tomorrow.

Benjamin Franklin
Poor Richard's Almanack, 1757

A self-made man? Yes—and worships his creator.

William Cowper (1731–1800)

I love those who yearn for the impossible.

Johann Wolfgang von Goethe (1749–1832)
Faust II

The deed is everything, the glory nothing.

Johann Wolfgang von Goethe
Faust II

Jack of all trades and master of none.

Maria Edgeworth (1767–1849)
Popular Tales, 1800

Daniel Webster struck me much like a steam engine in trousers.

Sydney Smith (1771–1845)
Lady Holland's Memoir, 1855

If you choose to represent the various parts in life by holes upon a table, of different shapes—some circular, some triangular, some square, some oblong—and the persons acting these parts by bits of wood of similar shapes, we shall generally find that the triangular person has got into the square hole, the oblong into the triangular, and a square person has squeezed himself into the round hole. The officer and the office, the doer and the thing done, seldom fit so exactly that we can say they were almost made for each other.

Sydney Smith
Sketches of Moral Philosophy, 1850

Trying to fit a square peg in a round hole.

Anonymous, probably from Sydney Smith (above)

A round man cannot be expected to fit in a square hole right away. He must have time to modify his shape.

Mark Twain (1835–1910)
More Tramps Abroad, 1897

Business, you know, may bring money, but friendship hardly ever does.

Jane Austen (1775–1817)
Emma, 1815

Men of genius do not excel in any profession because they labor in it, but they labor in it because they excel.

William Hazlitt (1778–1830)
Characteristics, 1821–1822

The busy have no time for tears.

Lord Byron (1788–1824)
The Two Foscari, 1821

Go, little one. There are good trades in this world. Let the rest of us languish in the misery in which we are doomed to die. This is a time when fortunes are made by those who have the wit, and that you have. Tonight or tomorrow, find a good house that may open its doors to you. Go with what God has given you and what I may add to that.

Alexandre Dumas the Elder (1802–1870)
Reporting the words of Marie-Antoine Carême's father to his son,
the great chef-to-be (1784–1833), one of fifteen children whom the
father couldn't feed and whom he abandoned in the street at age
eleven. Quoted in Auden, *A Certain World*, 1970

Whoso would be a man must be a nonconformist.

Ralph Waldo Emerson (1803–1882)
Self-Reliance, 1841

To be great is to be misunderstood.

Ralph Waldo Emerson
Self-Reliance

There are geniuses in trade as well as in war, or the state, or letters; and the reason why this or that man is fortunate is not to be told. It lies in the man: that is all anybody can tell you about it.

Ralph Waldo Emerson
Character, 1841

Nothing astonishes men so much as common sense and plain dealing.

Ralph Waldo Emerson
Art, 1841

The reward of a thing well done, is to have done it.

Ralph Waldo Emerson
Nominalist and Realist, 1844

I trust a good deal to common fame, as we all must. If a man has good corn, or wood, or boards, or pigs, to sell, or can make better chairs or knives, crucibles or church organs than anybody else, you will find a broad hard-beaten road to his house, though it be in the woods. [*Journal,* February 1855]

If a man can write a better book, preach a better sermon, or make a better mousetrap than his neighbor, though he builds his house in the woods the world will make a beaten path to his door. [Attributed, in a lecture, by Yule and Keene (*Borrowings,* 1889)]

Ralph Waldo Emerson

The art of getting rich consists not in industry, much less in saving, but in a better order, in timeliness, in being at the right spot.

Ralph Waldo Emerson
The Conduct of Life, 1860

Everybody likes and respects self-made men. It's a great deal better to be made in that way than not to be made at all.

Oliver Wendell Holmes (1809–1894)
The Autocrat of the Breakfast Table, 1858

Money-getters are the benefactors of our race. To them . . . are we indebted for our institutions of learning, and of art, our academies, colleges and churches.

P. T. Barnum (1810–1891)

There's a sucker born every minute.

Attributed to P. T. Barnum

Ride on! rough-shod if need be, smooth-shod if that will do, but ride on! Ride on over all obstacles, and win the race!

Charles Dickens (1812–1870)
David Copperfield, 1849–1850

My guiding star always is, Get hold of portable property.

Charles Dickens
Great Expectations, 1860–1861

Money and goods are certainly the best of references.

Charles Dickens
Our Mutual Friend, 1864–1865

That's the state to live and die in! . . . R–r–rich!

Charles Dickens
Our Mutual Friend

The ability to convert ideas to things is the secret of outward success.

Henry Ward Beecher (1813–1887)
Proverbs from Plymouth Pulpit, 1887

In battle or business, whatever the game,
In law or in love, it is ever the same;
In the struggle for power, or the scramble for pelf,
Let this be your motto—Rely on yourself!
For, whether the prize be a ribbon or throne,
The victor is he who can go it alone!

John Godfrey Saxe (1816–1887)
"The Game of Life"

The happiest time in any man's life is when he is in red-hot pursuit of a dollar with a reasonable prospect of overtaking it.

Josh Billings [Henry Wheeler Shaw] (1818–1885)

Self-made men are most always apt to be a little too proud of the job.

Josh Billings

Success is not always a sure sign of merit, but it is a first-rate way to succeed.

Josh Billings

Whatever is not nailed down is mine. Whatever I can pry loose is not nailed down.

Attributed to Collis P. Huntington (1821–1900)

All or nothing.

Henrik Ibsen (1828–1906)
Brand, 1866

Entrepreneurs

The strongest man in the world is he who stands most alone.

Henrik Ibsen
An Enemy of the People, 1882

Don't you believe, too, Hilde, that there are a few, special, chosen people who've been graced with the power and ability to *want* something, *desire* something, *will* something—so insistently and so—so inexorably—that they *must* get it in the end? Don't you believe that?

Henrik Ibsen
The Master Builder, 1892

And listen, down there by the river! The factories are at work! *My* factories! All those I would have built! Listen to them at work. It's the night-shift. So, they work night and day. Listen, listen! The wheels whirling and the cylinders flashing—round and round! Can't you hear it, Ella?

Henrik Ibsen
John Gabriel Borkman, 1896

Oh, we all get run over—once in our lives. But one must pick oneself up again. And behave as if it was nothing.

Henrik Ibsen
John Gabriel Borkman

The history of progress is written in the lives of infidels.

Robert G. Ingersoll (1833–1899)
Speech in New York, 1 May 1881

The business man and the artist are like matter and mind. We can never get either pure and without some alloy of the other.

Samuel Butler (1835–1902)

Man must have an idol—the amassing of wealth is one of the worst species of idolatry—no idol more debasing than the worship of money. Whatever I engage in I must push inordinately; therefore should I be careful to choose that life which will be the most elevating in its character. To continue much longer overwhelmed by business cares and with most of my thoughts wholly upon the way to make money in the shortest time, must degrade me beyond hope of permanent recovery.

Andrew Carnegie (1835–1919)
In Josephson, *The Robber Barons,* 1934

Yes, Sir. Wherever a man has got a ship, or a bridge, or a dock, or a house, or a car, or a fence, or a pig-pen anywhere in God's universe to paint, that's the paint for him, and he's bound to find it out sooner or later. You pass a ton of that paint dry through a blast furnace, and you'll get a quarter of a ton of pig-iron. I believe in my paint. I believe it's a blessing to the world. When folks come in, and kind of smell around, and ask me what I mix it with, I always say, "Well, in the first place, I mix it with *Faith,* and after that I grind it up with the best quality of boiled linseed oil that money will buy."

> William Dean Howells (1837–1920)
> Lapham speaking, in *The Rise of Silas Lapham,* 1885

Anybody has a right to evade taxes if he can get away with it. No citizen has a moral obligation to assist in maintaining the government.

> J. P. Morgan (1837–1913)

MR. MORGAN: Because it was absolutely impossible for more than one party to negotiate—to make the same negotiation for the same lot of gold. It would only have made competition.
SENATOR VEST: If the gold was abroad I take it for granted that anybody could get hold of it who had the means to do so.
If you were actuated by the desire to prevent a panic, why were you not willing that other people should do it, if they wanted to?
MR. MORGAN: They could not do it.

> J. P. Morgan
> Testimony on 19 June 1896 before a congressional committee investigating the
> $62 million loan to the US Treasury by a banking syndicate headed by Morgan
> and August Belmont.

I want to proclaim a new doctrine: a complete separation of business and government.

> J. P. Morgan

I feel bound in honor when I reorganize a property and am morally responsible for its management, to protect it—and I generally do protect it.

> J. P. Morgan
> As quoted by Hovey, in Josephson, *The Robber Barons,* 1934
> The fight for control of Northern Pacific Railroad, 1901

I have ways of making money you know nothing of.

> John D. Rockefeller (1839–1937)
> In Abels, *The Rockefeller Billions,* 1965 [Said: 1872]

I believe the power to make money is a gift of God . . . to be developed and used to the best of our ability for the good of mankind. Having been endowed with the gift I possess, I believe it is my duty to make money and still more money, and to use the money I make for the good of my fellow man according to the dictates of my conscience.

John D. Rockefeller
In Josephson, *The Robber Barons*, 1934

A great man represents a great ganglion in the nerves of society, or, to vary the figure, a strategic point in the campaign of history, and part of his greatness consists in his being *there*.

Oliver Wendell Holmes, Jr. (1841–1935)
John Marshall, 1901

The money-getter who pleads his love of work has a lame defense, for love of work at money-getting is a lower taste than love of money.

Ambrose Bierce (1842–c. 1914)
Collected Works, 1912

A man who is very busy seldom changes his opinions.

Friedrich Wilhelm Nietzsche (1844–1900)
Human All-Too-Human, 1878

I will not go on the board of a company that I don't control.

Thomas A. Edison (1847–1931)
Said after his first and last board meeting, August 1892

Self-made men are very apt to usurp the prerogative of the Almighty and overwork themselves.

Edgar Wilson ("Bill") Nye (1850–1896)

Don't be afraid to lose a little money. It advertises our stores more than anything else could. . . . We always come out on top.

F. W. Woolworth (1852–1919)

People are always blaming their circumstances for what they are. I don't believe in circumstances. The people who get on in this world are the people who get up and look for the circumstances they want, and, if they can't find them, make them.

George Bernard Shaw (1856–1950)
Mrs. Warren's Profession, 1893

The reasonable man adapts himself to the world; the unreasonable one persists in trying to adapt the world to himself. Therefore all progress depends on the unreasonable man.

George Bernard Shaw
Man and Superman, 1903

The worst cliques are those which consist of one man.

George Bernard Shaw
Back to Methuselah, 1921

I am simply unable to understand the value placed by so many people upon great wealth. . . . I am delighted to show any courtesy to Pierpont Morgan or Andrew Carnegie or James J. Hill, but . . . the very luxurious, grossly material life of the average multimillionaire whom I know does not appeal to me in the least, and nothing could hire me to lead it.

Theodore Roosevelt (1858–1919)

I do not dislike but I certainly have no especial respect or admiration for and no trust in, the typical big moneyed men of my country. I do not regard them as furnishing sound opinion as respects either foreign or domestic business.

Theodore Roosevelt

History is more or less bunk. It's tradition. We don't want tradition. We want to live in the present and the only history that is worth a tinker's dam is the history we make today. [Reported in the *Chicago Tribune*, 1916]
    History is bunk. [Said in court, when suing the *Tribune*, 1919]
    I did not say it *was* bunk. It was bunk to *me* . . . I did not need it very bad. [Quoted in Nevins et al., *Ford* (1954–1963)]

Henry Ford (1863–1947)

Let a man start out in life to build something better and sell it cheaper than it has been built or sold before, let him have that determination and the money will roll in.

Henry Ford

What we call evil is simply ignorance bumping its head in the dark.

Henry Ford
Quoted in the *Observer*, 16 March 1930

Exercise is bunk. If you are healthy, you don't need it: if you are sick, you shouldn't take it.

Attributed to Henry Ford

That's enough, Charlie. Don't show me any more figures; I've got the smell of the thing now.

Henry Ford
To Charles Sorenson, his lieutenant

You furnish the pictures and I'll furnish the war.

William Randolph Hearst (1863–1951)
Cable to artist Frederic Remington in Cuba, 1898

Calvinists and Jews have the religious fervor necessary for capitalistic enterprise.

Werner Sombart (1863–1941)
Quoted in Appel, "Reminiscences in Retailing,"
Bulletin of the Business Historical Society, Inc.,
December 1938

The Great Principles on which we will build this Business are as everlasting as the Pyramids.

H. Gordon Selfridge (?1864–1947)
Announcement, Selfridge's

If Max [Beaverbrook] gets to Heaven he won't last long. He will be chucked out for trying to pull off a merger between Heaven and Hell . . . after having secured a controlling interest in key subsidiary companies in both places, of course.

H. G. Wells (1866–1946)
Quoted in Taylor, *Beaverbrook,* 1970

I would rather be an opportunist and float than go to the bottom with my principles round my neck.

Attributed to Stanley Baldwin (1867–1947)

My bees always remind me that hard work, thrift, sobriety, and an earnest struggle to live an upright Christian life are the first rungs of the ladder of success.

Sebastian S. Kresge (1867–1966)
His hobby of bee-keeping

Nobody works as hard for his money as the man who marries it.

Frank McKinney ("Kin") Hubbard (1868–1930)

The great man . . . walks across his century and leaves the marks of his feet all over it, ripping out the dates on his galoshes as he passes.

Stephen Leacock (1869–1944)
Literary Lapses, 1910

I am a great believer in luck, and I find the harder I work the more I have of it.

Stephen Leacock

Lord Finchley tried to mend the Electric Light
Himself. It struck him dead: And serve him right!
It is the business of the wealthy man
To give employment to the artisan.

Hilaire Belloc (1870–1953)
More Peers, 1911

I admit that a grocer's shop is one of the most romantic and thrilling things that I have ever happened upon, but the romance and thrill are centered in the groceries, not the grocer. The citron and spices and nuts and dates, the barreled anchovies and Dutch cheeses, the jars of caviar and the chests of tea, they carry the mind away to Levantine coast towns and tropic shores, to the Old World wharfs and quays of the Low Countries, to dusty Astrakhan and far Cathay; if the grocer's apprentice has any romance in him it is not a business education he gets behind the grocer's counter, it is a standing invitation to dream and to wander, and to remain poor.

Saki [H. H. Munro] (1870–1916)
"Clovis on the Alleged Romance of Business," *The Square Egg,* 1924

Cowperwood rose suddenly, straight and determined—a trick with him when he wanted to really impress anyone. He seemed to radiate force, conquest, victory. "Do you want to come in?"

"Yes, I do, Mr. Cowperwood!" exclaimed Sippens, jumping to his feet, putting on his hat and shoving it far back on his head. He looked like a chest-swollen bantam rooster.

Cowperwood took his extended hand.

Theodore Dreiser (1871–1945)
The Titan, 1914

I can't help from making money, that is all.

Helena Rubinstein (1871–1965)
In the *New York Journal-American,*
12 March 1958

The chief business of the American People is business.

Calvin Coolidge (1872–1933)

When a President said that "the business of America is business," he told us something about the degree to which a standard of living can do stand-in duty for a way of life.

Adlai E. Stevenson (1900–1965)

The megalomaniac differs from the narcissist by the fact that he wishes to be powerful rather than charming, and seeks to be feared rather than loved. To this type belong many lunatics and most of the great men of history.

Bertrand Russell (1872–1970)
The Conquest of Happiness, 1930

The Eternal Principles of Retailing: Headings of an Analysis of John Wanamaker's Success I Made at the Time of His Death in 1922

He was himself. In whatever he did, whatever he wrote, whatever he said, was the personality, the originality of John Wanamaker.

He dreamed dreams—and he dramatized them as they came to life.

He was true—to himself, to his people, to the public, to manufacturers.

He believed in himself—and in his business, in his people, and in the public.

He was always on the job.

He kept himself fit.

He dared to do.

He was free—and he made others free.

He was a merchant—and he made his store "buyers" merchants, with no more limitations than he placed on himself, the limitations that business laws and common prudence dictate.

He had the "third eye"—the spiritual eye that genius has.

He saw the good in others and developed it.

He accepted no limitations.

He thought and acted in large units.

Yet he was careful of details.

He usually did the unexpected.

He was hospitable—with open heart and mind.
He was youthful in his outlook.
He educated himself, and kept ever at it.
He was a good listener.
He concentrated on what he was doing.
He rarely forgot.
He rarely carried home business cares.

He never sacrificed creativeness to efficiency. His stores were often criticized as not being efficient—in the German sense of the term. He believed that creativeness is greater than efficiency and where efficiency interfered he sacrificed efficiency.

He always sought to break records—even at fishing in Florida.
He gave and he received.
He gave service to mankind.
He gave reverence and worship to his Maker.

> Joseph H. Appel (1873–1949)
> Address to the Business Historical Society, 1938

Intuition is reason in a hurry.

> Holbrook Jackson (1874–1948)

Big business does not lend itself readily to dishonesty and crookedness.

> Owen D. Young (1874–1962)
> General Electric

A fellow who is always declaring he's no fool usually has his suspicions.

> Wilson Mizner (1876–1933)

This is my final word. It is time for me to become an apprentice once more. I have not settled in which direction. But somewhere, sometime, soon.

> Lord Beaverbrook (1879–1964)
> Speech on 25 May 1964, his 85th birthday;
> his last public statement

Chaplin is no business man—all he knows is that he can't take anything less.

> Samuel Goldwyn (1882–1974)
> Quoted in Chaplin, *My Autobiography*, 1964

For years I have been known for saying "Include me out"; but today I am giving it up forever.

> Samuel Goldwyn
> Address at Balliol College, Oxford, 1 March 1945

Entrepreneurs

Yes, I'm going to have a bust made of them.

Attributed to Samuel Goldwyn
To: What beautiful hands your wife has.

I read part of it all the way through.

Attributed to Samuel Goldwyn

Obviously, in a plutocracy the natural hero is the man who robs a bank.

William Carlos Williams (1883–1963)
"Childe Harold to the Round Tower Came"

Go around asking a lot of damfool questions and taking chances. Only through curiosity can we discover opportunities, and only by gambling can we take advantage of them.

Clarence Birdseye (1886–1956)

Because it's there.

George Leigh Mallory (1886–1924)
[When asked why he wanted to climb Mount Everest]

Do you know a better way to meet people like the Saltonstalls?

Joseph P. Kennedy (1888–1969)
When asked why he wanted to be on the Board of Massachusetts Electric

All men dream: but not equally. Those who dream by night in the dusty recesses of their minds wake in the day to find that it was vanity: but the dreamers of the day are dangerous men, for they may act their dream with open eyes, to make it possible.

T. E. Lawrence (1888–1935)
Seven Pillars of Wisdom, 1926

The toughest thing about success is that you've got to keep on being a success.

Irving Berlin (1888–   )
In *Theatre Arts*, February 1958

I have no complex about wealth. I have worked hard for my money, producing things people need. I believe that the able industrial leader who creates wealth and employment is more worthy of historical notice than politicians and soldiers.

J. Paul Getty (1892–1976)
In *Time*, 24 February 1958

The meek shall inherit the earth, but not the mineral rights.

Attributed to J. Paul Getty

My forbears were successful crooks living on the slopes of Mount Ararat.

> Michael Arlen [Dikran Kuyumjian] (1895–1956)

The compensation of a very early success is a conviction that life is a romantic matter. In the best sense one stays young.

> F. Scott Fitzgerald (1896–1940)
> *The Crack-Up*, 1945

He was not the frock-coated and impressive type of millionaire which has become so frequent since the war. He was rather the 1910 model—a sort of cross between Henry VIII and "our Mr. Jones will be in Minneapolis on Friday."

> F. Scott Fitzgerald
> *Notebooks*

I like people and I like them to like me, but I wear my heart where God put it—on the inside.

> F. Scott Fitzgerald
> *The Last Tycoon*, 1941

I'm the unity.

> F. Scott Fitzgerald
> Monroe Starr in *The Last Tycoon*

Money itself isn't the primary factor in what one does. A person does things for the sake of accomplishing something. Money generally follows.

> Colonel Henry Crown (1896–   )
> In the *New York Times*, 21 February 1960

After a certain point money is meaningless. It ceases to be the goal. The game is what counts.

> Aristotle Onassis (1900–1975)
> Quoted in *Esquire*, 1969

"I am a business man," said old man Burbage. "What I want is results. So you will pardon me if I speak frankly. The trouble with your plays, Master Will, is that you leave far too many characters alive at the end of them." "Oh," said Shakespeare.

> Caryl Brahms (?1901–?1982) and S. J. Simon
> *No Bed for Bacon*

A self-made man is one who believes in luck and sends his sons to Oxford.

> Christina Stead (1902–1983)
> *House of all Nations*, 1938

It's a matter of having principles. It's easy to have principles when you're rich. The important thing is to have principles when you're poor.

> Ray A. Kroc (1902–1984)
> McDonald's

When this world makes having money so important, so essential to well-being, it's hardly reasonable to blame a man for anything he may have done to try to get himself a supply.

> James Gould Cozzens (1903–1978)
> *Selected Notebooks*

You can fool all the people all of the time if the advertising is right and the budget is big enough.

> Joseph E. Levine (1905–   )
> Joseph E. Levine Presents

Q. What's two and two?
Grade: Buying or selling?

> Lord Grade (1906–   )
> Associated Television

All my shows are great. Some of them are bad. But they are all great.

> Lord Grade
> Quoted in the *Observer*, 14 September 1975

The trouble with this business is that the stars keep ninety per cent of my money.

> Lord Grade
> Moss Empires

Much of the world's work, it has been said, is done by men who do not feel quite well. Marx is a case in point.

> John Kenneth Galbraith (1908–   )
> *The Age of Uncertainty*, 1977

Nothing is as powerless as a prophet whose time has come. He becomes a priest and vision turns into ritual. Or he becomes a celebrity who appears on the Late-Late Show or in the society column. The prophet whose time has come no longer shocks; he entertains.

> Peter F. Drucker (1909–)
> *Adventures of a Bystander*, 1978

The clue to Henry Luce as a person was his birth and childhood as a China missionary's son, who grew up 200 miles inland from the Chinese coast with almost no company except Chinese children. China rather than the America of his ancestry molded Luce—he did not come to live in America until he entered Yale as an almost grown man. And whether he knew it or not (probably not, as introspection was not his strongest trait) his human relations, his way of managing, his system of control, were those of the Chinese ruler who remains far from the scene of action and takes no direct part, but who makes sure that no one else can become a threat by organizing countervailing officials, bureaucratic factions, and competing personal networks.

> Peter F. Drucker
> *Adventures of a Bystander*

Mrs. Thicknesse and I agreed that a business of his own was probably the only solution for him because he was obviously unemployable.

> Peter de Vries (1910–)
> *Comfort Me with Apples*, 1956

I, too, have been to the Huntington

A railroad baron in the West
Built this nest,

With someone else's pick and shovel
Built this hovel,

And bought these statues semi-nude,
Semi-lewd,

Where ladies' bosoms are revealed,
And concealed,

And David equally with Venus
Has no penis.

> J. V. Cunningham (1911–1985)
> *The Collected Poems and Epigrams*, 1971

Few people of attainments take easily to a plan of self-improvement. Some discover very early their perfection cannot endure the insult. Others find their intellectual pleasure lies in the theory, not the practice. Only a few stubborn ones will blunder on, painfully, out of the luxuriant world of their pretensions into the desert of mortification and reward.

> Patrick White (1912–   )
> *Voss*, 1957

I have always thought it would be easier to redeem a man steeped in vice and crime than a greedy, narrow-minded, pitiless merchant.

> Albert Camus (1913–1960)

I started at the top and worked my way down.

> Orson Welles (1915–1985)
> Quoted in Halliwell,
> *The Filmgoer's Book of Quotes*

He was a self-made man who owed his lack of success to nobody.

> Joseph Heller (1923–   )
> *Catch-22*, 1961

As hard as I've struggled, I'm one man who can say that my dream has come true.

> John Z. DeLorean (1925–   )
> TV commercial

Money is God in action.

> Frederick J. Eikerenkoetter II [Reverend Ike] (1925–   )

It is a paradox of the acquisitive society in which we now live, that although private morals are regulated by law, the entrepreneur is allowed considerable freedom to use and abuse the public in order to make money.

> Gore Vidal (1925–   )
> In *Esquire*, 1968

Whenever a friend succeeds, a little something in me dies.

> Gore Vidal
> Quoted in London *Sunday Times Magazine*, 16 September 1973

Money Talks

The great corporations of this country were not founded by ordinary people. They were founded by people with extraordinary energy, intelligence, ambition, aggressiveness. All those factors go into the primordial capitalist urge.

Daniel Patrick Moynihan (1927–   )
US Senate

Nothing is ever accomplished by a reasonable man.

J. Fred Bucy (1928–   )
Texas Instruments

The Third World never sold a newspaper.

Rupert Murdoch (1931–   )
Quoted in the *Observer*, 1 January 1978

There are six critical things you've got to have before you can get a company going. You need a concept of the enterprise in terms of the product or service you're going to deliver. You must have technical know-how in the business you're getting into; at least, *somebody* in the company must have it. You have to have physical resources. Frequently you attain them with money, but sometimes you don't; for example, they might already be in your basement shop. That's why I don't say "capital." You have to have contacts. That is totally neglected in the business literature. Everybody knows you have to have bankers, lawyers and accountants. But not only those. If you want to be successful, you can't operate in a vacuum. You have to have other people to put pieces into it. It's important for the would-be entrepreneurs to know that. Many of them want their own businesses because they hate everybody and want to be alone. They want to be successful hermits, and you can't do that. Then, next, you have to have customer orders. As obvious as that is, students don't think of it when I ask what things you need. Those five characteristics are in my book. The sixth was pointed out to me by a student. And it should have been so obvious because it has thwarted me personally. And that is *time*.

Karl H. Vesper (1932–   )
University of Washington

Making money is fun, but it's pointless if you don't use the power it brings.

John Bentley (1940–   )

Spend whatever it takes to build the best. Then, let people know about it. In New York, there is no limit to how much money people will spend for the very best, not second best, the very best.

Donald J. Trump (1946–   )
Quoted in the New York Times Magazine, 8 April 1984

When as a young and unknown man I started to be successful I was referred to as a gambler. My operations increased in scope and volume. Then I was known as a speculator. The sphere of my activities continued to expand and presently I was known as a banker. Actually I had been doing the same thing all the time.

Sir Ernest Cassel

Selznick gave the impression that he stormed through life demanding to see the manager—and that, when the manager appeared, Selznick would hand him a twenty-page memo announcing his instant banishment to Elba.

Lloyd Shearer
Quoted in Behlmer, Memo from David O. Selznick, 1972

MANAGERS

In an interview in the *Chicago Tribune*, Peter F. Drucker once said:

> Management is not being brilliant. Management is being conscientious. Beware the genius manager. Management is doing a very few simple things and doing them well. You put brilliant people into staff roles. But for criss sakes don't let them ever make decisions, because the secret of management is never to make a decision which ordinary human beings can't carry out. . . . Work is craftsmanship. Management is craftsmanship. Most of the time it is hard work to get a very few simple things across so that ordinary people can do it.

The quotations in this section are about the person who works hard "to get a very few simple things across" and whose behavior and opinions help us understand the effort. Also, since the craft of the manager asks for intelligent guesswork, some quotations here offer free advice.

Daniel Fitzpatrick cartoon in a 1937 issue of Collier's *maga-*
zine.

Our voices swell in admiration;
Of T. J. Watson proudly sing.
He'll ever be our inspiration,
To him our voices loudly ring.

Anonymous
From IBM company songbook

He who would climb the ladder must begin at the bottom.

English proverb

Without a shepherd sheep are not a flock.

Russian proverb

And Moses chose able men out of all Israel, and made them
heads over the people, rulers of thousands, rulers of hundreds,
rulers of fifties, and rulers of ten.
   And they judged the people at all seasons: the hard causes they
brought unto Moses, but every small matter they judged themselves.

Bible: Exodus 18:25–26

Let another man praise thee, and not thine own mouth.

Bible: Proverbs 27:2

Accuse not a servant unto his master.

Bible: Proverbs 30:10

Cast thy bread upon the waters: for thou shalt find it after many
days.

Bible: Ecclesiastes 11:1

Be not ignorant of any thing in a great matter or a small.

Bible: Ecclesiasticus 5:15

The cautious seldom err.

Confucius (551–479 B.C.)
The Confucian Analects

The superior man acts before he speaks, and afterwards speaks according to his actions.

> Confucius
> *The Confucian Analects*

Those who conduct public business make use of men not at all differing in nature from those whom the managers of private affairs employ; and those who know how to employ them, conduct either private or public affairs judiciously, while those who do not know, will err in the management of both.

> Xenophon (c. 430–c. 355 B.C.)
> Quoting Socrates (469–399 B.C.)
> *The Anabasis*

Never promise more than you can perform.

> Publilius Syrus (First Century B.C.)
> *Sententiae*

Do not ask for what you will wish you had not got.

> Seneca (c. 4 B.C.–A.D. 65)
> *Epistles*

I was shipwrecked before I got aboard.

> Seneca
> *Epistles*

You roll my log, and I will roll yours.

> Seneca
> *Apocolocyntosis*

It is a true proverb, that if you live with a lame man you will learn to limp.

> Plutarch (46–120)
> *Morals*

Remember that you ought to behave in life as you would at a banquet. As something is being passed around it comes to you; stretch out your hand, take a portion of it politely. It passes on; do not detain it. Or it has not come to you yet; do not project your desire to meet it, but wait until it comes in front of you. So act toward children, so toward a wife, so toward office, so toward wealth.

> Epictetus (c. 50–120)
> *Encheiridion*

Young men are fitter to invent than to judge, fitter for execution than for counsel, and fitter for new projects than for settled business.

> Francis Bacon (1561–1626)
> *Of Youth and Age,* 1625

He that is not handsome at twenty, nor strong at thirty, nor rich at forty, nor wise at fifty, will never be handsome, strong, rich, or wise.

> George Herbert (1593–1633)
> *Jacula Prudentum,* 1651

Everyone complains of his memory, and no one complains of his judgment.

> François, Duc de La Rochefoucauld (1613–1680)
> *Maximes,* 1664

It takes great skill to know how to conceal one's skill.

> La Rochefoucauld
> *Maximes*

Beware, as long as you live, of judging people by appearances.

> Jean de la Fontaine (1621–1695)
> *Fables,* 1668

I bend but do not break.

> La Fontaine
> *Fables*

Thanks be to God, since my leaving drinking of wine, I do find myself much better, and do mind my business better, and do spend less money, and less time lost in idle company.

> Samuel Pepys (1633–1703)
> *Diary,* 26 January 1662

A man who is master of patience is master of everything else.

> George Savile, Marquess of Halifax (1633–1695)
> *Political, Moral and Miscellaneous Reflections,* 1750

A man watches himself best when others watch him too.

> George Savile, Marquess of Halifax
> *Political, Moral and Miscellaneous Reflections*

Money Talks

He that leaveth nothing to chance will do few things ill, but he will do very few things.

George Savile, Marquess of Halifax
Political, Moral and Miscellaneous Reflections

Suspicion is rather a virtue than a fault, as long as it doth like a dog that watcheth, and doth not bite.

A wise man will keep his suspicions muzzled, but he will keep them awake.

George Savile, Marquess of Halifax
Political, Moral and Miscellaneous Reflections

There ought to be a great difference between the memory and the stomach; the last is to admit everything, the former should have the faculty of rejecting.

George Savile, Marquess of Halifax
Political, Moral and Miscellaneous Reflections

'Tis good to have men in awe, but dangerous to have them afraid of us.

George Savile, Marquess of Halifax
Political, Moral and Miscellaneous Reflections

A man in business must put up many fronts if he loves his own quiet.

William Penn (1644–1718)
Some Fruits of Solitude, 1693

He is worth gold that can win it.

James Kelly
Scottish Proverbs, 1721

To govern mankind one must not overrate them.

Lord Chesterfield (1694–1773)

Few people do business well who do nothing else.

Lord Chesterfield
Letters, 7 August 1749

Trade could not be managed by those who manage it if it had much difficulty.

Samuel Johnson (1709–1784)
To Hester Thrale, 16 November 1779

Managers

'Tis easy to resign a toilsome place,
But not to manage leisure with a grace;
Absence of occupation is not rest,
A mind quite vacant is a mind distress'd.

> William Cowper (1731–1800)
> "Retirement," in *Poems*, 1782

Take two managers and give them the same number of laborers, and let these laborers be equal in all respects. Let both managers rise equally early, go equally late to rest, be equally active, sober and industrious, and yet, in the course of the year, one of them, without pushing the hands that are under him more than the other, shall have performed infinitely more work.

> George Washington (1732–1799)

That one hundred and fifty lawyers should do business together ought not to be expected.

> Thomas Jefferson (1743–1826)
> *Autobiography;* on the US Congress, 6 January 1821

Thinking is more interesting than knowing, but less interesting than looking.

> Johann Wolfgang von Goethe (1749–1832)

To measure up to all that is demanded of him, a man must overestimate his capacities.

> Johann Wolfgang von Goethe

Two o'clock in the morning courage: I mean unprepared courage.

> Napoleon Bonaparte (1769–1821)
> From *Las Cases, Mémorial de Ste-Hélène,* 1823
> [Said: December 1815]

A load of cares lies like a weight of guilt upon the mind: so that a man of business often has all the air, the distraction and restlessness and hurry of feeling of a criminal.

> William Hazlitt (1778–1830)

There is always room at the top.

> Attributed to Daniel Webster (1782–1852)

The man who is above his business may one day find his business above him.

> Daniel Drew (1797–1879)

Money Talks

Love is the business of the idle, but the idleness of the busy.
Edward George Bulwer-Lytton (1803–1873)

Keep cool: it will be all one a hundred years hence.
Ralph Waldo Emerson (1803–1882)
Montaigne; or, The Skeptic, 1850

My father taught me to work; he did not teach me to love it.
Abraham Lincoln (1809–1865)

He's tough, ma'am, tough, is J. B. Tough and devilish sly!
Charles Dickens (1812–1870)
Dombey and Son, 1848

It is very easy to manage our neighbor's business, but our own sometimes bothers us.
Josh Billings [Henry Wheeler Shaw] (1818–1885)

Nothing is more humiliating than to see idiots succeed in enterprises we have failed in.
Gustave Flaubert (1821–1880)
L'Éducation sentimentale, 1870

There is the greatest practical benefit in making a few failures early in life.
T. H. Huxley (1825–1895)
On Medical Education, 1870

Perhaps the most valuable result of all education is the ability to make yourself do the thing you have to do, when it ought to be done, whether you like it or not; it is the first lesson that ought to be learned; and however early a man's training begins, it is probably the last lesson that he learns thoroughly.
T. H. Huxley
Technical Education, 1877

You scratch my back & Ile scratch your back.
Artemus Ward [Charles Farrar Browne] (1834–1867)
In "One of Mr. Ward's Business Letters," *Complete Works,* 1898

Mr. Morgan buys his partners: I grow my own.
Andrew Carnegie (1835–1919)
In Hendrick, *Life of Andrew Carnegie,* 1932

That is not what I asked you. I asked you to tell me how it *could* be done legally. Come back tomorrow or the next day and tell me how it can be done.

J. P. Morgan (1837–1913)
To ex-Judge Ashbel Green, 1885

There is nothing rigid or absolute in management affairs; it is all a question of proportion. . . . Compounded of tact and experience, proportion is one of the foremost attributes of the manager.

Henri Fayol (1841–1925)
General and Industrial Management, 1949

The only prize much cared for by the powerful is power. The prize of the general is not a bigger tent, but command.

Oliver Wendell Holmes, Jr. (1841–1935)
Law and the Court, 1913

Young man, the secret of my success is that at an early age I discovered I was not God.

Oliver Wendell Holmes, Jr.
Reply to a reporter, on his ninetieth birthday, 1931

Keep the faculty of effort alive in you by a little gratuitous exercise every day. That is, be systematically ascetic or heroic in little unnecessary points, do every day or two something for no other reason than that you would rather not do it, so that when the hour of dire need draws nigh, it may find you not unnerved and untrained to stand the test.

William James (1842–1910)
The Principles of Psychology, 1890

They say Wilson has blundered. Perhaps he has but I notice he usually blunders forward.

Thomas A. Edison (1847–1931)
Quoted in Dos Passos, *Mr. Wilson's War,* 1962

You don't learn to hold your own in the world by standing on guard, but by attacking, and getting well hammered yourself.

George Bernard Shaw (1856–1950)
Getting Married, 1908

Whether you think Jesus was God or not, you must admit that he was a first-rate political economist.

George Bernard Shaw
Androcles and the Lion, 1916

One man that has a mind and knows it can always beat ten men who haven't and don't.

George Bernard Shaw
The Apple Cart, 1929

Success covers a multitude of blunders.

George Bernard Shaw

We have witnessed in modern business the submergence of the individual within the organization, and yet the increase to an extraordinary degree of the power of the individual, of the individual who happens to control the organization. Most men are individuals no longer so far as their business, its activities, or its moralities are concerned. They are not units but fractions.

Woodrow Wilson (1856–1924)
Speech at Chattanooga, 31 August 1910

You shall judge of a man by his foes as well as by his friends.

Joseph Conrad (1857–1924)
Lord Jim, 1900

Facing it—always facing it—that's the way to get through. Face it! That's enough for any man!

Joseph Conrad

The best executive is the one who has sense enough to pick good men to do what he wants done, and self-restraint enough to keep from meddling with them while they do it.

Theodore Roosevelt (1858–1919)

The business ability of the man at the head of any business concern, big or little, is usually the factor which fixes the gulf between striking success and hopeless failure.

Theodore Roosevelt

The authority to issue an order involves the responsibility of seeing that the order is carried out.

Henry L. Gantt (1861–?)
Quoted in Schell, *The Technique of Executive Control,* 1926

I don't care a damn for your loyal service when you think I am right; when I really want it most is when you think I am *wrong.*

Attributed to General Sir John Monash (1865–1931)

The value of anything is not what you get paid for it, nor what it cost to produce, but what you can get for it at an auction.

William Lyon Phelps (1865–1943)
In the *National Observer,* 1969

Lots of folks confuse bad management with destiny.

Frank McKinney ("Kin") Hubbard (1868–1930)

You may help a lame dog over a stile, but he is still a lame dog on the other side.

Ernest Newman (1868–1959)
In Heyworth, ed., *Berlioz, Romantic and Classic: Writings by Ernest Newman,*
1972

He can be called a remarkable man who stands out from those around him by the resourcefulness of his mind, and who knows how to be restrained in the manifestations which proceed from his nature, at the same time conducting himself justly and tolerantly towards the weaknesses of others.

George Gurdjieff (1872–1949)
Meetings with Remarkable Men (tr., 1969)

Mrs. Walgreen portrayed her husband as possessing a canny modesty: "He used to come home and remark, 'Well, today I hired another man who is smarter than I am.' I would comment that nobody in the drug business was smarter than he was. But Charles would say, 'The only really smart thing about me is that I know enough to hire men who are smarter than I am.'"

Charles Walgreen (1873–1939)

A man looking at a hippopotamus may sometimes be tempted to regard a hippopotamus as an enormous mistake; but he is also bound to confess that a fortunate inferiority prevents him personally from making such mistakes.

G. K. Chesterton (1874–1936)
Charles Dickens, 1903

There is a great man who makes every man feel small. But the real great man is the man who makes every man feel great.

G. K. Chesterton
Charles Dickens

Where does a wise man kick a pebble? On the beach. Where does a wise man hide a leaf? In the forest.

G. K. Chesterton
The Innocence of Father Brown, 1911

The true leader is always led.

Carl Gustav Jung (1875–1961)
Quoted in the *Guardian Weekly,* 30 October 1976

We need to teach the highly educated person that it is not a disgrace to fail and that he must analyze every failure to find its cause. He must learn how to fail intelligently, for failing is one of the greatest arts in the world.

Charles F. Kettering (1876–1958)

Be nice to people on your way up because you'll meet 'em on your way down.

Wilson Mizner (1876–1933)
[Also attributed to Jimmy Durante (1893–1980)]

You're a mouse studying to be a rat.

Wilson Mizner
Remark

To govern is not to write resolutions and distribute directives; to govern is to control the implementation of the directives.

Joseph Stalin (1879–1953)
Quoted in McInnes,
The Communist Parties of Western Europe

If you don't drive your business you will be driven out of business.

B. C. Forbes (1880–1954)

It is a sin to believe evil of others, but it is seldom a mistake.

H. L. Mencken (1880–1956)

It is hard to believe that a man is telling the truth when you know you would lie if you were in his place.

H. L. Mencken

It often happens that I wake at night and begin to think about a serious problem and decide I must tell the Pope about it. Then I wake up completely and remember I am the Pope.

Pope John XXIII [Angelo Giuseppe Roncalli] (1881–1963)
Quoted in Fesquet, *Wit and Wisdom of Good Pope John*

As a rule, from what I've observed, the American Captain of Industry doesn't do anything out of business hours. When he has put the cat out and locked up the office for the night, he just relapses into a state of coma from which he emerges only to start being a Captain of Industry again.

> P. G. Wodehouse (1881–1975)
> *My Man Jeeves*, 1919

When I make a mistake it's a beaut!

> Fiorello H. La Guardia (1882–1947)
> Comment on an indefensible appointment

The buck stops here.

> Harry S. Truman (1884–1972)
> Sign on his desk

A President either is constantly on top of events or, if he hesitates, events will soon be on top of him. I never felt that I could let up for a single moment.

> Harry S. Truman
> *Memoirs*, 1955

I do not consider that efficiency need be mated to extreme delicacy or precision of touch. . . . It should possess a sweeping gesture—even if that gesture may at moments sweep the ornaments from the mantelpiece.

> Harold Nicolson (1886–1968)
> *Small Talk*, 1937

Your business is not to clear your conscience
But to learn how to bear the burdens on your conscience.
With the future of the others you are not concerned.

> T. S. Eliot (1888–1965)
> *The Cocktail Party*, 1950

Don't affect the quality of calmness. It will give an appearance of false dignity which is only amusing.

> Erwin H. Schell (1889–1965)
> *The Technique of Executive Control*, 1926

Don't vacillate. A poor plan persevered in is better than a good one shifted while being performed.

> Erwin H. Schell
> *The Technique of Executive Control*

209

Never be unreceptive to facts, however discouraging, disappointing, or injurious to your personal welfare they may appear to be.

Erwin H. Schell
The Technique of Executive Control

Remember that when an employee enters your office he is in a strange land.

Erwin H. Schell
The Technique of Executive Control

The executive is too prone to expect more in the way of knowledge and mental adaptability than is fair and reasonable to the employee.

Erwin H. Schell
The Technique of Executive Control

There is a requisite *dignity* in every position of authority which the occupant should respect and maintain. Dignity in office is a symbol of assurance that the responsibilities which accompany authority are not being treated lightly.

Erwin H. Schell
The Technique of Executive Control

Factors Influencing the Changing Philosophy of Corporate Management

Management's constant desire to widen its world by exploring the future.

Management's search for new devices which provide for flow patterns rather than periodicity in managerial operation.

Management's awareness of the new fitness of risk as a part of progress.

Management's acceptance of alacrity as an important newcomer in today's list of corporate virtues.

Management's discovery of untapped resources found in men at machines and, especially, the new resources of ingenuity and creativeness now so essential to competitive advantage.

Management's recognition of improvement as an innate desire of man.

Management's growing appreciation of the values of persuasiveness as applied to production no less than marketing or financial relationships.

Management's discovery that growth is the hope of every individual.

Management's realization that growing industrial complexity is a product of maturity and that there is a place for faith that all human problems can be solved.

Management's realization that since man's beginning his progress has in large measure rested upon the use of ever-better tools.

Management's recognition of morale as a kind of reserve that may only be earned—never bought.

Management's conviction that corporate continuity of employment, which permits employees to reach the limit of their potentialities, is a worthy objective.

Erwin H. Schell
Management Thought and Action, 1967

Yet administration demands *more than a method of thought*—it demands *a philosophy.*

Yet administration is *more than a task*—it is a *manner of living.* Yet administration *is more than a kind of doing*—it is a *kind of being.*

Yet long-term administration is *more than an affair of mind, body, and estate*—it is an *affair of the spirit.*

Yet I say that administration *is more than a form of leadership;* it is a *form of trusteeship.*

Erwin H. Schell
Management Thought and Action

The little affair of operational command is something that anybody can do.

Adolf Hitler (1889–1945)
Quoted in Bullock, *Hitler,* 1952

Nothing great will ever be achieved without great men, and men are great only if they are determined to be so.

Charles de Gaulle (1890–1970)
Le Fil de L'Épée, 1934

The perfection preached in the Gospels never yet built up an empire. Every man of action has a strong dose of egotism, pride, hardness, and cunning. But all of those things will be forgiven him, indeed, they will be regarded as high qualities, if he can make of them the means to achieve great ends.

Charles de Gaulle
Le Fil de L'Épée

Deliberation is the work of many men. Action, of one alone.

Charles de Gaulle
Les Mémoires de Guerre, 1954

Money Talks

There is one thing about being President—nobody can tell you when to sit down.

Dwight D. Eisenhower (1890–1969)
Quoted in the *Observer*, 9 August 1953

Three characteristics of top executives are: slow speech, impressive appearance, and a complete lack of sense of humor.

Johnson O'Connor (1891–   )
Human Engineering Laboratory

Going to work for a large company is like getting on a train. Are you going sixty miles an hour or is the train going sixty miles an hour and you're just sitting still?

J. Paul Getty (1892–1976)

God, give us grace to accept with serenity the things that cannot be changed, courage to change the things which should be changed and the wisdom to distinguish the one from the other.

Reinhold Niebuhr (1892–1971)
The Serenity Prayer, 1934

At the very highest level there is very little knowledge. They do not understand the opinion of the masses. They are very busy from morning until evening, but they do not examine people and they do not investigate matters. Their bureaucratic manner is immense. They beat their gongs to blaze the way. They cause people to become afraid just by looking at them.

Mao Tse-tung (1893–1976)

You might as well fall flat on your face as lean over too far backward.

James Thurber (1894–1961)
Fables for Our Time, 1940

I wanted to focus some public attention on the country's forgotten man—the corporation executive paid around $20,000 a year. After taxes and educating his children and perhaps one major illness, he reaches the age of 55 without saving a penny. There's something wrong with the system when a man who does everything he should do ends up in that spot.

John O. Ekblom (1894–1966)
On rejecting a $110,000 bonus at Hupp Corporation
New York Herald Tribune, 26 June 1959

Beware of inherited wealth. The job of getting is better than spending. I have often marveled at the fact that so many large Eastern businesses are headed by Western boys. Is it because the son of the well-to-do Eastern family is exposed to social temptations which sap his energies and dull his perceptions, thus causing him to be outrun in life's race despite his heritage of accomplishment and family connections? A debutante party is certainly not a fitting prelude to a busy day, nor is a night at the Stork Club. The Western boy at work in New York, bolstered, perhaps, by a little quiet homework, keen and fresh each morning, has proved himself tough competition for the man who wears the club tie. This business of how a young man spends his evenings is a part of that thin area between success and failure.

Robert R. Young (1897–1958)
New York Central Railroad
Quoted in *Newsweek,* 20 June 1955

We know what happens to people who stay in the middle of the road. They get run over.

Aneurin Bevan (1897–1960)
Quoted in the *Observer,* 9 December 1953

I am first and foremost a catalyst. I bring people and situations together.

Armand Hammer (1898–   )
Occidental Petroleum

The finest plans have always been spoiled by the littleness of them that should carry them out. Even emperors can't do it all by themselves.

Bertolt Brecht (1898–1956)
Mother Courage, 1949

A good manager is a man who isn't worried about his own career but rather the careers of those who work for him. My advice: Don't worry about yourself. Take care of those who work for you and you'll float to greatness on their achievements.

H. S. M. Burns (1900–1971)
Shell Oil
In Elliott, *Men at the Top,* 1959

Management is 85% of the problem.

W. Edwards Deming (1900–   )

Money Talks

A well-adjusted executive is one whose intake of pep pills over-balances his consumption of tranquilizers just enough to leave him sufficient energy for the weekly visit to his psychiatrist.

> Attributed to Arthur "Red" Motley (1900–)
> US Chamber of Commerce

An expert is someone who knows some of the worst mistakes that can be made in his subject, and how to avoid them.

> Werner Heisenberg (1901–1976)
> *Physics and Beyond,* 1971

As one retiring chief executive said to his successor, "Yesterday was the last day you heard the truth from your subordinates."

> Robert N. McMurry (1901–)
> "Clear Communications for Chief Executives,"
> *Harvard Business Review,* 1965

Not all chief executives are temperamentally capable of accepting and assimilating information which happens to conflict with their personal values and predilections.

> Robert N. McMurry
> "Clear Communications for Chief Executives,"
> *Harvard Business Review*

Teams of laborers built the pyramids and teams of craftsmen the medieval cathedrals. Now, for the first time, however, management itself has become a team effort.

> Crawford H. Greenewalt (1902–)
> Du Pont

The rushed existence into which industrialized, commercialized man has precipitated himself is actually a good example of an inexpedient development caused entirely by competition between members of the same species. Human beings of today are attacked by so-called *manager diseases,* high blood pressure, renal atrophy, gastric ulcers, and torturing neuroses: they succumb to barbarism because they have no more time for cultural interests.

> Konrad Lorenz (1903–)

Never forget that only dead fish swim with the stream.

> Malcolm Muggeridge (1903–)

Management is now where the medical profession was when it decided that working in a drug store was not sufficient training to become a doctor.

Lawrence A. Appley (1904–   )
American Management Association
In Elliott, *Men at the Top*, 1959

I think in the 1980s there are going to be fewer people in offices. Offices are a tremendous waste of time for chief executives and they create 60 per cent of all the work that takes place in them. I can be away from my office for three weeks, and things get done. But if I come in for one day, everything stops. Everyone wants to ask me what to do. In most cases, the boss is busy because he is in. He should be out where the rubber hits the road, working with people and watching them.

Lawrence A. Appley
American Management Association

To an ever-growing extent the managers are no longer, either as individuals or legally or historically, the same as capitalists. There is a combined shift: through changes in the technique of production, the functions of management become more distinctive, more complex, more specialized, and more crucial to the whole process of production, thus serving to set off those who perform those functions as a separate group or class in society; and at the same time those who formerly carried out what functions there were of management, the *bourgeoisie,* themselves withdraw from management, so that the difference in function becomes also a difference in the individuals who carry out that function.

James Burnham (1905–   )
The Managerial Revolution, 1941

When I've had a rough day, before I go to sleep I ask myself if there's anything more I can do right now. If there isn't, I sleep sound.

Lester L. Colbert (1905–   )
Chrysler
Quoted in *Newsweek,* 22 August 1955

The business executive is by profession a decision maker. Uncertainty is his opponent. Overcoming it is his mission. Whether the outcome is a consequence of luck or of wisdom, the moment of decision is without doubt the most creative and critical event in the life of the executive.

John D. McDonald (1906–   )
"How Businessmen Make Decision,"
Fortune, August 1955

To be a success in industry . . . takes a damn lot of energy. Who is going to put it out? It is the guy who when he isn't striving gets tense or anxious.

James N. Farr (1907–   )

Decision-making is one of the most important components for an executive—to make a decision, not to have a cliffhanger. You have to say either yes or no, even though a yes or no may be wrong at the time. You can't leave people in a vacuum. Be definitive, that's important. I can say yes or no. I'm sure I've been wrong a great many times; but in the overall average, it's worked out.

Helen Meyer (1907–   )
Dell Publishing

You can delegate authority, but you can never delegate responsibility for delegating a task to someone else. If you picked the right man, fine, but if you picked the wrong man, the responsibility is yours—not his.

Richard E. Krafve (1907–1974)
Raytheon
Quoted in the *Boston Sunday Globe,* 22 May 1960

To govern is to choose.

Attributed to Pierre Mendès-France (1907–   )

I'd much rather have that fellow inside my tent pissing out, than outside my tent pissing in.

Lyndon B. Johnson (1908–1973)
When asked why he kept J. Edgar Hoover as head of the FBI

The salary of the chief executive of the large corporation is not a market award for achievement. It is frequently in the nature of a warm personal gesture by the individual himself.

John Kenneth Galbraith (1908–   )
Annals of an Abiding Liberal, 1980

You are being paid to Think. Never forget that, because if anyone ever asks you what the blazes you're doing that's the answer—Being paid to think.

It is also your job to organize. Remember that the hallmark of a good Organizer is that he never *does* anything himself. He has Delegated his work so perfectly that there is nothing left to do.

Mark Spade [Nigel Balchin] (1908–1970)
How to Run a Bassoon Factory, 1936

Management by objectives works if you know the objectives. Ninety percent of the time you don't.

Peter F. Drucker (1909–   )

Management is not being brilliant. Management is being conscientious. Beware the genius manager. Management is doing a very few simple things and doing them well. You put brilliant people into staff roles. But for criss sakes don't let them ever make decisions, because the secret of management is never to make a decision which ordinary human beings can't carry out. . . . Work is craftsmanship. Management is craftsmanship. Most of the time it is hard to get a very few simple things across so that ordinary people can do it.

Peter F. Drucker
Claremont College Graduate School

Whenever you see a successful business, someone once made a courageous decision.

Peter F. Drucker

In an automated business the intuitive manager is obsolete; and experience under automation will not be a very reliable guide. To be a manager in an automated business, of course, a man need not have a formal education, let alone a degree; indeed it would be hard to find an institution of learning where he could acquire today the education he needs to be a manager tomorrow. But, in the sense of being able to handle systematic knowledge, he will have to be *highly* educated.

Peter F. Drucker
America's Next Twenty Years, 1955

The executive exists to make sensible exceptions to general rules.

Elting E. Morison (1909–   )

People ask me, "How can you take all the pressure on a job like this?" And I think I can answer for all chief executives: We love it. Any man in the top spot will say things like: "It's tough—tough and hard." But boy, take that pressure away from them, and they burst.

Fred J. Borch (1910–   )
General Electric

I don't believe in just ordering people to do things. You have to sort of grab an oar and row with them. My philosophy is to stay as close as possible to what's happening. If *I* can't solve something, how the hell can I expect my managers to?

> Harold S. Geneen (1910–   )
> International Telephone & Telegraph

Father taught us that opportunity and responsibility go hand in hand. I think we all act on that principle; on the basic human impulse that makes a man want to make the best of what's in him and what's been given him.

> Laurance S. Rockefeller (1910–   )

You can overcome all prejudice in this world if you make money for someone. They'll forgive your religion and everything. That's really the answer.

> William Bernbach (1911–1982)
> Doyle Dane Bernbach

Do not summon people to your office—it frightens them. Instead go to see them in *their* offices. This makes you visible throughout the agency. A chairman who never wanders about his agency becomes a hermit, out of touch with his staff.

> David Ogilvy (1911–   )
> Ogilvy & Mather

When the president does it, that means it is not illegal.

> Richard M. Nixon (1913–   )
> TV interview with David Frost, 20 May 1977

Happy is the man with a wife to tell him what to do and a secretary to do it.

> Lord Mancroft (1914–   )
> Quoted in the *Observer,* 18 December 1966

There is no way you can lead a large organization unless your people have independently come to a judgment that you're trustworthy, have a good sense of values and don't hand them a lot of baloney.

> Irving S. Shapiro (1916–   )
> Du Pont

There are a lot of young bucks waiting to be chief.

> Arjay Miller (1916–   )
> Ford Motor
> Stanford Business School

Never complain. Never explain.

> Henry Ford II (1917–   )

I think that is Number 1—the ability to handle uncertainty.

David A. Thomas (1917–   )
Cornell School of Business

Today's businessman must have the genius of an Einstein, the memory of an elephant and the education of a lawyer, scientist and educator all wrapped in one.

Russell B. Long (1918–   )
US Senate

One man, no matter how brilliant, can't be a successful corporation. A successful corporation is a group effort. The man at the top can help shape and define the company's goals; he can create an environment that gets people working together creatively; and he can act as umpire. He might know it all, but he can't run it all alone.

Harold V. Gleason (1919–   )
Franklin National Bank

So many people wanted to see Hopkins that it was necessary to fit them in whenever possible. First there were all the people who wanted to see him on company business—production people, research men, the top entertainers who had to be flattered, advertising executives with big contracts, the owners of affiliated stations, promotion men, publicity experts, sponsors, writers who were great artists and had never written for television, but now were going to. There were also bankers, real estate men, investment experts, and lawyers who, under Hopkins' guidance, administered the holdings of the United Broadcasting Corporation. And in addition to all these people who wanted to see Hopkins, there were executives of the many corporations of which he was a director, and the men and women connected with the good works of which he was a trustee. Hopkins was a trustee of two universities, five hospitals, three public libraries, one fund for orphaned children, two foundations for the advancement of the arts and sciences, a home for the blind, a haven for crippled children, and a snug harbor for retired seamen. In addition to that, he was a member of committees and commissions studying variously conditions in South India, Public Health in the United States, Racial Segregation, Higher Standards for Advertising, the Parking Problem in New York City, Farm Subsidies, Safety on the Highways, Freedom of the Press, Atomic Energy, the House Rules of the City Club, and a Code of Decency for Comic Books.

Sloan Wilson (1920–   )
The Man in the Gray Flannel Suit, 1955

We're the least-managed company in the world. My colleagues have as much say as I do, and sometimes more. I make marvelous decisions that are promptly overriden by them, and they do it without bashfulness or shame, but with reason. Seventy-five per cent of the time they are right. That's a high batting average, and it comes from having good people who are participating and having fun. As a result, we've got a hell-on-wheels management.

> Henry A. Walker, Jr. (1922–)
> Amfac

Room at the Top.

> John Braine (1922–)
> Title of book, 1957

We haven't anything that isn't for sale. Swift must either perform, or it won't be there.

> Donald P. Kelly (1922–)
> Esmark

I can say I'm the nicest guy in the world, but if the perception is something different, well, the world runs on perceptions. A chief executive officer has to discover what is effective—how he can make people listen, how he can be persuasive, how he can lead and motivate. If a CEO can't, then he's not very good—he'll be eaten up by the troops.

> Alden W. Clausen (1923–)
> Bank of America

There cannot be a crisis next week. My schedule is already full.

> Henry Kissinger (1923–)
> Quoted in *Time*, 24 January 1977

If you can keep your head when all about you are losing theirs, it's just possible you haven't grasped the situation.

> Jean Kerr (1923–)
> *Please Don't Eat the Daisies*, 1957

I've heard people say really often—I bet once a week—"I wouldn't want your job for all the money in the world." And I never respond to that. I don't know what the hell the response is. I love my job. They look upon it as a position that just grinds you and kills you off. I don't. Maybe that's the difference. In fact, maybe that's why the guys that say things like that will never get my job.

> Lee A. Iacocca (1924–)
> Ford Motor

That's the badge; that's the score-keeping, boys.

Lee A. Iacocca
Chrysler
Of his stock options and money; quoted in the *New York Times*, 23 December
1984

If I had to sum up in one word what makes a good manager, I'd say decisiveness. You can use the fanciest computers to gather the numbers, but in the end you have to set a timetable and act. And I don't mean rashly. I'm sometimes described as a flamboyant leader and a hip-shooter, a fly-by-the-seat-of-the-pants operator. But if that were true, I could never have been successful in this business.

Lee A. Iacocca
Iacocca, 1984

We're doing a little diversifying. But we have to live or die by cars and trucks.

Lee A. Iacocca
Chrysler
TV coverage of strike settlement, 28 October 1985

I got the empty feeling that what I was doing there might be nothing more than perpetuating a gigantic fraud.

John Z. DeLorean (1925–   )
On his running of GM's Chevrolet Division, 1971,
which he quit in 1973
"How Moral Men Make Immoral Decisions," in *On A Clear Day You Can See
General Motors— John Z. Delorean's Look Inside The Automobile Giant*, 1979

The more complicated and powerful the job, the more rudimentary the preparation for it. You cultivate the essential virtues: high purpose, intelligence, decency, humility, fear of the Lord, and the passion for freedom.

William F. Buckley, Jr. (1925–   )
National Review, 23 April 1963
Of the Presidency

Show me a country, a company or an organization that is doing well and I'll show you a good leader. Show me a country or a company that is not doing well and I'll show you a bad leader.

Joseph E. Brooks (1928–   )
Lord & Taylor

Teaching administration in the classroom is like trying to teach swimming without letting your students go near the water. At Harvard the students are placed in a dense fog and encouraged to wave their arms; at M.I.T. we teach hydrodynamics and make them do pushups.

John D. C. Little (1928–   )

A committee is an animal with four back legs.

John le Carré (1931–   )
Tinker, Tailor, Soldier, Spy, 1974

Businesses aren't run by geniuses. It is a matter of putting one foot after another in a logical fashion. The trick is in knowing what direction you want to go.

James R. Barker (1935–   )
Moore & McCormack

Business education reflects exactly what people in the business world want. We've designed organizations that reward people who think very narrowly and behave very narrowly. Why aren't management textbooks funny? It's because they don't have much realism to them. If they had much realism to them, they'd be funny as hell.

Jerry Harvey (1935–   )
George Washington University

I can provide leadership, but each of the owners is going to have to pick up an oar and start rowing the same way. [The current situation:] Some owners facing in different directions, some with big oars and some with little oars, and some with no oars in the water at all.

Peter V. Ueberroth (1937–   )
[On his job as Baseball Commissioner. Quoted in the *Wall Street Journal*, 18 October 1985

There is too much emphasis on management technique, as opposed to knowing and seeing what the heck is happening.

Henry Mintzberg (1939–   )
McGill University

Selecting the Executive Committee "Superman" at Du Pont; "Other Specifications" Expressed by Board Members Who Were Interviewed:
His head should be screwed on right.

He should be an individualist—we don't want go-alongers.

He should balance independence of opinion with the grace to submit to the will of the majority.

He should have ideas but be willing to see them turned down without waiting for an opportunity later to say "I told you so."

He should have a specialty and as much else as he can bring with him.

He should be a self-starter willing to be an adviser—with all that the term implies and all that it doesn't imply.

We want men who won't be earth-bound by logic but have the instinct or intuition to do the right thing whether logical or not.

We should have forbearance, and recognize that the other fellow has strong convictions, too.

He should have profound tolerance, and avoid getting provoked.

He needs personality, a fine mind, and a quick wit.

> William H. Mylander
> "Management by Executive Committee,"
> *Harvard Business Review,* 1955

There's one thing to be said for inviting trouble: it generally accepts.

> Mae Maloo
> Quoted in *Reader's Digest,* September 1976

Give me a good idea and capable men, and I can't fail. That combination is worth more than money in the bank. Money in the bank can earn only a fraction of its own value. The right men and ideas working together can multiply earnings.

> John G. Berry
> Kenilworth Steel

Hard work: Answering yes or no, on imperfect information.

> Lord Bowen
> Quoted in Chamberlain, *Politics From Inside*

Conspicuous personality is a requirement of great leadership.

> Eugene E. Jennings

HUMAN
RESOURCES

In this book, human resources are the people who do the work—"white collar, blue collar, no collar," as President Eisenhower put it. As the quotes in this section imply, a great deal of ink has been spilled to prove that the social sciences are real and that social engineering is possible; a great many statistics on human (and animal) behavior are used to predict habits in the workplace. Predictability is at the heart of profitability: if the task and the person who does it are inefficient, the workforce isn't working. "Be happy in your work," demands Saito of his captive workforce in Pierre Boulle's *The Bridge Over the River Kwai*. But, in that marvelous fiction, labor and their leaders must be satisfied—with respectful treatment, fair groundrules, and a do-able task. Not until hierarchy and the dignity of work are established, is a "proper bridge" built over the Kwai. The efficient manager of human resources hopes that, unlike the bridge over the River Kwai, his efforts do not come to an unprofitable end.

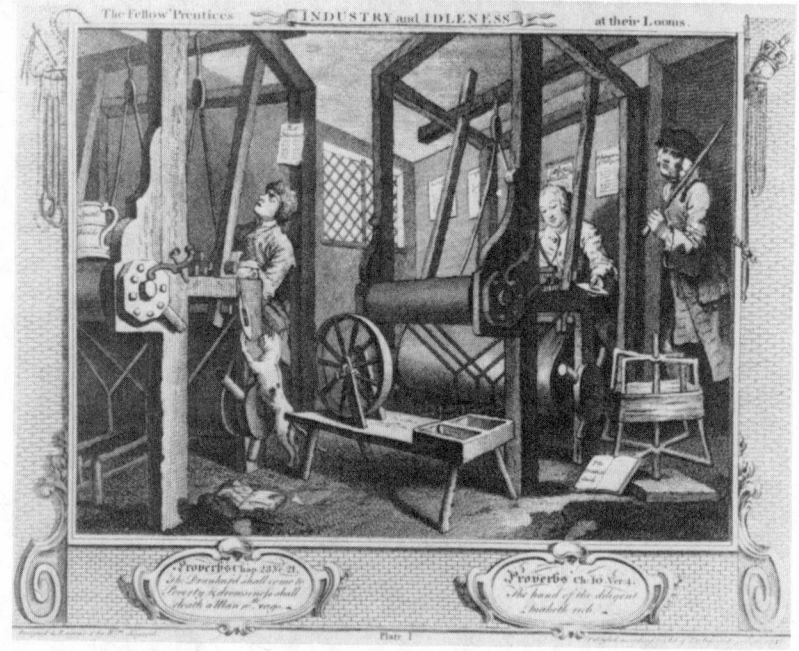

The Fellow 'Prentices at Their Looms, *by William Hogarth (1697–1764). From* **Industry and Idleness,** *1747.*

The Law of Labor:
No pains, no gains; no sweat, no sweet.

Anonymous

You cannot throw a crowd of men together and expect to have a successful organization any more than you may place a man, a woman and children within a house and expect a happy family.

Anonymous

Oh, why don't you work
Like other men do?
How the hell can I work
When there's no work to do?

Anonymous
Hallelujah, I'm a Bum, c. 1970

Saturday's child has to work for its living.

Anonymous nursery rhyme

Six long months have passed
Since I have slept in bed.
I ain't eat a square meal o'vittles in three long weeks;
Money thinks I'm dead.

American Black song

All I want of you is a little seevility, and that of the commonest goddamnedest kind. [Mate of a whaler to his captain; in Zephaniah W. Pease, *The History of New Bedford,* 1918]
    All I want out of you is silence, and damn little of that.

Anonymous
Traditional version of what the skipper said

There are foolish people, but no foolish trades.

French proverb

A man at work at his trade is the equal of the most learned doctor.

Hebrew proverb

Live with wolves, howl like a wolf.

Russian proverb

If your enemy turns to flee, give him a silver bridge.

Spanish proverb

The man who has a trade may go anywhere.

Spanish proverb

A skillful trade is better than an inherited fortune.

Welsh proverb

If the rich could hire other people to die for them, the poor could make a wonderful living.

Yiddish proverb

Not even God is wise enough.

Yoruba proverb

Be content with your wages.

Bible: Luke 3:14

For the laborer is worthy of his hire.

Bible: Luke 10:7

Gold is tried with a touchstone, and men by gold.

Ascribed to Chilon (Sixth century B.C.)

By nature, men are nearly alike; by practice, they get to be wide apart.

Confucius (551–479 B.C.)
The Confucian Analects

The superior man cannot be known in little matters, but he may be entrusted with great concerns. The small man may not be entrusted with great concerns, but he may be known in little matters.

Confucius
The Confucian Analects

The superior man is distressed by his want of ability.

Confucius
The Confucian Analects

What the superior man seeks is in himself. What the mean man seeks is in others.

> Confucius
> *The Confucian Analects*

If a man insisted always on being serious, and never allowed himself a bit of fun and relaxation, he would go mad or become unstable without knowing it.

> Herodotus (c. 485–c. 425 B.C.)
> *Histories*

The arts which we call mechanical . . . are injurious to the bodily health of workmen and overseers, in that they compel them to be seated and indoors, and in some cases also all the day before a fire. And when the body grows effeminate, the mind also becomes weaker and weaker.

> Xenophon (c. 430–c. 355 B.C.)
> *The Economist*

Hidden worth differs little from buried indolence.

> Horace (65–8 B.C.)
> *Odes,* 23 B.C.

No man is happy who does not think himself happy.

> Publilius Syrus (First Century B.C.)
> *Sententiae*

No man can enjoy happiness without thinking that he enjoys it.

> Samuel Johnson (1709–1784)

No one knows what he can do till he tries.

> Publilius Syrus
> *Sententiae*

When a building is about to fall down, all the mice desert it.

> Pliny the Elder (23–79)
> *Natural History*

Rats desert a sinking ship.

> Anonymous proverb

Love the little trade which you have learned, and be content with it.

> Marcus Aurelius (121–180)
> *Meditations*

Nothing is impossible to a willing heart.

> John Heywood (c. 1497–c. 1580)
> *Proverbs*, 1546

The insolence of office, and the spurns
That patient merit of the unworthy takes.

> William Shakespeare (1564–1616)
> *Hamlet*, 1600–1601

The ebb'd man . . . Comes dear'd by being lack'd.

> William Shakespeare
> *Antony and Cleopatra*, 1606

The "value" or "worth" of a man, is, as of all other things, his price; that is to say, so much as would be given for the use of his power.

> Thomas Hobbes (1588–1679)
> *Leviathan*, 1651

I have laid aside business, and gone a-fishing.

> Izaak Walton (1593–1683)
> *The Compleat Angler*, 1653–1655

Who is more busy than he that hath least to do?

> John Clarke (1609–1676)
> *Paroemiologia Anglo-Latina*, 1639

The gratitude of most men is merely a secret desire to receive greater benefits.

> François, Duc de La Rochefoucauld (1613–1680)
> *Maximes*

We give nothing so freely as advice.
We may give advice, but we can never prompt behavior.

> La Rochefoucauld
> *Maximes*

He that serves God for money will serve the Devil for better wages.

> Sir Roger L'Estrange, from Aesop (1616–1704)
> *Fables*, 1692

People who make no noise are dangerous.

> Jean de La Fontaine (1621–1695)
> *Fables*, 1678–1679

An ill workman quarrels with his tools.

John Ray (1627–1705)
English Proverbs, 1670

Few men would be deceived if their conceit of themselves did not help the skill of those that go about it.

George Savile, Marquess of Halifax (1633–1695)
Political, Moral and Miscellaneous Reflections, 1750

It is a general fault that we dislike men only for the injuries they do to us, and not for those they do to mankind. Yet it will be hard to give a good reason why a man who hath done a deliberate injury to one, will not do it to another.

George Savile, Marquess of Halifax
Political, Moral and Miscellaneous Reflections

It is a general mistake to think the men we like are good for everything, and those we do not, good for nothing.

George Savile, Marquess of Halifax
Political, Moral and Miscellaneous Reflections

It is from shortness of thought that men imagine there is any great variety in the World.

George Savile, Marquess of Halifax
Political, Moral and Miscellaneous Reflections

It is the fools and knaves that make the wheels of the World turn. They *are* the World; those few who have sense or honesty sneak up and down single, but never go in herds.

George Savile, Marquess of Halifax
Political, Moral and Miscellaneous Reflections

No man is so much a fool as not to have wit enough sometimes to be a knave; not any so cunning as a knave, as not to have weakness sometimes to play the fool.

George Savile, Marquess of Halifax
Political, Moral and Miscellaneous Reflections

Money is the best bait to fish for man with.

Thomas Fuller (1654–1734)
Gnomologia, 1732

Money is the sinew of love as well as of war.

Thomas Fuller
Gnomologia

231

They may be false who languish and complain
But they who sigh for money never feign.

> Lady Mary Wortley Montagu (1689–1762)
> Letter to James Steuart, 27 November 1759

Patience is a most necessary quality for business; many a man would rather you heard his story than grant his request.

> Lord Chesterfield (1694–1773)

An empty bag cannot stand upright.

> Benjamin Franklin (1706–1790)
> *Poor Richard's Almanack*, 1740

When men are employed, they are best contented; for on the days they worked they were good-natured and cheerful, and, with the consciousness of having done a good day's work, they spent the evening jollily; but on our idle days they were mutinous and quarrelsome.

> Benjamin Franklin
> *Autobiography*, 1771–1867

I never knew a man of merit neglected; it was generally his own fault that he failed of success.

> Samuel Johnson (1709–1784)

And having looked to Government for bread, on the very first scarcity they will turn and bite the hand that fed them.

> Edmund Burke (1729–1797)
> *Thoughts and Details on Scarcity*, 1800

I suppose there is not a man in the world who, when he becomes a knave for a thousand thalers, would not rather have remained honest for half the money.

> Georg Christoph Lichtenberg (1742–1799)
> *Reflections*, 1799

Never fear the want of business. A man who qualifies himself well for his calling, never fails of employment.

> Thomas Jefferson (1743–1826)

Man errs as long as he strives.

> Johann Wolfgang von Goethe (1749–1832)
> *Faust I*, 1808–1832

For I have been a man, and that means to have been a fighter.

> Johann Wolfgang von Goethe
> *West-Östlicher Diwan*, 1819

Power over a man's subsistence amounts to power over his will.

Alexander Hamilton (1755–1804)

Labor in this country is independent and proud. It has not to ask the patronage of capital, but capital solicits the aid of labor.

Daniel Webster (1782–1852)
Speech, 2 April 1824

Let woman then go on—not asking favors, but claiming as a right the removal of all hindrances to her elevation in the scale of being—let her receive encouragement for the proper cultivation of her powers, so that she may enter profitably into the active business of life. . . .

Lucretia Mott (1793–1880)
Speech, 17 December 1849

Man is a tool-using animal. . . . Without tools he is nothing, with tools he is all.

Thomas Carlyle (1795–1881)
Sartor Resartus, 1833–1834

"A fair day's wages for a fair day's work": it is as just a demand as governed men ever made of governing. It is the everlasting right of man.

Thomas Carlyle
Past and Present, 1843

Weighed in the balances of the sanctuary, or even in the clumsy scales of human justice, there is no equity in the allotments which assign to one man but a dollar a day, with working, while another has an income of a dollar a minute, without working.

Horace Mann (1796–1859)
"Great Wealth a Misfortune,"
The Bankers' Magazine and Statistical Register, March 1850

We must hold a man amenable to reason for the choice of his daily craft or profession. It is not an excuse any longer for his deeds that they are the custom of his trade. What business has he with an evil trade? Has he not a *calling* in his character?

Ralph Waldo Emerson (1803–1886)
Spiritual Laws, 1841

We boil at different degrees.

Ralph Waldo Emerson
Eloquence, 1870

Every really able man, in whatever direction he works . . . if you talk sincerely with him, considers his work, however much admired, as far short of what it should be.

Ralph Waldo Emerson
Immortality, 1875

A man who raises himself by degrees to wealth and power, contracts, in the course of this protracted labor, habits of prudence and restraint which he cannot afterwards shake off. A man cannot gradually enlarge his mind as he does his house.

Alexis de Tocqueville (1805–1859)
Democracy in America, 1840

The bad workmen who form the majority of the operatives in many branches of industry are decidedly of opinion that bad workmen ought to receive the same wages as good.

John Stuart Mill (1806–1873)
On Liberty, 1859

Labor is prior to, and independent of, capital. Capital is only the fruit of labor; and could never have existed if labor had not first existed. Labor is the superior of capital, and deserves much the higher consideration. Capital has its rights, which are as worthy of protection as any other rights.

Abraham Lincoln (1809–1865)
First Annual Message to Congress, 3 December 1861

Wages ought not to be insufficient to support a frugal and well-behaved wage-earner.

Pope Leo XIII [Gioacchino Pecci] (1810–1903)
Rerum novarum, 1891

I only know two sorts of boys. Mealy boys, and beef-faced boys.

Charles Dickens (1812–1870)
Oliver Twist, 1837–1838

My life is one demd horrid grind.

Charles Dickens
Nicholas Nickleby, 1838–1839

Young men passed above his head, and rose and rose; but he was always at the bottom.

Charles Dickens
Dombey and Son, 1848

You'll find us rough, sir, but you'll find us ready.

> Charles Dickens
> *David Copperfield,* 1849–1850

The mass of men lead lives of quiet desperation.

> Henry David Thoreau (1817–1862)
> *Walden,* 1854

Now in order that people may be happy in their work, these three things are needed: They must be fit for it: they must not do too much of it: and they must have a sense of success in it—not a doubtful sense, such as needs some testimony of others for its confirmation, but a sure sense, or rather knowledge, that so much work has been done well, and fruitfully done, whatever the world may say or think about it.

> John Ruskin (1819–1900)
> *Pre-Raphaelitism,* 1851

That country is the richest which nourishes the greatest number of noble and happy human beings.

> John Ruskin
> *Unto This Last,* 1862

Which of us . . . is to do the hard and dirty work for the rest— and for what pay? Who is to do the pleasant and clean work, and for what pay?

> John Ruskin
> *Sesame and Lilies,* 1865

Labor disgraces no man; unfortunately you occasionally find men disgrace labor.

> Ulysses S. Grant (1822–1885)
> Speech at Midland International Arbitration Union,
> Birmingham, England, 1877

Nothing can move a man who is paid by the hour; how sweet the flight of time seems to his calm mind.

> Charles Dudley Warner (1829–1900)

By this time they had reached the Astor House.

Phil jumped out first, and assisted Mr. Carter to descend.

He took Mr. Carter's handbag, and followed him into the hotel.

Mr. Carter entered his name in the register.

"What is your name?" he asked—"Philip Brent?"

"Yes, sir."

"I will enter your name, too."

"Am I to stay here?" asked Phil, in surprise.

"Yes; I shall need a confidential clerk, and for the present you will fill that position. I will take two adjoining rooms—one for you."

Phil listened in surprise.

"Thank you, sir," he said.

Horatio Alger, Jr. (1834–1899)
The Errand Boy (conclusion), 1888

You must capture and keep the heart of the original and supremely able man before his brain can do its best.

Andrew Carnegie (1835–1919)
"The Secret of Business Is the Management of Men,"
The World's Work, June 1903

If you pick up a starving dog and make him prosperous, he will not bite you. This is the principal difference between a dog and a man.

Mark Twain (1835–1910)
Pudd'nhead Wilson, 1894

Training is everything. The peach was once a bitter almond; cauliflower is nothing but cabbage with a college education.

Mark Twain
Pudd'nhead Wilson

We do not deal much in facts when we are contemplating ourselves.

Mark Twain

Question: Do you consider ten dollars a week enough for a longshoreman with a family to support?

Answer: If that's all he can get, and he takes it, I should say that is enough.

J. P. Morgan (1837–1913)

Wanamaker's Code of Labor Relations

(a) An admission as a fundamental principal that workers are entitled to further considerations beyond legal wages, covering their welfare and their education.

(b) To see that employees are not overreached or overlooked, and making it possible that there shall be nothing between a man and success but himself.

(c) To provide education to employees as the only means of doing what legislation or combination [i.e., unions] cannot do, the improvement of their earning capacity, and thereby assisting to remove the antagonisms of labor and capital, adding to the sum of human happiness.

(d) That the education provided shall not include the dead languages or other unuseful studies to the detriment of the practical and technical everyday work studies that aid in making a better living.

(e) That the education must at the same time go toward the development of character in order to enable a man to better engineer his life to a higher living and greater happiness, as well as to earn his daily bread.

(f) To keep foremost the observance of the spirit as well as the letter of the laws that govern our business transactions and relations to each other.

(g) A fixed plan of retirement of employees on retired pay to give rest and recreation to the old and chances to the younger people for promotion.

(h) A Court of Appeal, chosen by the employees, to hear and adjust impartially any complaint the employees desire to lay before such a court of reference.

John Wanamaker (1838–1922)
Golden Book of the Wanamaker Stores, Jubilee Year, 1861–1911,
edited by Appel and Hodges, 1911–13

It is but a truism that labor is most productive where its wages are largest. Poorly paid labor is inefficient labor, the world over.

Henry George (1839–1897)
Progress and Poverty, 1879

The Forgotten Man . . . delving away in patient industry, supporting his family, paying his taxes, casting his vote, supporting the church and the school . . . but he is the only one for whom there is no provision in the great scramble and the big divide. Such is the Forgotten Man. He works, he votes, generally he prays—but his chief business in life is to pay. . . .

William Graham Sumner (1840–1910)
Speech: The Forgotten Man, 1883

Money Talks

All forms of personal excellence, superiority, skill and distinguished attainment constitute natural monopolies and find their reward under applications of the monopoly principle.

> William Graham Sumner
> *A Group of Natural Monopolies*, 1892

The rights and interests of the laboring man will be protected and cared for—not by the labor agitators, but by the Christian men to whom God in his infinite wisdom has given the control of the property interests of this country.

> George F. Baer (1842–1914)
> Letter to a critic, coal-strike dispute, 1902

As a cure for worrying, work is better than whiskey.

> Thomas A. Edison (1847–1931)
> Interview on Prohibition

Mistrust a subordinate who never finds fault with his superior.

> John Churton Collins (1848–1908)
> In Logan Pearsall Smith, *A Treasury of English Aphorisms*, 1928

I do not value the labor movement only for its ability to give higher wages, better clothes, and better homes—its ultimate goal is to be found in the progressively evolving life possibilities of those who work. There are such wonderful possibilities in the life of each man and woman! No human being is unimportant. My inspiration comes in opening opportunities that all alike may be free to live life to the fullest.

> Samuel Gompers (1850–1924)
> *Seventy Years of Life and Labor*, 1925

A successful man cannot realize how hard an unsuccessful man finds life.

> Edgar Watson Howe (1853–1937)
> *Country Town Sayings*, 1911

There are moments when art attains almost to the dignity of manual labor.

> Oscar Wilde (1854–1900)

The youth of America is their oldest tradition. It has been going on now for three hundred years.

> Oscar Wilde
> *A Woman of No Importance*, 1893

He is a barbarian, and thinks that the customs of his tribe and island are the laws of nature.

> George Bernard Shaw (1856–1950)
> *Caesar and Cleopatra*, 1901

When a stupid man is doing something he is ashamed of, he always declares it is his duty.

> George Bernard Shaw
> *Caesar and Cleopatra*

A lifetime of happiness! No man alive could bear it: it would be hell on earth.

> George Bernard Shaw
> *Man and Superman*, 1903

A man who has no office to go to—I don't care who he is—is a trial of which you can have no conception.

> George Bernard Shaw
> *The Irrational Knot*, 1905

There are only two qualities in the world: efficiency and inefficiency; and only two sorts of people: the efficient and the inefficient.

> George Bernard Shaw
> *John Bull's Other Island*, 1907

No: I don't want no gold and no diamonds. I'm a good girl, I am.

> George Bernard Shaw
> *Pygmalion*, 1916

Men like conventions because men made them.

> George Bernard Shaw

There are not competent people enough in the world to go around; somebody must get the incompetent lawyers and doctors.

> George Bernard Shaw

You can't hold a man down without staying down with him.

> Attributed to Booker T. Washington (1856–1915)

I am a friend of the workingman, and I would rather be his friend than be one.

> Clarence Darrow (1857–1938)

239

Failure is instructive. The person who really thinks learns quite as much from his failures as from his successes.

John Dewey (1859–1952)

I like work; it fascinates me; I can sit and look at it for hours.

It is impossible to enjoy idling thoroughly unless one has plenty of work to do.

Jerome K. Jerome (1859–1927)
Idle Thoughts of an Idle Fellow, 1889

Every man who is high up likes to feel that he has done it all himself; and the wife smiles, and lets it go at that. It's our only joke. Every woman knows that.

James M. Barrie (1860–1937)
What Every Woman Knows, 1908

The man who is employed for wages is as much a businessman as his employer.

William Jennings Bryan (1860–1925)

We always think every other man's job is easier than our own. And the better he does it, the easier it looks.

Eden Phillpots (1862–1960)

About the only job left that a woman can beat a man is in female impersonator in vaudeville.

O. Henry [William Sydney Porter] (1862–1910)
The Hand that Rules the World

The best investment a young man starting out in business could possibly make is to give all his time, all his energies to work, just plain, hard work.

Charles Schwab (1862–1939)

I have gone through some rather dark chapters in American industrial history. It is a great joy to realize that humanity rules today; that industry has awakened to the fact that the employer, in engaging men's services, is entitled to use them but not to abuse them. . . . Let us hope that the new order which we find in industry will hasten the day when we shall cease altogether to talk about a separation between labor and capital and begin to think of ourselves as contributing to a cooperative undertaking in the advancement of which every supervisor and every employee is an important and essential factor.

Charles Schwab

What can a union give them, that they don't already have?
Henry Ford (1863–1947)
Quoted in Livesay, *American Made,* 1979
Having paid his workers $5 a day when the going rate was $2

Liberating them from the necessity of work so that they can devote their energies to subversive activities.
Henry Ford
Quoted in Livesay, *American Made*
Of his opposition to unions and union leadership, whose salaries were financed
by workers' union dues

The human race, in its intellectual life, is organized like the bees: the masculine soul is a worker, sexually atrophied, and essentially dedicated to impersonal and universal arts; the feminine is a queen, infinitely fertile, omnipresent in its brooding industry, but passive and abounding in intuitions without method and passions without justice.
George Santayana (1863–1952)
The Life of Reason, 1905–1906

"You're a Christian?" "Church of England," said Mr. Polly. "Mm," said the employer, a little checked. "For good all round business work, I should have preferred a Baptist."
H. G. Wells (1866–1946)
The History of Mr. Polly, 1910

Capital still pats Labor on the back—with an ax.
Finley Peter Dunne [d.b.a. Mr. Dooley] (1867–1936)

The constable has three sons, two self-sustaining and one employed by the city.
Frank McKinney ("Kin") Hubbard (1868–1930)

I had therefore to advise the laborers to go on strike. Before I did so, I came in very close contact with them and their leaders, and explained to them the conditions of a successful strike:
1. Never resort to violence,
2. Never to molest blacklegs [scabs],
3. Never to depend upon alms, and
4. To remain firm, no matter how long the strike continued, and to earn bread, during the strike, by any other honest labor.
Mohandas Karamchand Gandhi (1869–1948)
The Story of My Experiments With Truth, 1929

There is but one bargain that the I.W.W. will make with the employing class—*complete surrender of all controls of industry to the organized workers.*

Bill Haywood (1869–1928)
Founding of the International Workers of the World, Chicago, 1905

You cannot make a man by standing a sheep on its hind legs. But by standing a flock of sheep in that position you can make a crowd of men.

Max Beerbohm (1872–1956)
Zuleika Dobson, 1911

The madman is not the man who has lost his reason. The madman is the man who has lost everything except his reason.

G. K. Chesterton (1874–1936)
Orthodoxy, 1909

It seems a pity that psychology should have destroyed all our knowledge of human nature.

G. K. Chesterton
Quoted in the *Observer,* 9 December 1934

There is no room now for the dilettante, the weakling, for the shirker, or the sluggard. The mine, the factory, the dockyard, the salt sea waves, the fields to till, the home, the hospital, the chair of the scientist, the pulpit of the preacher—from the highest to the humblest tasks, all are of equal honor; all have their part to play.

Winston Churchill (1874–1965)
Speech to Canadian Senate and House of Commons, 1941

Personally I'm always ready to learn, although I do not always like being taught.

Winston Churchill
Quoted in the *Observer,* 9 November 1952

By working faithfully eight hours a day, you may eventually get to be a boss and work twelve hours a day.

Robert Frost (1874–1963)

The reason why worry kills more people than work is that more people worry than work.

Robert Frost

The world is full of willing people: some willing to work, the rest willing to let them.

Robert Frost

There are only two classes in society: those who get more than they earn, and those who earn more than they get.

Holbrook Jackson (1874–1948)

You sparkle with larceny.

Wilson Mizner (1876–1933)
Remark

When you see some girls marry, you realize how they must hate to work for a living.

Helen Rowland (1876–?)

There's a longer lease for the old gang in letting the youngsters in than in keeping them out, isn't there?

Harley Granville-Barker (1877–1946)
The Secret Life, 1923

Most of the people living in New York have come here from the farm to try to make enough money to go back to the farm.

Don Marquis (1878–1937)

Personnel selection is decisive. People are our most valuable capital.

Joseph Stalin (1879–1953)
Quoted in Solzhenitsyn, *The Love Girl and the Innocent,* 1969

There is no inherent mechanism in our present system which can with certainty prevent competitive sectional bargaining for wages from setting up a vicious spiral of rising prices under full employment.

Sir William Henry Beveridge (1879–1963)
Full Employment in a Free Society, 1945

There is more credit and satisfaction in being a first-rate truck driver than a tenth-rate executive.

B. C. Forbes (1880–1954)

The average male gets his living by such depressing devices that boredom becomes a sort of natural state to him.

H. L. Mencken (1880–1956)
In Defense of Women

Business succeeds rather better than the state in imposing its restraints upon individuals, because its imperatives are disguised as choices.

Walton H. Hamilton (1881–1958)

Men are like wine. Some turn to vinegar, but the best improve with age.

Pope John XXIII [Angelo Giuseppe Roncalli] (1881–1963)
Quoted in Brenan, *Thoughts in a Dry Season,* 1978

The average man . . . is always waiting for something to happen to him instead of setting to work to make things happen. For one person who dreams of making fifty thousand pounds, a hundred people dream of being left fifty thousand pounds.

A. A. Milne (1882–1956)
If I May, 1920

We're overpaying him but he's worth it.

Samuel Goldwyn (1882–1974)

How'm I gonna do decent pictures when all my good writers are in jail? . . . Don't misunderstand me, they all ought to be hung.

Samuel Goldwyn
Quoted by Dorothy Parker
In *Writers at Work: First Series,* 1958

Anybody who goes to see a psychiatrist ought to have his head examined.

Attributed to Samuel Goldwyn

Every director bites the hand that lays the golden egg.

Attributed to Samuel Goldwyn

To get along, go along. [*Or:* The way to get along is to go along.]

Attributed to Sam Rayburn (1882–1961)
US House

Go with the flow.

American saying

These unhappy times call for the building of plans . . . that build from the bottom up and not from the top down, then put their faith once more in the forgotten man at the bottom of the economic pyramid.

Franklin D. Roosevelt (1882–1945)
Radio address, 7 April 1932

He had insomnia so bad that he couldn't sleep when he was working.

> Arthur ("Bugs") Baer (1885–1969)

He had reasons for not working; he said your body was only a machine and he was no mechanic.

> Arthur ("Bugs") Baer

Large scale collective bargaining . . . is merely a seductive name for bilateral monopoly, and means either adjudication of conflicts in terms of power, or deadlock and stoppage, usually injuring outside people more than the immediate parties to the dispute.

> Frank Hyneman Knight (1885–1974)
> *Freedom and Reform,* 1947

Market competition is the only form of organization which can afford a large measure of freedom to the individual.

> Frank Hyneman Knight
> *Freedom and Reform*

Considering how bad men are, it is wonderful how well they behave.

> Salvador de Madariaga (1886–1978)
> *Morning without Noon*

The House with the Seven Gables is gone, consumed by fire,
And in the evenings businessmen from Boston
Sit in the beautiful houses, mobbed by cars.

> Edwin Muir (1887–1959)
> "Salem, Massachusetts"

And the wind shall say "Here were decent godless people;
Their only monument the asphalt road
And a thousand lost golf balls."

> T. S. Eliot (1888–1965)
> *The Rock,* 1934

All cases are unique, and very similar to others.

> T. S. Eliot
> *The Cocktail Party,* 1950

The will is never free—it is always attached to an object, a purpose. It is simply the engine in the car—it can't steer.

> Joyce Cary (1888–1957)
> In *Writers at Work: First Series,* 1958

Money Talks

To the casual reader the lesson of [Horatio Alger's] stories was not that hard work brings in but a pittance, or that the way to succeed is to stand in with the men who have the capital, but something quite different. The lesson was that capital comes as a reward from heaven to him who labors mightily and uses his head all the time. Work, save, be a good boy, shun the fleshpots, and presently the mining stock will fall into your lap and all will be well.

Frederick Lewis Allen (1890–1954)
"Horatio Alger, Jr." [1834–1899], *The Saturday Review of Literature,*
17 September 1938

The graveyards are full of indispensable men.

Attributed to Charles de Gaulle (1890–1970)

Union leaders who convince the workman that his employer is his natural enemy serve only the Marxian doctrine.

Herbert V. Kohler (1891–1968)
Kohler

There is no substitute for talent. Industry and all the virtues are of no avail.

Aldous Huxley (1894–1963)
Point Counter Point, 1928

There is a good deal of solemn cant about the common interests of capital and labor. As matters stand, their only common interest is that of cutting each other's throat.

Brooks Atkinson (1894–1984)
Once Around the Sun, 1951

Anybody who has any doubt about the ingenuity or the resourcefulness of a plumber never got a bill from one.

George Meany (1894–1980)

Just as the skilled carpenter, the skilled mechanic, the skilled dressmaker have in some degree survived the first industrial revolution, so the skilled scientist and the skilled administrator may survive the second. However, taking the second revolution as accomplished, the average human being of mediocre attainments or less has nothing to sell that it is worth anyone's money to buy.

Norbert Wiener (1894–1964)
Cybernetics, 1948

Among the working classes one of the unforgivable words of abuse is "bastard"—because they take bastardy seriously.

> Robert Graves (1895–   )
> *Occupation: Writer,* 1950

To be mad is not easy,
Will earn him no money,
But a niche in the news.

> Robert Graves
> "The Halls of Bedlam"

I got my job by hollering, and no day passes but what I holler about something.

> Leon Henderson (1895–?)
> Quoted in Schlesinger, *The Coming of the New Deal,* 1959

One of those men who reach such an acute limited excellence at twenty-one that everything afterward savors of anti-climax.

> F. Scott Fitzgerald (1896–1940)
> *The Great Gatsby,* 1925

There are only the pursued, the pursuing, the busy, and the tired.

> F. Scott Fitzgerald
> *The Great Gatsby*

Thirty—the promise of a decade of loneliness, a thinning list of single men to know, a thinning briefcase of enthusiasm, thinning hair.

> F. Scott Fitzgerald
> *The Great Gatsby*

It is in the thirties that we want friends. In the forties we know they won't save us any more than love did.

> F. Scott Fitzgerald
> *Notebooks,* 1945

Familiarity with women employees is likely to be a costly affair for the male supervisor.

> Lydia G. Giberson, M.D. (1899–?)
> *The Foreman's Handbook,* 1949

Now is no time to think of what you do not have. Think of what you can do with that there is.

> Ernest Hemingway (1899–1961)

The world breaks everyone and afterward many are strong at the broken places. But those that will not break it kills. It kills the very good and the very gentle and the very brave impartially. If you are none of these you can be sure that it will kill you too but there will be no special hurry.

> Ernest Hemingway
> *A Farewell to Arms*, 1929

Time is the least thing we have of.

> Ernest Hemingway
> In *The New Yorker*, Profile by Lillian Ross, 13 May 1950

A man can be destroyed but not defeated.

> Ernest Hemingway
> *The Old Man and the Sea*, 1952

Actors are cattle.

> Attributed to Alfred Hitchcock (1899–1980)

The bonus is really one of the great give-aways in business enterprise. It is the annual salve applied to the conscience of the rich and the wounds of the poor.

> E. B. White (1899–   )
> *One Man's Meat*, 1944

In the tiny space of twenty years, we have bred a whole generation of working Americans who take it for granted that they will never be out of a job or go a single year without a salary increase.

> K. K. DuVall (1900–?)
> Chicago Merchandise National Bank
> Quoted in *Time*, 10 September 1956

Modern man lives under the illusion that he knows what he wants, while he actually wants what he is supposed to want.

> Erich Fromm (1900–1980)
> *Escape from Freedom*, 1941

No private business monopoly, producer organization or cartel wields the market (and physical) power or commands the discipline over its members which many unions have achieved.

> Gottfried Haberler (1900–   )
> *Economic Growth and Stability*, 1974

Many of the job failures, nervous breakdowns, and "battles with the bottle" almost certainly have their causes in vocational misplacement and subsequent mishandling by well-intentioned but often unqualified personnel people.

> Robert N. McMurry (1901–)
> "Clear Communications for Chief Executives,"
> *Harvard Business Review,* 1965

McMurry's Law of Diminishing Competence: In any supervisory hierarchy *weakness begets greater weakness.*

McMurry's Law of Allegiance to Strength: Where two agencies are competing for employee allegiance and loyalty, the one with the strongest, most aggressive, and decisive representative will nearly always win out.

> Robert N. McMurry
> "Clear Communications for Chief Executives,"
> *Harvard Business Review*

Why did you keep me on tiptoe so long if you weren't going to kiss me?

> Tom Matthews (1901–)
> Quoted in the *Observer,* 19 May 1963
> To Henry Luce, who had decided against a
> British edition of *Time*

Things that are bad for business are bad for the people who work for business.

> Thomas E. Dewey (1902–1971)

A fool in a high station is like a man on the top of a high mountain—everything appears small to him and he appears small to everybody.

> Leander W. Matsch (1902–)

I am inclined to think the corporation that is not in the business of human development may not be in any business. At least, not for long.

> William S. Vaughn (1902–)
> Eastman Kodak

If two men on the same job agree all the time, then one is useless. If they disagree all the time, then both are useless.

> Darryl F. Zanuck (1902–1979)
> Quoted in the *Observer,* 23 October 1949

This business of petty inconvenience and indignity, of being kept waiting about, of having to do everything at other people's convenience, is inherent in working-class life. A thousand influences constantly press a working man into a *passive* role. He does not act, he is acted upon.

> George Orwell [Eric Arthur Blair] (1903–1950)
> *The Road to Wigan Pier,* 1937

To the ordinary working man, the sort you would meet in any pub on Saturday night, Socialism does not mean much more than better wages and shorter hours and nobody bossing you about.

> George Orwell
> *The Road to Wigan Pier*

I'm fat, but I'm thin inside. Has it ever struck you that there's a thin man inside every fat man, just as they say there's a statue inside every block of stone?

> George Orwell
> *Coming Up for Air,* 1939

Imprisoned in every fat man a thin one is wildly signaling to be let out.

> Cyril Connolly (1903–1974)
> *The Unquiet Grave,* 1945

Enclosing every thin man, there's a fat man demanding elbowroom.

> Evelyn Waugh (1903–1966)
> *Officers and Gentlemen,* 1955

Money is paper blood.

> Attributed to Bob Hope (1903–)

It is a mark of many famous people that they cannot part with their brightest hour.

> Lillian Hellman (1905–1984)
> *Pentimento,* 1973

One of the worst things about life is not how nasty the nasty people are. You know that already. It is how nasty the nice people can be.

> Anthony Powell (1905–)
> *The Kindly Ones,* 1962

Human Resources

It is the characteristic excellence of the strong man that he can bring momentous issues to the fore and make a decision about them. The weak are always forced to decide between alternatives they have not chosen themselves.

Dietrich Bonhoeffer (1906–1945)
Letters and Papers from Prison

Go very light on vices such as carrying on in society. The social ramble ain't restful.

Satchel Paige (c. 1906–1982)
How to Keep Young, 1953

Was he free? Was he happy? The question is absurd:
Had anything been wrong, we should certainly have heard.

W. H. Auden (1907–1973)
"The Unknown Citizen," in *Another Time,* 1940

To a worker, leisure means simply the hours he needs to relax and rest in order to work efficiently. He is therefore more likely to take too little leisure than too much; workers die of coronaries and forget their wives' birthdays. To the laborer, on the other hand, leisure means freedom from compulsion, so that it is natural for him to imagine that the fewer hours he has to spend laboring, and the more hours he is free to play, the better.

What percentage of the population in a modern technological society are, like myself, in the fortunate position of being workers? At a guess I would say sixteen per cent, and I do not think that figure is likely to get bigger in the future.

Technology and the division of labor have done two things: by eliminating in many fields the need for special strength or skill, they have made a very large number of paid occupations which formerly were enjoyable work into boring labor, and by increasing productivity they have reduced the number of necessary laboring hours. It is already possible to imagine a society in which the majority of the population, that is to say, its laborers, will have almost as much leisure as in earlier times was enjoyed by the aristocracy. When one recalls how aristocracies in the past actually behaved, the prospect is not cheerful. Indeed, the problem of dealing with boredom may be even more difficult for such a future mass society than it was for aristocracies. The latter, for example, ritualized their time; there was a season to shoot grouse, a season to spend in town, etc. The masses are more likely to replace an unchanging ritual by fashion which it will be in the economic interest of certain people to change as often as possible. Again, the masses cannot go in for hunting, for very soon there would be no animals left to hunt. For other aristocratic amusements like gambling, dueling, and warfare, it may be only too easy to find equivalents in dangerous driving, drug-taking, and senseless acts of violence. Workers seldom commit acts of violence, because they can put their aggression into their work, be it physical like the work of a smith, or mental like the work of a scientist or an artist. The role of aggression in mental work is aptly expressed by the phrase "getting one's teeth into a problem."

W. H. Auden
A Certain World, 1970

He was so punctual, you could regulate
The sun by him.

Christopher Fry (1907–   )
The Lady's Not for Burning, 1948

There are two main sorts of incentive—the sort where people get something nice if they work hard, and the sort where they get something nasty if they don't. In these enlightened days we only use the first sort.*
  * Of course we still fire people who don't work hard enough, but we don't usually consider that an incentive any more.

Mark Spade [Nigel Balchin] (1908–1970)
How to Run a Bassoon Factory, 1936

The world is made of people who never quite get into the first team and who just miss the prizes at the flower show.

Jacob Bronowski (1908–1974)
The Face of Violence, 1954

We have to understand the world can only be grasped by action, not by contemplation. The hand is more important than the eye. . . . The hand is the cutting edge of the mind.

Jacob Bronowski
The Ascent of Man, 1973

One of the best ways of avoiding necessary and even urgent tasks is to seem to be busily employed on things that are already done.

John Kenneth Galbraith (1908–   )
The Affluent Society, 1958

What we need is hatred. From it are our ideas born.

Jean Genet (1910–   )
The Blacks, 1960

252

All English shop assistants are Miltonists. A Miltonist firmly believes that "they also serve who only stand and wait."

> George Mikes (1912–   )
> *How to be Inimitable,* 1960

There was a disturbance in my heart, a voice that spoke there and said, *I want, I want, I want!* It happened every afternoon, and when I tried to suppress it it got even stronger. . . . It never said a thing except *I want, I want, I want!*

> Saul Bellow (1915–   )
> *Henderson the Rain King,* 1959

This book is about the organization man. . . . I can think of no other way to describe the people I am talking about. They are not the workers, nor are they the white-collar people in the usual, clerk sense of the word. These people only work for the Organization. The ones I am talking about *belong* to it as well.

> William H. Whyte, Jr. (1917–   )
> *The Organization Man,* 1956

For reasons of protocol, organization men publicly extol human relations for the beneficial effects it casts downward, but privately they spend most of their time talking about using it upward.

> William H. Whyte, Jr.
> *The Organization Man*

A corporation prefers to offer a job to a man who already has one, or doesn't immediately need one. The company accepts you if you are already accepted. To obtain entry into paradise, in terms of employment, you should be in a full state of grace.

> Alan Harrington (1919–   )
> *Life In the Crystal Palace,* 1959

Lateral Arabesque—a pseudo-promotion consisting of a new title and a new work place.

> Laurence J. Peter (1919–   ) and Raymond Hull (1919–   )
> *The Peter Principle,* 1969

The Peter Principle: In a Hierarchy Every Employee Tends to Rise to his Level of Incompetence.

Work is accomplished by those employees who have not yet reached their level of incompetence.

Competence, like truth, beauty and contact lenses, is in the eye of the beholder.

> Laurence J. Peter and Raymond Hull
> *The Peter Principle*

A lot of workers and middle-class people are losing their afflu-ence, and they're not going to give it up easily. If they see this as the result of monopolistic behavior, damned if they won't fight the money folks in this country and make the liberals in Congress look like John Birch Society members.

George C. Wallace (1919–   )

Without some strikes, we might not have been able to compete in the marketplace.

Roy H. Holdt (1920–   )
White Consolidated Industries

I'm not a humanitarian, you know. I believe that people should be treated well, but I also believe it's the way to run a business. It's the only way you're going to provide yourself with contented, trained people in the future.

Aanon Michael Rosholt (1920–   )
Barlow Rand (South Africa)
On his treatment of employees

The number of laws of executive and organizational behavior to be collected increases in proportion to the number already col-lected.

Thomas L. Martin, Jr. (1921–   )

We don't have any problem, the union has a problem.

James D. Finley (1922–   )
J. P. Stevens

I subscribe to the thought that most people have a finite reservoir of intellectual material to add to an enterprise and that when it's gone, it's gone. Then you have to put somebody else's reservoir to work.

John W. Hanley (1922–   )
Monsanto

A word needs to be said on the emerging principle of consumer sovereignty as it affects trade issues—that is, the proposition that the consumer has an inalienable, top-priority right to $4 Korean shoes, regardless of the conditions under which they are made, the human, social and economic cost of lost American jobs, and of who really gets the $4. This principle is mostly expounded by those who get their shoes at Gucci.

Lane Kirkland (1922–   )
AFL-CIO

The only way to convert the heathen is to travel into the jungle.
Lane Kirkland
AFL-CIO

Even when he cheated he couldn't win, because the people he cheated against were always better at cheating too.
Joseph Heller (1923–   )
Catch-22, 1961

I think that maybe in every company today there is always at least one person who is going crazy slowly.
Joseph Heller

There was only one catch and that was Catch-22, which specified that a concern for one's own safety in the face of dangers that were real and immediate was the process of a rational mind.
Joseph Heller
Catch-22

The organization of any bureaucracy is very much like a septic tank. The really big chunks always rise to the top.
John Imhoff (1923–   )

Consider the history of labor in a country in which, spiritually speaking, there are no workers, only candidates for the hand of the boss's daughter.
James Baldwin (1924–   )
The Fire Next Time, 1963

Mr. Reuther may deplore General Motors' hold on the automobile industry, as rising on 60 per cent. He has never been heard to deplore his own control over the automobile industry, which rises on 100 per cent.
William F. Buckley, Jr. (1925–   )
On The Right, 27 January 1966
Of Walter Reuther

But when I don't smoke I scarcely feel as if I'm living. I don't feel as if I'm living unless I'm killing myself.
Russell Hoban (1925–   )
Turtle Diary, 1975

I think we exaggerate the flexibility and freshness of young people. Advanced age can be conducive to conceptual skills that are extraordinarily important. Experience obviously helps, except when it causes us to see new events as mere repetitions of the past.

Ross Webber (1934–)
Wharton School

The remarkable thing about the human mind is its range of limitations.

Celia Green (1935–)
The Decline and Fall of Science, 1976

A birthday is a big event in everybody's life. It should be a holiday—with pay.

Michael Darling
News summaries, 18 January 1954

To me, the most important element in management is the human being. You can have the best plans in the world, you can have the most marvelous equipment. But it is people that carry out the plans and use the equipment. Without willing workers, you have nothing. So the first essential is to treat people with consideration.

Yoshiki Yamasaki
Toyo Kogyo, Mazda

COMMUNI-CATIONS

Communication is essential to business. Without communication there would be no marketing, no functioning of human resources, no production and operations—no business. External and internal, public and private, spoken, written, gestured—communications are lifeblood to enterprise. When we communicate effectively, we get results.

Successful communicators have an answer to the question: HOW does WHO communicate WHAT to WHOM, and WHY? (And WHERE? And WHEN?) The "gospel" printed at the beginning of this section was the editor's effort to analyze management communication for his students at Harvard Business School in 1981. Many of the quotes in this section serve to elucidate the fourteen principles of the "gospel."

Advertisement, circa 1920.

The Management Communication Gospel, According to RWK

1. *Know who you are and what you want.* And assume that the world knows neither—until you let it know.
2. *Honor the language:* its words; its grammar; its beauty, its rhythm, its flexibility. Resist gibberish. "My dear friend, clear your *mind* of cant."

   [Dr. Johnson]
3. *Read critically.* I.e., *Read, and read appreciatively.* Not everything printed is accurate, or right, or useful, or worth repeating.
4. *Ask questions.* It is in the answers to questions that our knowledge consists.

   [Aristotle]
5. *Carry your learning lightly.* No one likes a bully or a bore.
6. *Prize simplicity.* Simplicity implies single-mindedness, or attention to the matter at hand. It also suggests maturity and civility. [Simplicity ≠ simplemindedness.]
7. When introducing what you have to say, *Identify persons, places and things.* People like to know—or soon need to be reminded of—who's who and what's what.
8. *Define your terms.* People want to know what you mean, not suppose that you mean something or other.
9. *Analyze; don't summarize.* The world is more interested in how you see things and what they mean to you—less in what it already knows, or would just as soon forget.
10. *Speak/write in the active voice.* "I take responsibility for what I'm saying," not "Responsibility is being taken for what's been said by me."
11. *Write in the present tense.* Present yourself and represent what you're writing about in the present tense for the reader to read presently—unless you're reporting actions or events for the sake of noting that they happened or occurred in the past. E.g., "I *am writing* to tell you that we *have* completed our survey." [Present & present perfect.] E.g., "I *wrote* her that we *had completed* our survey." [Past & past perfect.]
12. *Spell correctly and conventionally.* Spelling is one indication of literacy.
13. *Punctuate intelligently.* Success may not actually hang on a

259

comma or a hand gesture, but intelligently punctuated communications do invite intelligent responses.
14. *Revise. Edit. Proofread*. The product should be ready, pol-
ished, whole.

Before you trust a man, eat a peck of salt with him.

Anonymous, derived from Cicero

Call upon a man of business during hours of business only to
transact your business. Then go about your business and give him
time to attend to his business.

Anonymous

Committee: A group of men who keep minutes and waste hours.

Anonymous

When I hear artists or authors making fun of businessmen I
think of a regiment in which the band makes fun of the cooks.

Anonymous

"While there is currently an increasing trend towards strict
adherence to principles of public morality," the board's special
counsel informed the stockholders, "it cannot yet be said that it
must always override all other considerations."

Anonymous
Fruehauf

You must ask much to get a little.

Anonymous

If you have no money, be polite.

Danish proverb

Money is more eloquent than a dozen members of parliament.

Danish proverb

One bag of money is stronger than two bags of truth.

Danish proverb

It takes two to make a bargain.

English proverb

Money talks.

English proverb

Communications

Mention money and the whole world is silent.

German proverb

No bargain without wine.

Latin saying

When money speaks the truth is silent.

Russian proverb

The closed mouth swallows no flies.

Spanish proverb

Speak silver, reply gold.

Swahili proverb

Money is the best messenger.

Yiddish proverb

Let thy speech be short, comprehending much in few words.

Bible: Ecclesiasticus 32:8

It is a foolish thing to make a long prologue, and to be short in the story itself.

Bible: II Maccabees 2:32

It is this simplicity that makes the uneducated more effective than the educated when addressing popular audiences.

Aristotle (384–322 B.C.)
Rhetoric

A plausible impossibility is always preferable to an unconvincing possibility.

Aristotle
Poetics

It is a hard matter, my fellow citizens, to argue with the belly, since it has no ears.

Cato the Elder (234–149 B.C.)

The belly has no ears nor is it to be filled with fair words.

François Rabelais (c. 1494–1553)
Gargantua and Pantagruel, 1548

A hungry stomach cannot hear.

Jean de La Fontaine (1621–1695)
Fables, 1678–1679

Money Talks

A hungry man is not a free man.

Adlai E. Stevenson (1900–1965)
Speech, Kasson, Minnesota, 6 September 1952

Once a word has been allowed to escape, it cannot be recalled.

Horace (65–8 B.C.)
Epistles

The people are a many-headed beast.

Horace
Epistles

There is harmony in discord.

Horace
Epistles

You have played enough; you have eaten and drunk enough. Now it is time for you to depart.

Horace
Epistles

Grammarians dispute—and the case is still before the courts.

Horace
Epistles (Ars Poetica)

If you wish me to weep, you yourself must first be grief-stricken.

Horace
Epistles (Ars Poetica)

It is when I struggle to be brief that I become obscure.

Horace
Epistles (Ars Poetica)

A good reputation is more valuable than money.

Publilius Syrus (First century B.C.)
Sententiae

Not every question deserves an answer.

Publilius Syrus
Sententiae

He who receives a benefit with gratitude repays the first installment on his debt.

Seneca (c. 4 B.C.–A.D. 65)
Moral Essays

Communications

Hear the other side.

St. Augustine (354–430)
De Duabus Animabus

Reading maketh a full man, conference a ready man, and writing an exact man.

Francis Bacon (1561–1626)
Of Studies, 1625

Good words are worth much, and cost little.

George Herbert (1593–1633)
Jacula Prudentum, 1651

Where the drink goes in, there the wit goes out.

George Herbert
Jacula Prudentum

Words are women, deeds are men.

George Herbert
Jacula Prudentum

Bare words are no good bargain.

John Clarke (1609–1676)
Paroemiologia Anglo-Latina, 1639

Quarrels would not last so long if the fault were only on one side.

François, Duc de La Rochefoucauld (1613–1680)
Maximes, 1664

To establish ourselves in the world, we have to do all we can to appear established.
To succeed in the world, we do everything we can to appear successful.

La Rochefoucauld
Maximes

Make every bargain clear and plain,
That none may afterward complain.

John Ray (1627–1705)
English Proverbs, 1670

A patient hearer is a sure speaker.

George Savile, Marquess of Halifax (1633–1695)
Political, Moral and Miscellaneous Reflections, 1750

If men would think how often their own words are thrown at their heads, they would less often let them go out of their mouths.

George Savile, Marquess of Halifax
Political, Moral and Miscellaneous Reflections

Men are angry when others do not hear them, yet they have more reason to be afraid when they do.

George Savile, Marquess of Halifax
Political, Moral and Miscellaneous Reflections

There is so much wit necessary to make a skillful hypocrite that the faculty is fallen amongst bunglers, who make it ridiculous.

George Savile, Marquess of Halifax
Political, Moral and Miscellaneous Reflections

Proper words in proper places, make the true definition of a style.

Jonathan Swift (1667–1745)
Letter to a Young Clergyman, 1720

God send some money, for they are little thought of that want it, quoth the Earl of Eglinton at his prayer.

James Kelly
Scottish Proverbs, 1721

Without some dissimulation no business can be carried on at all.

Lord Chesterfield (1694–1773)
Letters, 22 May 1749

Blame-all and Praise-all are two blockheads.

Benjamin Franklin (1706–1790)
Poor Richard's Almanack, 1734

If you would not be forgotten,
As soon as you are dead and rotten,
Either write things worth reading,
Or do things worth the writing.

Benjamin Franklin
Poor Richard's Almanack, 1738

A word to the wise is enough, and many words won't fill a bushel.

Benjamin Franklin
Poor Richard's Almanack, 1758

Communications

Speaking of Turkeys . . .

I wish the bald eagle had not been chosen as the representative of our country; he is a bird of bad moral character; like those among men who live by sharping and robbing, he is generally poor, and often very lousy.

The turkey is a much more respectable bird, and withal a true original native of America.

Benjamin Franklin
Letter to Sarah Bache, 1784

Money will say more in one moment than the most eloquent lover in years.

Henry Fielding (1707–1754)
The Miser, 1733

Attack is the re-action; I never think I have hit hard, unless it rebounds.

Samuel Johnson (1709–1784)
In Boswell, *Life of Johnson,* 1791
[Said: 2 April 1775]

Knowledge is of two kinds. We know a subject ourselves, or we know where we can find information upon it.

Samuel Johnson
In Boswell, *Life of Johnson*
[Said: 18 April 1775]

Clear your *mind* of cant.

Samuel Johnson
In Boswell, *Life of Johnson*
[Said: 15 May 1783]

Don't *attitudenize.*

Samuel Johnson

Sir, the insolence of wealth will creep out.

Samuel Johnson

One says a lot in vain, refusing;
The other mainly hears the "No."

Johann Wolfgang von Goethe (1749–1832)
Iphigenie auf Tauris, 1787

The shepherd always tries to persuade the sheep that their interests and his own are the same.

Stendhal [Marie Henri Beyle] (1783–1842)

Money Talks

Free trade, one of the greatest blessings which a government can confer on a people, is in almost every country unpopular.

Thomas Babington Macaulay (1800–1859)
Essay on Mitford's History of Greece, 1824

Speak what you think today in hard words and tomorrow speak what tomorrow thinks in hard words again, though it contradict everything you said today.

Ralph Waldo Emerson (1803–1882)
Self-Reliance, 1841

I hate quotations. Tell me what you know.

Ralph Waldo Emerson
Journal, May 1849

Whatever was required to be done, the Circumlocution Office was beforehand with all the public departments in the art of perceiving—How Not To Do It.

Charles Dickens (1812–1870)
Little Dorrit, 1857–1858

The public be damned. I am working for my stockholders. If the public want the train, why don't they pay for it?

William H. Vanderbilt (1821–1885)
To a reporter's question about the Chicago Limited, a fast, extra-fare mail train
that was being eliminated: "Don't you run it for the public benefit?"

Commerce is the great civilizer. We exchange ideas when we exchange fabrics.

Robert G. Ingersoll (1833–1899)
Reply to the Indianapolis clergy

I an anxyus to skewer your infloounce.

Artemus Ward [Charles Farrar Browne] (1834–1867)
Works, 1898
From "One of Mr. Ward's Business Letters"

We must fetch the public sumhow. We must wurk on their feelins.

Artemus Ward
Works
From "One of Mr. Ward's Business Letters"

Communications

The advantage of doing one's praising for oneself is that one can lay it on so thick and exactly in the right places.

Samuel Butler (1835–1902)
The Way of All Flesh, 1903

I do not mind lying, but I hate inaccuracy.

Samuel Butler
Notebooks, 1912

One of the most striking differences between a cat and a lie is that a cat has only nine lives.

Mark Twain (1835–1910)
Pudd'nhead Wilson, 1894

It were not best that we should all think alike; it is difference of opinion that makes horse races.

Mark Twain
Pudd'nhead Wilson

Always do right. This will gratify some people, and astonish the rest.

Mark Twain
To the Young People's Society,
Greenpoint Presbyterian Church, Brooklyn, 1901

A powerful agent is the right word. Whenever we come upon one of those intensely right words in a book or a newspaper the resulting effect is physical as well as spiritual, and electrically prompt.

Mark Twain
Essay on William Dean Howells, 1906

Its name is Public Opinion. It is held in reverence. It settles everything. Some think it is the voice of God.

Mark Twain
Europe and Elsewhere

Don't talk to me about appealing to the public. I am done with the public, for the present anyway. The public reads the headlines and that is all. The story itself is fair and shows the facts. That would be all right if the public read the facts. But it does not. It reads the headlines and listens to the demagogues and that's the stuff public opinion is made of.

J. P. Morgan (1837–1913)

To know when one's self is interested, is the first condition of interesting other people.

Walter Pater (1839–1894)
Marius the Epicurean, 1885

What is everybody's business is nobody's business—except the journalist's.

Joseph Pulitzer (1847–1911)

Half the time when men think they are talking business, they are wasting time.

Edgar Watson Howe (1853–1937)

He knew the precise psychological moment when to say nothing.

Oscar Wilde (1854–1900)
The Picture of Dorian Gray, 1891

There is only one thing in the world worse than being talked about, and that is not being talked about.

Oscar Wilde
The Picture of Dorian Gray

Experience is the name everyone gives to their mistakes.

Oscar Wilde
Lady Windermere's Fan, 1892

In matters of grave importance, style, not sincerity, is the vital thing.

Oscar Wilde
The Importance of Being Earnest, 1893

Three addresses always inspire confidence, even in tradesmen.

Oscar Wilde
The Importance of Being Earnest

There are no secrets better kept than those secrets that everybody guesses.

George Bernard Shaw (1856–1950)
Mrs. Warren's Profession, 1893

Effectiveness of assertion is the alpha and omega of style.

George Bernard Shaw
Man and Superman, 1903

Titles distinguish the mediocre, embarrass the superior, and are disgraced by the inferior.

> George Bernard Shaw
> *Man and Superman*

What really flatters a man is that you think him worth flattering.

> George Bernard Shaw
> *John Bull's Other Island,* 1907

The nauseous sham goodfellowship our democratic public men get up for shop use.

> George Bernard Shaw
> *Back to Methuselah,* 1921

A man never tells you anything until you contradict him.

> George Bernard Shaw

The trouble, Mr. Goldwyn, is that you are only interested in art and I am only interested in money.

> George Bernard Shaw
> When declining to sell
> Samuel Goldwyn screen rights to his plays

The truth is the one thing that nobody will believe.

> George Bernard Shaw

Sears, Roebuck & Co. Chicago. Capital and Surplus: Over Five Million Dollars Fully-Paid. Reference By Special Permission: First National Bank, Chicago. Corn Exchange Nat'l Bank, Chicago. National City Bank, New York. Second National Bank, Boston. We Have No Agents or Solicitors—Persons Claiming to be Our Representatives are Swindlers.

> Sears' catalogue (cover copy), 1905

I have always found that the man whose second thoughts are good is worth watching.

> James M. Barrie (1860–1937)
> *What Every Woman Knows,* 1908

It is more important that a proposition be interesting than that it be true.

> Alfred North Whitehead (1861–1947)
> *Adventures of Ideas,* 1933

With the sense of sight, the idea communicates the emotion, whereas, with sound, the emotion communicates the idea, which is more direct and therefore more powerful.

Alfred North Whitehead
Dialogues of Alfred North Whitehead, 1943

Insistence of hard-headed clarity issues from sentimental feeling, as it were a mist cloaking the perplexities of fact. Insistence on clarity at all costs is based on sheer superstition as to the mode in which human intelligence functions.

Alfred North Whitehead

It is a profoundly erroneous truism, repeated by all copy-books and by eminent people when they are making speeches, that we should cultivate the habit of thinking what we are doing. The precise opposite is the case. Civilization advances by extending the number of important operations which we can perform without thinking about them.

Alfred North Whitehead

A straw vote only shows the way the hot air blows.

O. Henry [William Sydney Porter] (1862–1910)
A Ruler of Men, 1913

Business today consists in persuading crowds.

Gerald Stanley Lee (1862–?)
Crowds, 1913

Most people who have been done a favor consider it an opportunity to show their incorruptibility rather than their gratitude. This is not only considerably cheaper morally, but it sometimes increases their pride so much that pretty soon they look down on their benefactor.

Arthur Schnitzler (1862–1931)

Nothing succeeds like—failure.

Oliver Herford (1863–1935)

They are only ten. [Said to have been posted in *The Times'* offices to remind the staff of their public's mental age]

Lord Northcliffe (1865–1922)

You can always tell a Harvard man, but you can't tell him much.

Attributed to James Barnes (1866–1936)

What the proprietorship of these papers is aiming at is power, and the power without responsibility—the prerogative of the harlot through the ages.

Stanley Baldwin (1867–1947)
Of Beaverbrook *(Daily Express, Evening Standard)*
and Rothermere *(Daily Mail),* 1931

Good God, that's done it. He's lost us the tarts' vote.
[Duke of Devonshire's remark at same 1931 by-election meeting.]

When you frame a sentence don't do it as if you were loading a shotgun but as if you were loading a rifle. Don't fire in such a way and with such a load that you will hit a lot of things in the neighborhood besides, but shoot with a single bullet and hit that one thing alone.

Joseph Ruggles Wilson (1867–1903)
Quoted in Dos Passos, *Mr. Wilson's War,* 1962

Some people pay a compliment as if they expected a receipt.
Frank McKinney ("Kin") Hubbard (1868–1930)

The Socratic manner is not a game at which two can play. Please answer my question to the best of your ability.

Max Beerbohm (1872–1956)
Zuleika Dobson, 1911

To say that a man is vain means merely that he is pleased with the effect he produces on other people. A conceited man is satisfied with the effect he produces on himself.

Max Beerbohm
Quia Imperfectum

Business will be better or worse.

Calvin Coolidge (1872–1933)

Every man speaks of public opinion, and means by public opinion, public opinion minus his opinion.

G. K. Chesterton (1874–1936)
Heretics, 1905

There is no such thing on earth as an uninteresting subject; the only thing that can exist is an uninterested person.

G. K. Chesterton
Heretics

Journalism largely consists in saying "Lord Jones Dead" to people who never knew Lord Jones was alive.

> G. K. Chesterton
> *The Wisdom of Father Brown,* 1914

Here is the answer which I will give to President Roosevelt. . . . Give us the tools, and we will finish the job.

> Winston Churchill (1874–1965)
> Radio broadcast, 9 February 1941

We have finished the job, what shall we do with the tools?

> Emperor Haile Selassie (1891–1975)
> To Churchill

I do not resent criticism, even when, for the sake of emphasis, it parts for the time with reality.

> Winston Churchill
> Speech in the House of Commons, 22 January 1941

When you have to kill a man it costs nothing to be polite.

> Winston Churchill
> *The Grand Alliance,* 1950

Short words are best and the old words when short are best of all.

> Winston Churchill
> Saying

This is the sort of English up with which I will not put.

> Attributed to Winston Churchill

An aphorism is never exactly truthful. It is either a half-truth or a truth and a half.

> Karl Kraus (1874–1936)
> *Sprüche and Widersprüche,* 1909

Speech is the Mother, not the handmaid, of Thought.

> Karl Kraus
> *Sprüche and Widersprüche*

The Americans who are the most efficient people on earth . . . have invented so wide a range of pithy and hackneyed phrases that they can carry on an amusing and animated conversation without giving a moment's reflection to what they are saying and so leave their minds free to consider the more important matters of big business and fornication.

> W. Somerset Maugham (1874–1965)
> *Cakes and Ale,* 1930

272

I won't take my religion from any man who never works except with his mouth.

Carl Sandburg (1878–1967)

Slang is a language that takes off its coat, spits on its hands, and goes to work.

Carl Sandburg

It is difficult to get a man to understand something when his salary depends upon his not understanding it.

Upton Sinclair (1878–1968)

The first Rotarian was the first man to call John the Baptist Jack.

H. L. Mencken (1880–1956)

I am afraid of this word Reality, not connoting an ordinarily definable characteristic of the things it is applied to, but used as though it were some kind of celestial halo.

Sir Arthur Stanley Eddington (1882–1944)
The Nature of the Physical World, 1928

In two words: im-possible.

Samuel Goldwyn (1882–1974)
In Johnston, *The Great Goldwyn*, 1937

Tell me, how did you love my picture?

Attributed to Samuel Goldwyn

What we want is a story that starts with an earthquake and works its way up to a climax.

Samuel Goldwyn

A verbal contract isn't worth the paper it's written on.

Attributed to Samuel Goldwyn

If Roosevelt were alive he'd turn in his grave.

Attributed to Samuel Goldwyn

I'll give you a definite maybe.

Attributed to Samuel Goldwyn

It's more than magnificent—it's mediocre.

Attributed to Samuel Goldwyn

Too caustic? To hell with cost; we'll make the picture anyway.

Attributed to Samuel Goldwyn

You ought to take the bull between the teeth.
Attributed to Samuel Goldwyn

The very people who have done the breaking through are themselves often the first to try to put a scab on their achievement.
Igor Stravinsky (1882–1971)
In Craft, *Conversations with Igor Stravinsky*, 1959

[Of Lloyd George] Watching the company, with six or seven senses not available to ordinary men, judging character, motive, and subconscious impulse, perceiving what each was thinking and even what each was going to say next, and compounding with telepathic instinct the argument or appeal best suited to the vanity, weakness, or self-interest of his immediate auditor.
John Maynard Keynes (1883–1946)
Economic Consequences of the Peace, 1919

There is no harm in being sometimes wrong—especially if one is promptly found out.
John Maynard Keynes
Essays in Biography, 1933

Worldly wisdom teaches that it is better for the reputation to fail conventionally than to succeed unconventionally.
John Maynard Keynes
The General Theory of Employment, Interest and Money, 1936

No matter how thin you slice it, it's still baloney.
Attributed to Rube Goldberg (1883–1970)

I do not object to people looking at their watches when I am speaking. But I strongly object when they start shaking them to make sure they are still going.
Lord Birkett (1883–1962)

I sit here all day trying to persuade people to do the things they ought to have sense enough to do without my persuading them. . . . That's all the powers of the President amount to.
Harry S. Truman (1884–1972)
Quoted in Neustadt, *Presidential Power*, 1960, 1968

I take the view, and always have done, that if you cannot say what you have to say in twenty minutes, you should go away and write a book about it.
Lord Brabazon (1884–1964)
Reported in the press, June 1955

Many promising reconciliations have broken down because, while both parties came prepared to forgive, neither party came prepared to be forgiven.

Charles Williams (1886–1945)

The man who has cured himself of B.O. and halitosis, has learned French to surprise the waiter, and the saxophone to amuse the company, may find that people still avoid him because they do not like him.

Heywood Broun (1888–1939)
Quoted in Brogan,
The American Character, 1944

How to Win Friends and Influence People.

Dale Carnegie (1888–1955)
Title of book, 1936

When dealing with people, let us remember we are not dealing with creatures of logic. We are dealing with creatures of emotion, creatures bristling with prejudices and motivated by pride and vanity.

Dale Carnegie
How to Win Friends and Influence People

There is only one way under high Heaven to get anybody to do anything. Did you ever stop to think of that? Yes, just one way. And that is by making the other person want to do it. Remember, there is no other way.

Dale Carnegie
How to Win Friends and Influence People

Six Ways to Make People Like You

Rule 1: Become genuinely interested in other people.
Rule 2: Smile.
Rule 3: Remember that a man's name is to him the sweetest and most important sound in the English language.
Rule 4: Be a good listener. Encourage others to talk about themselves.
Rule 5: Talk in terms of the other man's interests.
Rule 6: Make the other person feel important—and do it sincerely.

Dale Carnegie
How to Win Friends and Influence People

Everything that can be said can be said clearly.

Ludwig Wittgenstein (1889–1951)
Tractatus Logico-philosophicus, 1921

Money Talks

All propaganda has to be popular and has to adapt its spiritual level to the perception of the least intelligent of those towards whom it intends to direct itself.

Adolf Hitler (1889–1945)
Mein Kampf, 1933

Only constant repetition will finally succeed in imprinting an idea on the memory of the crowd.

Adolf Hitler
Mein Kampf

The great masses of people . . . will more easily fall victims to a big lie than to a small one.

Adolf Hitler
Mein Kampf

Is Moby-Dick the whale or the man?

Harold Ross (1892–1951)
The New Yorker

If you don't want prosperity to falter, then Buy, Buy, Buy—on credit, of course. In other words, the surest way of bringing on a rainy day is to prepare for it.

Joseph Wood Krutch (1893–1970)
Human Nature and the Human Condition, 1959

One script writer, apparently forgetting that General Mills was the sponsor of his serial, had one of his women characters go temporarily blind because of an allergy to chocolate cake. There was hell to pay, and the writer had to make the doctor in charge of the patient hastily change his diagnosis.

James Thurber (1894–1961)

Flattery is all right—if you don't inhale.

Adlai E. Stevenson (1900–1965)
Speech, 1 February 1961

Chief executives repeatedly fail to recognize that for communication to be effective, it must be two-way: *there has to be feedback to ascertain the extent to which the message has actually been understood, believed, assimilated, and accepted.* This is a step few companies ever take (perhaps because they fear to learn how little of the message has actually been transmitted).

Robert N. McMurry (1901–   )
"Clear Communications for Chief Executives,"
Harvard Business Review, 1965

Communications

Good communications start at the top. If the chief executive cannot face reality, he cannot expect that his subordinates will expose him to it. It takes a man of courage and resolution to accept reality in its less roseate aspects. Such men are rare.

Robert N. McMurry
"Clear Communications for Chief Executives,"
Harvard Business Review

For God's sake don't say yes until I've finished talking.

Darryl F. Zanuck (1902–1979)
Quoted in French, *The Movie Moguls,* 1969, 1970

Just fancy yourself as a banker—and discovering outside your plate glass façade an ever-lengthening column of men and women, all having bankbooks and checks clutched in their hands. Fancy those who would be best known to you, the ones with the biggest balances, pushing to the head of the line—there to bargain excitedly with the depositors holding the places nearest the wickets of the paying tellers. Even that won't give you a hint of what a banker's dread is like unless you heighten the effect with a swarm of hoarse-throated newsboys, each with his cry pitched to a hysterical scream; and then give the hideous concert an overtone of sound from the scuffling feet of a mob.

Frank A. Vanderlip, Jr. (1907–   )
Filiorum

"My door is always open—bring me your problems." This is guaranteed to turn on every whiner, lackey and neurotic on the property.

Robert F. Six (1907–   )
Continental Airlines

Wealth has never been a sufficient source of honor in itself. It must be advertised, and the normal medium is obtrusively expensive goods.

John Kenneth Galbraith (1908–   )
The Affluent Society, 1958

These men of the technostructure are the new and universal priesthood. Their religion is business success; their test of virtue is growth and profit. Their bible is the computer printout; their communion bench is the committee room. The sales force carries their message to the world, and a message is what it is often called.

John Kenneth Galbraith
The Age of Uncertainty, 1977

Industrial relations are like sexual relations. It's better between two consenting parties.

> Vic Feather [Lord Feather] (1908–1976)
> Quoted in the *Guardian Weekly,* 8 August 1976

We have seen too much success to have become obsessed with failure.

> Lyndon B. Johnson (1908–1973)
> Quoted in *National Review,* 31 December 1963

If people in a group want to interrupt serious discussion with some diversion or personal expression—let them. Then bring them back to the agenda. Committees work best when the talk swings between the personal and the purposeful.

> Irving Lee (1909–   )
> *How to Talk with People,* 1952

What is important here is not that men disagree, but that they become disagreeable about it.

> Irving Lee
> *How to Talk with People*

I once asked Paul Garrett what his primary assignment was when Alfred Sloan had hired him as the first public relations man in General Motors, shortly after *Fortune* had been launched [1930]. "To keep *Fortune* away from GM," was his reply. And there were many tales around of attempts by managements to persuade or even bribe *Fortune* editors and writers to cancel a planned story on their company.

> Peter F. Drucker (1909–   )
> *Adventures of a Bystander,* 1978

"This is Thomas Watson," said the voice on the telephone. "I want to speak to the writer of the story on my company." "I am afraid, Mr. Watson," I said, "that the writer is not available. You will have to discuss the story with me; I am the editor in charge of it." "I don't want to discuss the story," said Mr. Watson, "I want to speak to the writer personally." "Give me your message," I said, "and I'll see that he gets it." "Tell that young man," said Watson, "that I want him to join IBM as our director of public relations; he can name his own salary." I thought this might be one of the "persuasion" attempts of which I had heard. "You realize, Mr. Watson," I said, "that the story will come out in the magazine whether the writer stays on the staff or not." "Of course," said Watson, "and if the story does not appear, I withdraw my offer." "Mr. Watson," I said, "have you read the story?" "Of course," he said, quite irritated, "I always read what's written about me and my company." "And you still want the writer as your director of public relations?" "Of course," said Watson, "at least he takes me seriously!"

Peter F. Drucker
Adventures of a Bystander
When he was editing *Fortune*'s tenth anniversary issue, 1940

The medium is the message. This is merely to say that the personal and social consequences of any medium . . . result from the new scale that is introduced into our affairs by each extension of ourselves or by any new technology.

Marshall McLuhan (1911–1980)
Understanding Media, 1964

There is a basic principle that distinguishes a hot medium like radio from a cool one like the telephone, or a hot medium like the movie from a cool one like TV. A hot medium is one that extends one single sense in "high definition." High definition is the state of being well filled with data. A photograph is, visually, "high definition." A cartoon is low definition simply because very little visual information is provided. Telephone is a cool medium, or one of low definition, because the ear is given a meagre amount of information. Hot media are, therefore, low in participation, and cool media are high in participation or completion by the audience.

Marshall McLuhan
Understanding Media

The new electronic interdependence recreates the world in the image of a global village.

Marshall McLuhan
The Medium Is the Message, 1967

For you have learned, not what to say,
But how the saying must be said.

J. V. Cunningham (1911–1985)
"To a Friend, on her Examination for the Doctorate in English,"
The Collected Poems and Epigrams, 1971

Most of the people who are writing advertising today have never had to sell anything to anybody. They've never seen a consumer.

David Ogilvy (1911–   )
Ogilvy & Mather

There is a strong correlation between people's attitudes toward big business and the amount of correct economic information they have.

M. L. Frankel (1912–   )
Joint Council on Economic Education

You have only three real friends: Jesus Christ, Sears, Roebuck, and Gene Talmadge.

Eugene Talmadge (1913–   )
US Senate
To the voters of Georgia

I wish some people in high places would stop talking the three-martini lunch. I happen to think that the three-martini lunch is the epitome of American efficiency. Where else can you get an earful, a bellyful and a snootful at the same time?

Gerald R. Ford (1913–   )

Your mind must always go, even while you're shaking hands and going through all the maneuvers. I developed the ability long ago to do one thing while thinking another.

Richard M. Nixon (1913–   )

Shakespeare, in the familiar lines, divided great men into three classes: those born great, those who achieve greatness, and those who have greatness thrust upon them. It never occurred to him to mention those who hire public relations experts and press secretaries to make themselves look great.

Daniel J. Boorstin (1914–   )
The Image, 1961, 1964

I think that cars today are almost the exact equivalent of the great Gothic cathedrals: I mean the supreme creation of an era, conceived with passion by unknown artists, and consumed in image if not in usage by a whole population which appropriates them as a purely magical object.

Roland Barthes (1915–1980)
Mythologies

As far as criticism is concerned, we don't resent that unless it is absolutely biased, as it is in most cases.

John Vorster (1915–   )
Quoted in the *Observer*, 9 November 1969

Communications

The responsiveness of a firm to the consumer is directly proportionate to the distance on the organization chart from the consumer to the chairman of the board.

Virginia H. Knauer (1915–   )
US Office of Consumer Affairs

I give them a chance once a year to work me over, and that's enough.

James D. Finley (1916–   )
J. P. Stevens
Of talking to the press and the public at the annual stockholders' meeting

People very rarely think in groups; they talk together, they exchange information, they adjudicate, they make compromises. But they do not think; they do not create.

William H. Whyte, Jr. (1917–   )
The Organization Man, 1956

The executive is very gregarious when he sees some practical utility to the gregariousness. But if he doesn't see that utility, good fellowship bores him to death.

William H. Whyte, Jr.
The Organization Man

It's most infrequent for businessmen and lawyers to read novels. Only women read novels—and now they're going professional.

Louis Auchincloss (1917–   )
Hawkins, Delafield & Wood
Quoted in the *New York Times,* 28 October 1985

But they could do better at teaching communication skills. And if the schools could concentrate on a little instruction in humility it would be helpful. You just don't come fresh out of business school ready to run a large corporation.

Reginald H. Jones (1917–   )
General Electric

We've long believed there's nothing to be gained by telling our competitors how we do things.

Edward G. Harness (1918–   )
Procter & Gamble

[Of public relations] I have found it to be the craft of arranging truths so that people will like you. Public-relations specialists make flower arrangements of the facts, placing them so that the wilted and less attractive petals are hidden by sturdy blooms.

Alan Harrington (1919–)

Papyromania—compulsive accumulation of papers.
  Papyrophobia—abnormal desire for "a clean desk."

Laurence J. Peter (1919–) and Raymond Hull (1919–)
The Peter Principle, 1969

And suppose we solve all the problems it presents? What happens? We end up with more problems than we started with. Because that's the way problems propagate their species. A problem left to itself dries up or goes rotten. But fertilize a problem with a solution—you'll hatch out dozens.

N. F. Simpson (1919–)
A Resounding Tinkle, 1957

There are many things which we do which don't seem to have any particular point or tangible result. Take today; a lot of time and energy has been spent on arranging for you to listen to me take a long time to declare open a building which everybody knows is open already.

Philip Mountbatten, Duke of Edinburgh (1921–)
Speech: Opening of Chesterfield College of Technology,
21 November 1958

Good communication is characterized by providing employees with information which *they want* and getting information to them *quickly* and through the channels *they prefer.*

Louis I. Gelfand (1922–)
Pillsbury
"Communicate Through Your Supervisor,"
Harvard Business Review, 1970

The businessman only wants two things said about his company—what he pays his public-relations people to say and what he pays his advertising people to say. He doesn't like anybody ever to look above, beyond or over that.

Don S. Hewitt (1922–)
CBS, *60 Minutes*

Communications

The advocates of consumerism, unionism, government intervention are exciting. We are the establishment. We are often dull.
> Louis T. Hagopian (1925–   )
> N. W. Ayer International

We cannot, after all, neglect to consider the challenge television has undertaken. It is more formidable by far than that of Scheherazade the slave girl, who, after all, was given a respite after her thousand and first tale. In undertaking to entertain us—indeed, to give us a choice of entertainment—every day and every night of every week of every month of every year, television has undertaken the job it simply cannot do to everyone's satisfaction.
> William F. Buckley, Jr. (1925–   )
> In *National Review*, 2 January 1960

I am often accused of an inordinate reliance on unusual words, and desire—as would you in my shoes, I think—to defend myself against the insinuation that I write as I do simply to prove that I have returned recently from the bowels of a dictionary with a fish in my mouth, establishing my etymological dauntlessness. Surely one must distinguish between those who plunder old tomes to find words which, in someone's phrase, should never be let out, belonging strictly to the zoo sections of the dictionary; and such others as Russell Kirk who use words because a) the words signify just exactly what the user means, and because b) the user deems it right and proper to preserve in currency words which in the course of history were coined as the result of a felt need.
> William F. Buckley, Jr.
> In *National Review*, 11 February 1964

[Commercialism is] doing well that which should not be done at all.
> Gore Vidal (1925–   )
> Quoted in the *Listener*, 7 August 1975

I think it's time for business to acknowledge—without apology—that we do represent a special interest, one that we believe is vitally important. We have the perfect right—in fact, the responsibility—to do what we can to correct the false impression that others have of us. But we must do this as *businessmen,* not as preservers of our great social and economic system.
> Daniel J. Crum (1926–   )
> Maytag

Twenty years ago, we were all bewitched by the concept of corporate image. It was innocent enough in the beginning. It makes perfect sense to find out as accurately as possible what the public thinks about a company or a product or a candidate. And it makes sense to respond to public priorities, to correct misconceptions, to present oneself to the public accurately. But then we began to perceive that image could be separated from reality—that an image could be shaped independent of reality. Business began to concern itself not with how to present itself to the public most accurately, but whether to maintain a "high profile" or a "low profile." We began to think more about the impact of alternative synthetic images than the authenticity of our image. . . . And so we in business, whether we like it or whether we deserve it or not, find ourselves in the public consciousness with the politicians and planners who make decisions in secret, who shade the truth, who view public opinion as something to be managed and manipulated. All this was based on a subliminal suspicion that the public could not be trusted with the whole truth.

> Preston Robert Tisch (1926–   )
> Loew's

The habit most worth cultivating is that of thinking clearly even though inspired.

> Thomas H. Uzzell (1932–   )

In my experience, the worst thing you can do to an important problem is discuss it.

> Simon Gray (1936–   )
> *Otherwise Engaged*, 1975

A company is judged by the president it keeps.

> James Hulbert (1942–   )

We are a noisy lot; and of what gets said among us, far more goes unheard and unheeded than seems possible.

> Wendell Johnson
> "The Fateful Process of Mr. A. Talking to Mr. B.,"
> *Harvard Business Review*, 1953

All echelons of the staff will coordinate the configuration of the plans with the requisite tailoring of the overview in order to expedite the functional objective.

> Capt. Scarrett Adams, USN

Universities don't teach our kids how our capitalistic system works. We are a nation of employees. We all work for somebody. 75 or 80 million of us. Yet nobody tells our kids how our system works, the means by which we make our living. Take the 500 top corporations. They have several hundred billion in capital, they hire 15 million people, and they only make a nickel on the dollar. Just think, some of these stupid kids want to destroy this Establishment. I'm going to tell them this, but I'm afraid they may laugh me right out of the building.

George Spatta
Clark Equipment

BUSINESS POLICY

Business Policy is at once the most secret and valuable of assets, for it is an internal ethic. Policy determines strategy—how to cope with competition and gain advantage—and it helps determine the name and nature of an industry. From the outside, an industry may seem harmonious; at least the companies that advertise within it seem to be hawking the same wares or making the same offers and claims. But in these days of conglomerates and multinationals, the internal struggles are wide and deep. Changes in organization—from centralized to decentralized control, and back again, for example—force constant reconsideration of business policy. And if competition were not enough to cope with, there is government regulation and, in many industries and for many reasons, the demand for public policy. The quotes in this section offer views on the formulation of policy and policy statements articulated by confident managers.

"THE AMERICAN BEAUTY ROSE CAN BE PRODUCED IN ALL ITS SPLENDOR ONLY BY SACRIFICING THE EARLY BUDS THAT GROW UP AROUND IT." — John D. Rockefeller, Jr.

John D. Rockefeller (1839–1937), pictured: John D. Rockefeller, Jr. (1874–1960), quoted out of context. Cartoon by Spencer in the Literary Digest, *6 May 1905.*

Don't worry about our future if we automate. Worry about our future if we don't automate.

Anonymous

We don't aspire to be a fashion leader, but we're fast followers.

Anonymous
K Mart

Forgive us for frantic buying and selling; for advertising the unnecessary and coveting the extravagant, and calling it good business when it is not good for you.

United Presbyterian Church
Litany for Holy Communion, 1968

Everybody's business is nobody's business.

English proverb

No progress is going back.

Latin proverb

Secrecy is the soul of business.

Spanish proverb

The fish dies because he opens his mouth.

Spanish proverb

Great gains are not won except by great risks.

Xerxes (died 465 B.C.)
Said to Artabanus, before the battle of Thermopylae (480 B.C.)
In Herodotus, *Histories*

Consider the little mouse, how wise an animal it is which never entrusts its life to one hole only.

Plautus (254–184 B.C.)
Truculentus

It is a bad plan that admits of no modification.

Publilius Syrus (First century B.C.)
Sententiae

Look for a tough wedge for a tough log.

> Publilius Syrus
> *Sententiae*

The business that trusts to luck is a bad business.

> Publilius Syrus
> *Sententiae*

You should hammer your iron when it is glowing hot.

> Publilius Syrus
> *Sententiae*

The best ideas are common property.

> Seneca (c.4 B.C.–A.D. 65)
> *Epistles*

Every time we began to form into teams we would be re-organized. I would learn later in life what a wonderful method this was to create the illusion of progress while causing confusion and demoralization.

> Petronius (First century A.D.)
> *Satyricon*

Conceal a flaw, and the world will imagine the worst.

> Martial (c.40–c.104)
> *Epigrams*

You get no prize for outrunning an ass.

> Martial
> *Epigrams*

He is a fool who leaves things close at hand to follow what is out of reach.

> Plutarch (46–120)
> *Morals*

When the iron is hot, strike.

> John Heywood (c.1497–c.1580)
> *Proverbs*, 1546

When the sun shineth, make hay.

> John Heywood
> *Proverbs*

Business Policy

Many strokes overthrow the tallest oaks.

John Lyly (c.1554–1606)
Euphues, 1579

One bird in the hand is worth two in the wood.

Thomas Lodge (c.1558–1625)
Rosalynde, 1590

In civil business; what first? Boldness; what second, and third? Boldness. And yet boldness is a child of ignorance and baseness.

Francis Bacon (1561–1626)
Of Boldness, 1625

First, all means to conciliate; failing that, all means to crush.

Cardinal Richelieu (1585–1642)

Great businesses turn on a little pin.

George Herbert (1593–1633)
Outlandish Proverbs, 1640

Trade is most vigorously carried on in every state and government by the heterodox part of the same; and such as profess opinions different from what are publicly established.

William Petty (1623–1687)
Political Arithmetick, 1672

Men by habit make irregular stretches of power, without discerning the consequence and extent of them.

George Savile, Marquess of Halifax (1633–1695)
Political, Moral and Miscellaneous Reflections, 1750

The most necessary thing in the World, and yet the least usual, is to reflect that those we deal with may know how to be as arrant knaves as ourselves.

George Savile, Marquess of Halifax
Political, Moral and Miscellaneous Reflections

The World is beholden to generous mistakes for the greatest part of the good that is done in it.

George Savile, Marquess of Halifax
Political, Moral and Miscellaneous Reflections

There is no little enemy.

Benjamin Franklin (1706–1790)
Poor Richard's Almanack, September 1733

The used key is always bright.

Benjamin Franklin
Poor Richard's Almanack, July 1744

The cat in gloves catches no mice.

Benjamin Franklin
Poor Richard's Almanack, February 1754

By pursuing his own interest [the individual] frequently promotes that of the society more effectually than when he really intends to promote it. I have never known much good done by those who affected to trade for the public good.

Adam Smith (1723–1790)
Wealth of Nations, 1776

Nobody ever saw a dog make a fair and deliberate exchange of one bone for another with another dog. Nobody ever saw one animal by its gestures and natural cries signify to another, this is mine, that yours; I am willing to give this for that.

Adam Smith
Wealth of Nations

Everything which is properly *business* we must keep carefully separate from *life*. Business requires earnestness and method; life must have a freer handling.

Johann Wolfgang von Goethe (1749–1832)
Elective Affinities, 1808

One never goes so far as when one doesn't know where one is going.

Johann Wolfgang von Goethe
Letter to Karl Friedrich Zelter, 1812

Whenever I hear people talking about "liberal" ideas, I am always astounded that men should so love to fool themselves with empty sounds. An idea should never be liberal: it must be vigorous, positive, and without loose ends so that it may fulfill its divine mission and be productive. The proper place for liberality is in the realm of emotions.

Johann Wolfgang von Goethe

One is weary of hearing about the omnipotence of money. I will say rather that, for a genuine man, it is no evil to be poor.

Thomas Carlyle (1795–1881)
Heroes and Hero Worship, 1840

Boldness, in business, is the first, second, and third thing.

Henry George Bohn (1796–1884)
Handbook of Proverbs, 1855

If you want a man to do fair work for you, let him have fair play.

George D. Prentice (1802–1870)

The ways of trade are grown selfish to the borders of theft, and supple to the borders (if not beyond the borders) of fraud.

Ralph Waldo Emerson (1803–1882)
Man the Reformer

All stealing is comparative. If you come to absolutes, pray who does not steal?

Ralph Waldo Emerson
Experience

We must scrunch or be scrunched.

Charles Dickens (1812–1870)
Our Mutual Friend, 1864–1865

I know of no more encouraging fact than the unquestionable ability of man to elevate his life by a conscious endeavor.

Henry David Thoreau (1817–1862)
Walden, 1854

In the long run men hit only what they aim at.

Henry David Thoreau
Walden

Not only is there but one way of *doing* things rightly, but there is only one way of *seeing* them, and that is seeing the whole of them.

John Ruskin (1819–1900)
The Two Paths

For the merchant, even honesty is a financial speculation.

Charles Baudelaire (1821–1867)
Intimate Journals, 1887

Boundless risk must pay for boundless gain.

William Morris (1834–1896)
The Earthly Paradise: The Wanderers, 1868

Tell the truth or trump—but get the trick.

Mark Twain (1835–1910)
Pudd'nhead Wilson, 1894

Habit is habit, and not to be flung out of the window by any man, but coaxed downstairs a step at a time.

Mark Twain
Pudd'nhead Wilson

Let us be thankful for the fools. But for them the rest of us could not succeed.

Mark Twain
Following the Equator, 1897

It is easier to stay out than to get out.

Mark Twain
Following the Equator

We need some imaginative stimulus, some not impossible ideal such as may shape vague hope, and transform it into effective desire, to carry us year after year, without disgust, through the routine work which is so large a part of life.

Walter Pater (1839–1894)
Marius the Epicurean, 1885

It is not competition, but monopoly, that deprives labor of its product. Wages, inheritance, gifts and gambling aside, every process by which men acquire wealth rests upon a monopoly, a prohibition, a denial of liberty.

Benjamin R. Tucker (1854–?)
Why I Am an Anarchist, 1892

My specialty is being right when other people are wrong.

George Bernard Shaw (1856–1950)
You Never Can Tell, 1898

There is nothing so bad or so good that you will not find Englishmen doing it; but you will never find an Englishman in the wrong. He does everything on principle. He fights you on patriotic principles; he robs you on business principles; he enslaves you on imperial principles.

George Bernard Shaw
The Man of Destiny, 1898

You see things; and you say, "Why?" But I dream things that never were; and I say, "Why not?"

George Bernard Shaw
Back to Methuselah, 1921

Men on the inside of business know how business is conducted.
Woodrow Wilson (1856–1924)

All business sagacity reduces itself in the last analysis to a judicious use of sabotage.
Thorstein Veblen (1857–1929)
The Nature of Peace, 1919

In life, as in a football game, the principle to follow is: Hit the line hard.
Theodore Roosevelt (1858–1919)
The Strenuous Life, 1900

The best way out is always through.
Robert Frost (1874–1963)
A Servant to Servants, 1914

Everything should be made as simple as possible, but not simpler.
Albert Einstein (1879–1955)
Quoted in *Reader's Digest,* October 1977

Time is a great legalizer, even in the field of morals.
H. L. Mencken (1880–1956)
A Book of Prefaces, 1917

Tell me to what you pay attention and I will tell you who you are.
José Ortega y Gasset (1883–1955)

Everybody's merging. It's the style. If you can't grow bigger, you have to get smaller. If you can't expand, suspend.
Sol Hurok (1888–1974)

In business a reputation for keeping absolutely to the letter and spirit of an agreement, even when it is unfavorable, is the most precious of assets, although it is not entered in the balance sheet.
Lord Chandos [Oliver Lyttelton, 1st Viscount] (1893–1972)

Bigness taxes the ability to manage intelligently. . . . The growth of bigness has resulted in ruthless sacrifices of human values. The disappearance of free enterprise has submerged the individual in the impersonal corporation. When a nation of shopkeepers is transformed into a nation of clerks, enormous spiritual sacrifices are made.
William O. Douglas (1898–1980)
US Supreme Court
To businessmen, 1963

Competition means decentralized planning by many separate persons.

> Friedrich August von Hayek (1899–   )
> *The Use of Knowledge in Society,*
> *in Individualism and Economic Order,* 1948

The man who offers a bribe gives away a little of his own importance; the bribe once accepted, he becomes the inferior, like a man who has paid for a woman.

> Graham Greene (1904–   )
> *The Comedians,* 1966

Hell, we look at a company with a problem the same way a surgeon looks at a patient with cancer. The earlier you get the damned thing, the less it's going to spread.

> Edward S. Reddig (1904–   )
> White Consolidated Industries

I don't meet competition, I crush it.

> Charles Revson (1906–1975)
> Revlon

Mr. American executive! Mr. American (labor) union member! As you enjoy the music on your symphonic Sony, as you take snaps of your family picnic with your Nikon or Yashica camera, as you bop along the highways in your Toyota, please think about the rigidities in American business and labor practice that cripple our ability to compete in world markets.

> S. I. Hayakawa (1906–   )
> San Francisco State College

Machines are beneficial to the degree that they eliminate the need for labor, harmful to the degree that they eliminate the need for skill.

> W. H. Auden (1907–1973)
> *A Certain World,* 1970

The true role of advertising is exactly that of the first salesman hired by the first manufacturer—to get business away from his competitors.

> Rosser Reeves (1910–1984)
> *Reality in Advertising,* 1961

We must not be hampered by yesterday's myths in concentrating on today's needs.

Harold S. Geneen (1910–   )
International Telephone & Telegraph

Like a patient suffering with fever, the Treasury's attitude toward reform comes in fits and starts, interspersed with periods of profound coma.

Henry S. Reuss (1912–   )
US House

Banking without risk-taking would be a sterile, even a parasitical, business.

Ellmore C. Patterson (1913–   )
Morgan Guaranty

The free-enterprise system in America has become one large chicken factory, where little chicks—the small companies—are grown to maturity and made marketable to satisfy the unending appetite of conglomerate corporate America.

Charles A. Vanik (1913–   )
US House

The nation's most important industries were created by merger and acquisition. Without them, we would probably still have to rely on the stagecoach lines, which would undoubtedly have been nationalized, and be talking about training programs for the horses to solve the problems in that system.

Ralph E. Ablon (1916–   )
Ogden

This company has never left its base. We seek to be anything but a conglomerate.

Edward G. Harness (1918–   )
Procter & Gamble

If you don't know where you are going, you will probably end up somewhere else.

Laurence J. Peter (1919–   ) and Raymond Hull (1919–   )
The Peter Principle, 1969

The watchword for Side-Issue Specialists is *Look after the molehills and the mountains will look after themselves.*

Laurence J. Peter and Raymond Hull
The Peter Principle

The key to success in business is understanding of the world about you and then making products to fit the needs of the times. A person who looks inward is bound to try to make the times try to fit his company's products.

Pieter C. Vink (1919–   )
North American Philips

A merger is an example of the timidity of American managers when faced with the choice between the adventure of capital investment and acquiring another company.

Robert Lekachman (1920–   )
Lehman College, CUNY

The American government is a rule of the people, by the people, for the boss.

Austin O'Malley (1920–   )

If you are going to develop a business, you had better not get too involved in details of an operation. You had better stay on the promotion side. I think that's why many small businessmen stay small. You know, it's like the garage mechanic who likes to stay under the car and the restaurant owner who never gets out of the kitchen.

Jay Van Andel (1924–   )
Amway

Large companies are not innovative. Hugeness destroys initiative.

Willard Mueller (1925–   )
University of Wisconsin

Free enterprise ended in the United States a good many years ago. Big oil, big steel, big agriculture avoid the open marketplace. Big corporations fix prices among themselves and drive out the small entrepreneur. In their conglomerate forms, the huge corporations have begun to challenge the legitimacy of the state.

Gore Vidal (1925–   )

If we can't do business observing certain absolute standards, we will simply demur from doing business. Instead of growing another $30-million in sales we'll grow a little less, but we'll sleep better for it.

W. Michael Blumenthal (1926–   )
Bendix

We're not a holding company. We're in a safe business, but I've got my people used to making money without growing. What's wrong with that?

Helmut Maucher (1928–   )
Nestlé
Quoted in *Forbes*, 13 February 1984

[Advertising] agencies have, more often than not, allowed the personality of the brand to derive not from the distilled essence of what the brand is, but from the personal lifestyle of the copywriter or the last movie the art director saw—or sometimes from the image the agency itself wants to project for new business purposes. Or sometimes from nothing at all except a demented compulsion to be "with it"—which inevitably involves expressionless teenyboppers wriggling to expressionless music. The same teenyboppers, I swear, in everybody's commercials. Where's the unique personality?

John E. O'Toole (1929–   )
Foote, Cone & Belding

We intend to operate every company we acquire. Forever.

David J. Primuth (1938–   )
Wickes

We will tackle the giants and set them back because we have a better product and better know-how of the marketplace. Being a smaller company we will out-maneuver them.

Thomas Casey
Tampax

I am not dealing with companies, I am dealing with people.

Leopold D. Silberstein
Penn-Texas

Excellence and size are fundamentally incompatible.

Robert C. Townsend
Avis

BOTTOM
LINE

The bottom line of the balance sheet has become a metaphor for a conclusion, stripped of its supporting arguments, its rationalization, and its qualifications. The quotations of this section express the "bottom lines" of many lives and times and enterprises. To paraphrase George Bernard Shaw ("The golden rule is that there is no golden rule"), the bottom line is that there is no bottom line to business. In a famous retort to the claim that only the bottom line shows the worth of the product, Edwin Land, founder of Polaroid, said, "The only thing that matters is the bottom line? What a presumptuous thing to say! The bottom line is in heaven" (1977). Not all businessmen would agree.

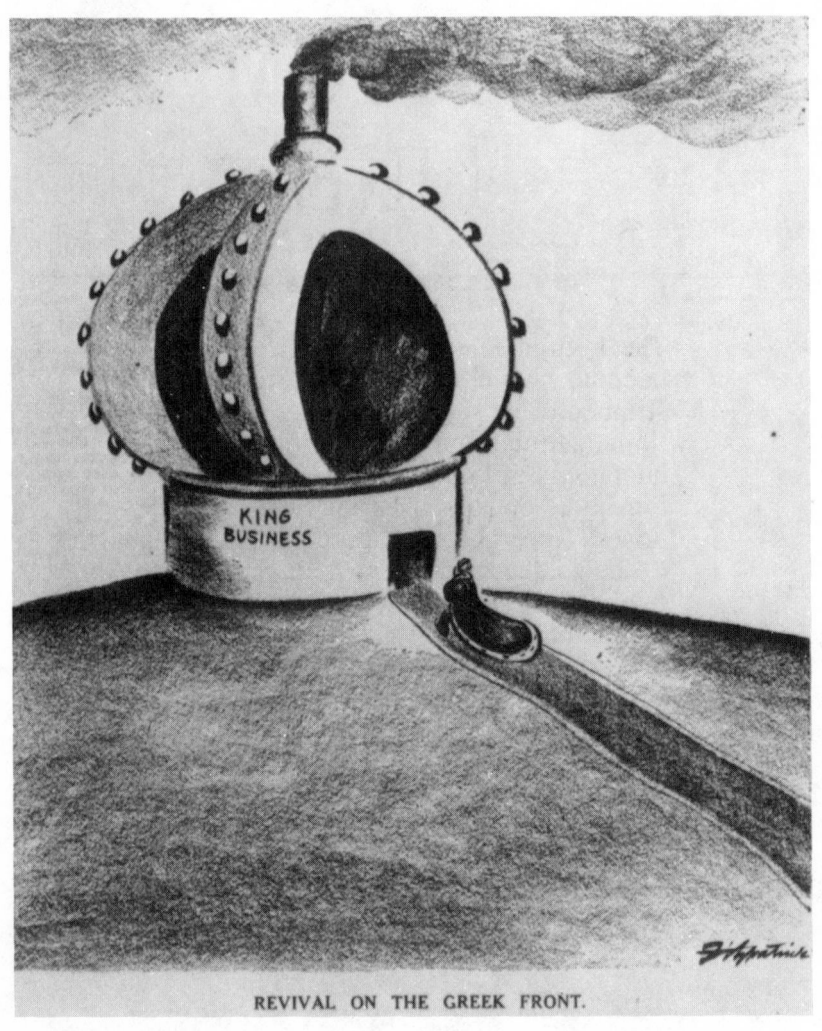

REVIVAL ON THE GREEK FRONT.

Cartoon by Fitzpatrick, in the Wisconsin State Journal, *6 November 1935.*

Business circles should be on the square.

Anonymous

He profits most who serves best.

Anonymous

Money never goes to jail.

Anonymous

The man who minds his own business usually has a good one.

Anonymous

There is no free lunch.

Anonymous

You don't make big fortunes by peddling little things in the street.

Anonymous

How I Made My Fortune

It was really quite simple. I bought an apple for five cents, spent the evening polishing it, and sold it the next day for 10 cents. With this I bought two apples, spent the evening polishing them, and sold them for 20 cents. And so it went until I had amassed $1.60. It was then that my wife's father died and left us a million dollars.

Anonymous capitalist to a young reporter, quoted by Bertell Ollman in the *New York Times,* 19 February 1984

Do you want to be happy or do you want a house in the Hamptons?

Anonymous student saying
Harvard Business School

That's the way the cookie crumbles.

American saying

Money is sweet balm.

Arabic proverb

He that is without money might as well be buried in rice with his mouth sewed up.

Chinese proverb

Every man to his trade.

English proverb

Money is a fruit that is always ripe.

English proverb

The busiest men have the most leisure.

English proverb

Who likes not his business, his business likes not him.

English proverb
In Hazlitt, *English Proverbs*, 1869

No money, no fear.

German proverb

Let business wait till tomorrow.

Greek proverb

Money makes the man.

Greek proverb

He who does not teach his son a trade teaches him to be a robber.

Hebrew proverb

Never be modest in eating or in business.

Hindu proverb

Bargain like a gypsy, but pay like a gentleman.

Hungarian proverb

Health without money is half sickness.

Italian proverb

No one fouls his hands in his own business.

Italian proverb

Money swore an oath that nobody who didn't love it should ever have it.

Irish proverb

Money smells good no matter what its source.

Latin proverb

Who hath money hath fear; who hath none hath sorrow.

Persian proverb

When I had money everyone called me brother.

Polish proverb

Money makes a man free ilka where. [*Ilka* = every]

Scottish proverb

Money makes and money mars.

Scottish proverb

Muck and money gae thegither.

Scottish proverb

Dawn comes no sooner for the early riser.

Spanish proverb

God helps those who get up early.

Spanish proverb

In the sweat of thy face shalt thou eat bread, till thou return unto the ground.

Bible: Genesis 3:19

It is not necessary that a man should earn his living by the sweat of his brow unless he sweats easier than I do.

Henry David Thoreau (1817–1862)
Walden, 1854

What is eating one's bread in the sweat of one's brow but making money? I will believe no man who tells me that he would not sooner earn two loaves than one—and if two, then two hundred. I will believe no man who tells me that he would sooner earn one dollar a day than two—and if two, then two hundred.

Anthony Trollope (1815–1882)
North America, 1862

He that trusteth in his riches shall fall.

Bible: Proverbs 11:28

Seest thou a man diligent in his business? He shall stand before kings.

Bible: Proverbs 22:29

Vanity of vanities, saith the Preacher, vanity of vanities; all is vanity.

What profit hath a man of all his labor which he taketh under the sun?

One generation passeth away, and another generation cometh: but the earth abideth for ever.

The sun also ariseth.

Bible: Ecclesiastes 1:2–5

Be not overwise in doing thy business.

Bible: Ecclesiasticus 10:26

There is no riches above a sound body.

Bible: Ecclesiasticus 30:16

Study to be quiet, and to do your own business.

Bible: 1 Thessalonians 4:11

Be instant in season, out of season.

Bible: 2 Timothy 4:2

While the sand is yet on your feet, sell.

Talmud

Never blush to tell an honest business.

Homer (c. 700 B.C.)

Badness you can get easily, in quantity: the road is smooth, and it lies close by. But in front of excellence the immortal gods have put sweat, and long and steep is the way to it, and rough at first. But when you come to the top, then it is easy, even though it is hard.

Hesiod (c. 700 B.C.)
Works and Days

Do not seek evil gains; evil gains are the equivalent of disaster.

Hesiod
Works and Days

At the beginning of a cask and at the end take your fill; in the middle be sparing.

Hesiod
Works and Days

Do it today; don't count on tomorrow.

> Horace (65–8 B.C.)
> *Odes*
> [Traditionally, *Carpe diem* = Seize the day]

Tomorrow's life is too late. Live today.

> Martial (c. 40–c. 104)
> *Epigrams*

A man who is always ready to believe what is told him will never do well, especially a businessman.

> Petronius (First century A.D.)
> *Satyricon*

Brief is the opportunity for gain.

> Martial
> *Epigrams,* 93

It is difficulties that show what men are.

> Epictetus (c. 50–120)
> *Discourses*

The good or ill of man lies within his own will.

> Epictetus
> *Discourses*

First say to yourself what you would be; and then do what you have to do.

> Epictetus
> *Discourses*

We all live in a state of ambitious poverty.

> Juvenal (c. 50–c. 130)
> *Satires*

Money is mourned with deeper sorrow than friends or kindred.

> Juvenal
> *Satires*

Avoid, as you would the plague, a clergyman who is also a man of business.

> St. Jerome (c. 342–420)
> *Letters*

Talk of nothing but business, and dispatch that business quickly.

> Aldus Manutius (1450–1515)
> On the door of the Aldine Press, Venice, c. 1490

Unto money be all things obedient.

Richard Taverner (1505?–1575)
Proverbs, 1539

The man of understanding has lost nothing, if he has—if he owns—himself.
The greatest thing in the world is to know how to be—to belong to—oneself.

Michel Eyquem de Montaigne (1533–1592)
Essays

He that will do right in gross must needs do wrong by retail.

Montaigne

Bargains made in speed are commonly repented at leisure.

George Pettie (1548–1589)
Petite Palace of Pettie His Pleasure, 1576

In all negotiations of difficulty, a man may not look to sow and reap at once; but must prepare business, and so ripen it by degrees.

Francis Bacon (1561–1626)

Money makes a man laugh.

John Selden (1584–1654)
Table Talk, 1689

The praise of ancient authors proceeds not from the reverence of the dead, but from the competition and mutual envy of the living.

Thomas Hobbes (1588–1679)
Leviathan, 1651

No lock will hold against the power of gold.

George Herbert (1593–1633)
Outlandish Proverbs, 1640

To be too busy gets contempt.

George Herbert
Outlandish Proverbs

He that lies with the dogs, riseth with fleas.

George Herbert
Jacula Prudentum, 1651

Bottom Line

He that stays does the business.

George Herbert
Jacula Prudentum

Let none admire
That riches grow in Hell; that soil may best
Deserve the precious bane.

John Milton (1608–1674)
Paradise Lost: Book I, 1667

Money brings honor, friends, conquest, and realms.

John Milton
Paradise Regained, 1671

Most people judge men only by their success or their good fortune.

François, Duc de La Rochefoucauld (1613–1680)
Maximes, 1664

In the adversity of our best friends, we find something that doth not displease us.

La Rochefoucauld
Maximes

It is impossible to please all the world and one's father.

Jean de La Fontaine (1621–1695)
Fables, 1668

In a calm sea every man is a pilot.

John Ray (1627–1705)
English Proverbs, 1670

The best of a bad bargain.

Samuel Pepys (1633–1703)
Diary, 14 August 1663

Most men that do thrive in the world do forget to take pleasure during the time that they are getting their estate, but reserve that till they have got one, and then it is too late for them to enjoy it.

Samuel Pepys
Diary, 10 March 1666

Ambition hath no mean. It is either upon all fours or upon tiptoes.

George Savile, Marquess of Halifax (1633–1695)
Political, Moral and Miscellaneous Reflections, 1750

There are only two ways of getting on in the world: by one's own industry, or by the stupidity of others.

Jean de La Bruyère (1645–1696)
Les Caractères, 1688

Men of business must not break their word twice.

Thomas Fuller (1654–1734)
Gnomologia, 1732

No man will take counsel, but every man will take money: therefore money is better than counsel.

Jonathan Swift (1667–1745)
Thoughts on Various Subjects, 1706

Censure is the tax a man pays to the public for being eminent.

Jonathan Swift
Thoughts on Various Subjects, 1711

If Heaven had looked upon riches to be such a valuable thing, it would not have given them to such a scoundrel.

Jonathan Swift
Letter to Miss Vanhomrigh, 12 August 1720

Vision is the art of seeing things invisible.

Jonathan Swift
Thoughts on Various Subjects, 1726

This maxim more than all the rest
Is thought too base for human breast;
"In all distresses of our friends
"We first consult our private ends,
"While nature kindly bent to ease us,
"Points out some circumstance to please us."

If this, perhaps, your patience move,
Let reason and experience prove.

We all behold with envious eyes,
Our equal raised above our size;
Who would not at a crowded show,
Stand high himself, keep others low?
I love my friend as well as you,
But would not have him stop my view;
Then let me have the higher post:
I ask but for an inch at most.

Jonathan Swift
Verses on the Death of Dr. Swift, 1731

How hard for real worth to gain its price.

Edward Young (1683–1765)
Love of Fame, 1728

Success generally depends upon knowing how long it takes to succeed.

Charles de Secondat, Baron de Montesquieu (1689–1755)
Pensées, c. 1750

Necessity never made a good bargain.

Benjamin Franklin (1706–1790)
Poor Richard's Almanack, 1735

Early to bed and early to rise, makes a man healthy, wealthy, and wise.

Benjamin Franklin
Poor Richard's Almanack

Experience keeps a dear school, but fools will learn in no other.

Benjamin Franklin
Poor Richard's Almanack, 1743

Drive thy business, or it will drive thee.

Benjamin Franklin
Poor Richard's Almanack, 1744

Success has ruined many a man.

Benjamin Franklin
Poor Richard's Almanack, 1752

Every state of society is as luxurious as it can be. Men always take the best they can get.

Samuel Johnson (1709–1784)
In Boswell, *Life of Johnson,* 1791
[Said: 14 April 1778]

I believe it is best to eat just as one is hungry: but a man who is in business, or a man who has a family, must have stated meals.

Samuel Johnson
In Boswell, *Life of Johnson*
[Said: 17 April 1778]

It is better to live rich, than to die rich.

Samuel Johnson
In Boswell, *Life of Johnson*
[Said: 17 April 1778]

Whatever you have, spend less.

> Samuel Johnson
> In Boswell, *Life of Johnson*
> [Said: 7 December 1782]

The contempt of money is no more a virtue than to wash one's hand is one; but one does not willingly shake hands with a man that never washes his.

> Horace Walpole (1717–1797)
> Letter to William Mason, 18 April 1777

Every man, as long as he does not violate the laws of justice, is left perfectly free to pursue his own interest his own way, and to bring both his industry and capital into competition with those of any other man or order of men.

> Adam Smith (1723–1790)
> *Wealth of Nations*, 1776

Secrecy and Dispatch may prove the Soul of success to an Enterprise.

> George Washington (1732–1799)
> Letter to David Cobb, 30 June 1781

Money, and not morality, is the principle of commercial nations.

> Thomas Jefferson (1743–1826)
> Letter to John Langdon, 1810

Half the things that people do not succeed in, are through fear of making the attempt.

> James Northcote (1746–1831)

A useless life is an early death.

> Johann Wolfgang von Goethe (1749–1832)
> *Iphigenie auf Tauris*, 1787

Let us live in as small a circle as we will, we are either debtors or creditors before we have had time to look round.

> Johann Wolfgang von Goethe
> *Elective Affinities*, 1808

One must *be* something to be able to *do* something.

> Johann Wolfgang von Goethe
> Conversation with Eckermann, 20 October 1828

If I work incessantly to the last, nature owes me another form of existence when the present one collapses.

Johann Wolfgang von Goethe
Letter to Eckermann, 4 February 1829

Genius begins great works; labor alone finishes them.

Joseph Joubert (1754–1824)
Pensées, 1810

Great things are done when men and mountains meet;
This is not done by jostling in the street.

William Blake (1757–1827)
Notebook, c. 1807–1809

The world is too much with us; late and soon,
Getting and spending, we lay waste our powers.

William Wordsworth (1770–1850)
"The World Is Too Much with Us," 1807

As for money, enough is enough; no man can enjoy more.

Robert Southey (1774–1843)
The Doctor, 1840

Adversity is sometimes hard upon a man; but for one man who can stand prosperity, there are a hundred that will stand adversity.

Thomas Carlyle (1795–1881)
Heroes and Hero Worship, 1841

Adversity, if a man is set down to it by degrees, is more supportable with equanimity by most people than any great prosperity arrived at in a single lifetime.

Samuel Butler (1835–1902)
The Way of All Flesh, 1903

Nothing great was ever achieved without enthusiasm.

Ralph Waldo Emerson (1803–1882)
Circles, 1841

The secret of success is constancy to purpose.

Benjamin Disraeli (1804–1881)
Speech, 24 June 1872

My old father used to have a saying: If you make a bad bargain, hug it all the tighter.

Abraham Lincoln (1809–1865)
Letter to Joshua Speed, 25 February 1842

But the jingling of the guinea helps the hurt that Honor feels.

> Alfred, Lord Tennyson (1809–1892)
> *Locksley Hall*, 1842

You pays your money and you takes your choice.

> *Punch*, 1846

The best business you can go into you will find on your father's farm or in his workshop. If you have no family or friends to aid you, and no prospect opened to you there, turn your face to the great West, and there build up a home and fortune.

> Horace Greeley (1811–1872)
> In Parton, *Life of Horace Greeley*, 1855

I haven't any time to make money, and I don't want any anyhow. Money is more trouble than it's worth.

> Horace Greeley
> [Said: c. 1860]

Less is more.

> Robert Browning (1812–1889)
> *Andrea del Sarto*, 1855
> Creed of the modern architect Ludwig Miës van der Rohe
> (1886–1969)

White shall not neutralize the black, nor good
Compensate bad in man, absolve him so:
Life's business being just the terrible choice.

> Robert Browning
> *The Ring and the Book*, 1868–1869

Take nothing on its looks; take everything on evidence. There's no better rule.

> Charles Dickens (1812–1870)
> *Our Mutual Friend*, 1864–1865

Beware of all enterprises that require new clothes.

> Henry David Thoreau (1817–1862)
> *Walden*, 1854

We do not ride on the railroad; it rides upon us.

> Henry David Thoreau
> *Walden*

Never work before breakfast; if you have to work before breakfast, get your breakfast first.

Josh Billings [Henry Wheeler Shaw] (1818–1885)

The great end of life is not knowledge but action.

T. H. Huxley (1825–1895)
Technical Education, 1877

He who has money has in his pocket those who have none.

Leo Tolstoi (1828–1910)
Money, 1895

Look into any man's heart you please, and you will always find, in every one, at least one black spot which he has to keep concealed.

Henrik Ibsen (1828–1906)
Pillars of Society, 1877

I am half inclined to think we are all ghosts, Mr. Manders. It is not only what we have inherited from our fathers that exists again in us, but all sorts of old dead ideas and all kinds of old dead beliefs and things of that kind. They are not actually alive in us; but there they are dormant, all the same, and we can never be rid of them.

Henrik Ibsen
Ghosts, 1881

Good devils and bad devils. Fair-haired devils and dark-haired devils. If only you always knew whether it's the fair or the dark that have got hold of you.

Henrik Ibsen
The Master Builder, 1892

The man who dies . . . rich dies disgraced.

Andrew Carnegie (1835–1919)
Wealth, June 1889

There is a great deal of truth in Andrew Carnegie's remark "The man who dies rich dies disgraced." I should add, the man who lives rich, lives disgraced.

Aga Khan III (1877–1957)
Memoirs, 1954

Be good and you will be lonesome.

Mark Twain (1835–1910)
Following the Equator, 1897

Never be a bear on the United States.

Attributed to Junius S. Morgan (1813–1890)
and J. P. Morgan (1837–1913)

The man who is a bear on the future of the United States will always go broke. [1895]

J. P. Morgan

To burn always with this hard, gemlike flame, to maintain this ecstasy, is success in life.

Walter Pater (1839–1984)
The Renaissance, 1873

The higher laws of religious or moral order envisage the individual only, or else interests which are not of this world, whereas management principles aim at the success of associations of individuals and at the satisfying of economic interests. Given that the aim is different, it is not surprising that the means are not the same. There is no identity, so there is no contradiction. Without principles one is in darkness and chaos; interest, experience and proportion are still very handicapped, even with the best principles. The principle is the lighthouse fixing the bearings but it can only serve those who already know the way to port.

Henri Fayol (1841–1925)
General and Industrial Management, 1917

We learn how to behave as lawyers, soldiers, merchants, or whatnot by being them. Life, not the parson, teaches conduct.

Oliver Wendell Holmes, Jr. (1841–1935)
Letter to Sir Frederick Pollock, 1926

The moral flabbiness born of the exclusive worship of the bitch-goddess SUCCESS. That—with the squalid cash interpretation put on the word success—is our national disease.

William James (1842–1910)
Letter to H. G. Wells, 11 September 1906

Success—"the bitch-goddess, Success" in William James's phrase—demands strange sacrifices from those who worship her.

Aldous Huxley (1894–1963)

Every step forward is made at the cost of mental and physical pain to someone.

Friedrich Wilhelm Nietzsche (1844–1900)
Genealogy of Morals, 1887

Be patient, wait, work, stick.

A. E. Rice
Small Talk About Business, 1892

There is no substitute for hard work.

Thomas A. Edison (1847–1931)
Life, 1932

Genius is one percent inspiration and ninety-nine percent perspiration.

Thomas A. Edison
Life

Genius is ten percent inspiration and fifty percent capital gains.

Howard Kandel

Nothing matters very much, and very few things matter at all.

Attributed to Arthur James Balfour (1848–1930)

In thousands of years there has been no advance in public morals, in philosophy, in religion or in politics, but the advance in business has been the greatest miracle the world has ever known.

Edgar Watson Howe (1853–1937)
The Blessing of Business, 1918

Genius is born, not paid.

Oscar Wilde (1854–1900)

Anyone who critically analyzes a business learns this: that success or failure of an enterprise depends usually upon one man.

Louis D. Brandeis (1856–1941)
Testimony before the Committee on Interstate
Commerce, 62nd Congress, 1911–1912

Life is just one damned thing after another.

Elbert Hubbard (1856–1915)
Thousand and One Epigrams

It is not true that life is one damn thing after another—it is one damn thing over another.

Edna St. Vincent Millay (1892–1950)
Letters

The principal object of management should be to secure the maximum prosperity for the employer, coupled with the maximum prosperity for each employee.

Frederick W. Taylor (1856–1915)
The Principles of Scientific Management, 1911

He who can, does. He who cannot, teaches.

George Bernard Shaw (1856–1950)
Man and Superman, 1903

Lack of money is the root of all evil.

George Bernard Shaw
Man and Superman

This is the true joy in life, the being used for a purpose recognized by yourself as a mighty one; the being thoroughly worn out before you are thrown on the scrap heap; the being a force of nature instead of a feverish selfish little clod of ailments and grievances complaining that the world will not devote itself to making you happy.

George Bernard Shaw
Man and Superman

Nothing knits man to man like the frequent passage from hand to hand of cash.

Walter R. Sickert (1860–1942)
In Auden, *A Certain World*, 1970

Worry is interest paid on trouble before it falls due.

William Ralph Inge (1860–1954)
Wit and Wisdom of Dean Inge

In nature there are no rewards or punishments; there are consequences.

Horace Annesley Vachell (1861–?)
The Face of Clay

Honesty pays, but it don't seem to pay enough to suit some people.

Frank McKinney ("Kin") Hubbard (1868–1930)

Bottom Line

As to democracy, fellow citizens,
Are you not prepared to admit
That I, who inherited riches and was to the manner
    born,
Was second to none in Spoon River
In my devotion to the cause of Liberty?
While my contemporary, Anthony Findlay,
Born in a shanty and beginning life
As a water carrier to the section hands,
Then becoming a section hand when he was grown,
Afterwards foreman of the gang, until he rose
To the superintendency of the railroad,
Living in Chicago,
Was a veritable slave driver,
Grinding the faces of labor,
And a bitter enemy of democracy.
And I say to you, Spoon River,
And to you, O Republic,
Beware of the man who rises to power
From one suspender.

> Edgar Lee Masters (1869–1950)
> "John Hancock Otis"
> *Spoon River Anthology,* 1915

Miniver scorned the gold he sought,
    But sore annoyed was he without it;
Miniver thought, and thought, and thought,
    And thought about it.

Miniver Cheevy, born too late,
    Scratched his head and kept on thinking;
Miniver coughed, and called it fate,
    And kept on drinking.

> Edwin Arlington Robinson (1869–1935)
> "Miniver Cheevy," 1910

The English have a proverb: "Conscience makes cowboys of us all."

> Saki [H. H. Munro] (1870–1916)
> *Wratislav*

To be clever enough to get all that money, one must be stupid enough to want it.

> G. K. Chesterton (1874–1936)
> *The Innocence of Father Brown,* 1911

The world will never starve for wonders; but only for want of wonder.

> G. K. Chesterton
> Inscription, General Motors Building, Century of
> Progress Exposition, Chicago

New roads: new ruts.

> Attributed to G. K. Chesterton

Nothing in life is so exhilarating as to be shot at without result.

> Winston Churchill (1874–1965)
> *The Malakand Field Force*, 1898

You will make all kinds of mistakes; but as long as you are generous and true, and also fierce, you cannot hurt the world or even seriously distress her. She was made to be wooed and won by youth.

> Winston Churchill
> *Roving Commission: My Early Life*, 1930

Never give in, never give in, never, never, never, never—in nothing, great or small, large or petty—never give in except to convictions of honor and good sense.

> Winston Churchill
> Address at Harrow School, 1941

Everyone has his day and some days last longer than others.

> Winston Churchill
> Speech in the House of Commons, January 1952

American business needs a lifting purpose greater than the struggle of materialism.

> Herbert Hoover (1874–1964)

As soon as an idea is accepted it is time to reject it.

> Holbrook Jackson (1874–1948)

In democracies, those who lead, follow; those who follow, lead.

> Holbrook Jackson

Sacrifice is a form of bargaining.

> Holbrook Jackson

Suffer fools gladly; they may be right.

> Holbrook Jackson

The typical man of any nation is the exception.

Holbrook Jackson

I really believe that more harm is done by old men who cling to their influence than by young men who anticipate it.

Owen D. Young (1874–1962)
General Electric
In the *New York Herald Tribune*, 12 July 1962

It is not the crook in modern business that we fear, but the honest man who does not know what he is doing.

Owen D. Young
General Electric

He worked like hell in the country so he could live in the city, where he worked like hell so he could live in the country.

Don Marquis (1878–1937)

The successful people are the ones who can think up things for the rest of the world to keep busy at.

Don Marquis

Common sense is the collection of prejudices acquired by age eighteen.

Albert Einstein (1879–1955)
In *Scientific American*, February 1976

If at first you don't succeed, try again. Then quit. No use being a damn fool about it.

W. C. Fields (1880–1946)
In Halliwell, *the Filmgoer's Book of Quotes*

Don't overestimate the decency of the human race.

H. L. Mencken (1880–1956)

You come into the world with nothing, and the purpose of your life is to make something out of nothing.

H. L. Mencken

What this country needs is a good five-cent nickel.

Franklin P. Adams [F.P.A.] (1881–1960)
Quoted in *Liberty*, 2 January 1943

The best you get is an even break.

Franklin P. Adams
Ballade of Schopenhauer's Philosophy

Scattergood sat on the porch of his store in the sunniest spot, twiddling his bare toes.

"The way to make money," he said to the mountain opposite, "is to let smarter folks'n you be make it for you—like I done."

Clarence Budington Kelland (1881–1964)
"Scattergood Baines—Invader," *Saturday Evening Post,*
30 June 1917

The world belongs to the Enthusiast who keeps cool.

William McFee (1881–?)

We have all passed a lot of water since then.

Samuel Goldwyn (1882–1974)
In French, *The Movie Moguls*

If you can't stand the heat, get out of the kitchen.

Harry S. Truman (1884–1972)
Saying

I've been rich and I've been poor. Believe me, rich is better.

Attributed to Sophie Tucker (c. 1884–1966)

The best of a bad job is all any of us make of it.

T. S. Eliot (1888–1965)
The Cocktail Party, 1950

Don't get mad, get even.

Attributed to Joseph P. Kennedy (1888–1969)

Only a fool holds out for the top dollar.

Joseph P. Kennedy

Competition brings out the best in products and the worst in people.

David Sarnoff (1891–1971)
In *Esquire,* 1964

The leader must know, must know that he knows, and must be able to make it abundantly clear to those about him that he knows.

Clarence B. Randall (1891–1967)
Inland Steel
Making Good in Management, 1964

Bottom Line

Never acquire a business you don't know how to run.

Robert W. Johnson (1893–1968)
Johnson & Johnson
In *Dun's Review,* December 1970

Make your top managers rich and they will make you rich.

Robert W. Johnson
Johnson & Johnson

Don't fight forces; use them.

R. Buckminster Fuller (1895–1983)
Shelter, 1932

Dare to be naïve.

R. Buckminster Fuller
Synergetics, 1975

The dinosaur's eloquent lesson is that if some bigness is good, an overabundance of bigness is not necessarily better.

Eric A. Johnston (1895–1963)
US Chamber of Commerce
In *Quote,* 23 February 1958

Success is feminine and like a woman; if you cringe before her, she will override you. So the way to treat her is to show her the back of your hand. Then maybe she will do the crawling.

William Faulkner (1897–1962)
Interview in *Writers at Work: First Series,* 1958

Experience isn't interesting till it begins to repeat itself—in fact, till it does that, it hardly *is* experience.

Elizabeth Bowen (1899–1973)
The Death of the Heart, 1938

Man's main task in life is to give *birth* to himself.

Erich Fromm (1900–   )
Man for Himself, 1947

Man, unlike any other thing organic or inorganic in the universe, grows beyond his work, walks up the stairs of his concepts, emerges ahead of his accomplishments.

John Steinbeck (1902–1968)
The Grapes of Wrath, 1939

Nice guys finish last.

> Leo Durocher (1906–   )

The size of General Motors is not the cause of its success, but the consequence of success.

> James M. Roche (1906–   )
> General Motors

There is only one way a business can earn a profit, and that is to make a product a consumer wants to buy, produce it efficiently, provide good service and treat the consumer honestly and fairly.

> James M. Roche
> General Motors

Don't look back. Something may be gaining on you.

> Satchel Paige (c. 1906–1982)
> *How to Keep Young*, 1953

Hindsight is always twenty-twenty.

> Billy Wilder (1906–   )
> In Colombo, *Colombo's Hollywood*

Life is a misery if you don't get more than you deserve.

> Harry Oppenheimer (1908–   )
> De Beers and Anglo American

I don't know what this country would do without big business. When I look at how far this country we all love has come—in food, in communications, in transportation—it's all due entirely to big business.

> Edwin H. Gott (1908–   )
> United States Steel

The monomaniac is unlikely to succeed. Most leave only their bleached bones in the roadless desert. But the rest of us, with multiple interests instead of a single mission, are certain to fail and to have no impact at all.

> Peter F. Drucker (1909–   )
> *Adventures of a Bystander*, 1978

Genius is born and made. This heel who mastered
By infinite pains his trade was born a bastard.

> J. V. Cunningham (1911–1985)
> *The Collected Poems and Epigrams*, 1971

American society has tried so hard and so ably to defend the practice and theory of production for profit and not primarily for use that now it has succeeded in making its jobs and products profitable and useless.

> Paul Goodman (1911–1972)
> *Growing Up Absurd*, 1960

Heart attacks are reserved for businessmen.

> Eugène Ionesco (1912–   )
> *Exit the King*, 1963

Winning isn't everything, it's the only thing. [Attributed to Vince Lombardi]
    Winning isn't everything, but wanting to win is.

> Vince Lombardi (1913–1970)
> Interview, 1962

Jobs just don't come into being without a companion capital formation to provide the facilities on which they can exist. And without an adequate profit opportunity, there is no way by which the necessary capital formation can occur.

> R. Heath Larry (1914–   )
> United States Steel

In this decade of the seventies, corporations must bear the cost of social responsibility or the consequences of evading it.

> David Rockefeller (1915–   )
> Chase Manhattan Bank

If economists were any good at business, they would be rich men instead of advisers to rich men.

> Kirk Kerkorian (1917–   )
> Metro-Goldwyn-Mayer

Capitalism was doomed ethically before it was doomed economically, a long time ago.

> Alexander Solzhenitsyn (1918–   )
> *Cancer Ward*, 1966

If the package doesn't say "New" these days, it better say "Seven Cents Off."

> Spencer Klaw (1920–   )
> In *Fortune*, 1963

The automobile changed our dress, manners, social customs, vacation habits, the shape of our cities, consumer purchasing patterns, common tastes and positions in intercourse.

> John Keats (1920–)
> *The Insolent Chariots*, 1958

The rest of the world most certainly does not owe us a living.

> Philip Mountbatten, Duke of Edinburgh (1921–)
> Speech to businessmen, 17 October 1961

You cannot turn the clock back, they all say. To the extent that is true, it is an observation so overbearingly banal as to suggest idiocy on the part of the man who makes it. To the extent that it is intended metaphorically, i.e., to say that one cannot change the course of things, then it is, in the cautious words of Professor Hayek, "among the most fatuous statements in modern language—what it seems to be saying is that one cannot profit from one's mistakes." But of course one *can* profit from one's mistakes: a great body of learning—all of empirical knowledge—develops from that general rule, which is embedded in so many of the little apothegms of our society, like "Once burnt, twice shy," "Experience is the best teacher," etc., etc.

> William F. Buckley, Jr. (1925–)
> *On the Right*, 28 May 1964

You must automate, emigrate or evaporate.

> James A. Baker (1927–)
> General Electric

The only place where success comes before work is in a dictionary.

> Vidal Sassoon (1928–)

The buck stops with the guy who signs the cheques.

> Rupert Murdoch (1931–)
> News America Publishing

Human wants are never satisfied.

> J. Willard Marriott, Jr. (1932–)
> Marriott

Industries and businesses that must operate in the market-place of free choice know that they must change, they must adapt, they must accommodate to changes in public attitudes—or they will surely die.

> William D. Ruckelshaus (1932–)
> US Environmental Protection Agency

Bottom Line

At some time in the life cycle of virtually every organization, its ability to succeed in spite of itself runs out.

Richard H. Brien
In the *Educational Record*, 1970

True, you can't take it with you, but then, that's not the place where it comes in handy.

Brendan Francis

The best way to help the poor is not to become one of them.

Laing Hancock

Our very business life is not to get ahead of others, but to get ahead of ourselves.

Attributed to Thomas L. Monson

You don't buy a stock because it has real value. You buy it because you feel there is always a greater fool down the street ready to pay more than you paid.

Donald J. Stocking
US Securities and Exchange Commission

The best route to the top is to own the company.

Lewis Bookwalter Ward
Harvard Business School

STANDARD REFERENCES

W. H. Auden. *A Certain World: A Commonplace Book.* New York: Viking, 1970.

John Bartlett. *Familiar Quotations,* 15th edition, edited by Emily Morison Beck. Boston: Little, Brown, 1980.

Edward C. Bursk, Donald T. Clark, and Ralph W. Hidy. *The World of Business,* 4 volumes. New York: Simon & Schuster, 1962.

J. M. and M. J. Cohen. *The Penguin Dictionary of Quotations.* Harmondsworth: Penguin, 1960. *The Penguin Dictionary of Modern Quotations.* Harmondsworth: Penguin, 1971, 1980.

Evan Esar. *The Dictionary of Humorous Quotations.* Garden City: Doubleday, 1949.

Robert I. Fitzhenry. *Barnes & Noble Book of Quotations.* New York: Barnes & Noble, 1981, 1983.

Rudolph Flesch. *The Book of Unusual Quotations.* New York: Harper, 1957.

Alex Groner. *The American Heritage History of American Business and Industry.* New York: American Heritage Publishing Co., 1972.

Leonard Louis Levenson. *Bartlett's Unfamiliar Quotations.* New York: Cowles, 1971.

Harold C. Livesay. *American Made: Men Who Shaped the American Economy.* Boston: Little, Brown, 1979.

H. L. Mencken. *A New Dictionary of Quotations on Historical Principles.* New York: Knopf, 1960.

Milton Moskowitz et al. *Everybody's Business: An Almanac.* New York: Harper & Row, 1980.

The Oxford Dictionary of Quotations. Oxford: Oxford University Press, 1941, 1979.

Alan F. and Jason R. Pater. *What They Said In—.* Beverly Hills, Cal.: Monitor, 1969–.

Burton Stevenson. *The Home Book of Proverbs, Maxims and Familiar Phrases.* New York: Macmillan, 1948.

Stevenson. *The Home Book of Quotations,* 10th edition. New York: Dodd, Mead, 1967.

INDEX

W

Wagner, C. Everett, 29
Walgreen, Charles, 207
Walker, Henry A., Jr., 220
Wallace, George C., 254
Wallace, Henry A., 114
Wallich, Henry C., 117
Walpole, Horace, 11, 312
Walter, Henry G., Jr., 26
Walton, Izaak, 9, 230
Wanamaker, John, 41, 159, 237
Ward, Artemus [Charles Farrar
    Browne], 204, 266
Ward, Lewis Bookwalter, 327
Warner, Charles Dudley, 15, 235
Washington, Booker T., 239
Washington, George, 58, 88, 157, 203,
    312
Waugh, Evelyn, 250
Wearly, William L., 98
Webber, Ross, 256
Webster, Daniel, 39, 90, 203, 233
Weeden, Donald E., 28
Weidenbaum, Murray L., 102
Welles, Orson, 193
Wells, Carolyn, 63
Wells, H. G., 19, 185, 241
Wernette, J. Philip, 67
West, Mae, 162
White, E. B., 42, 248
White, Patrick, 193
Whitehead, Alfred North, 19, 112, 135,
    269, 270
Whitehorn, Katharine, 148
Whitman, Walt, 133
Whitney, Eli, 131
Whyte, William H., Jr., 253, 281
Wiener, Norbert, 141, 246
Wight, Oliver W., 149

Wilde, Oscar, 18, 79, 134, 159, 238, 268,
    317
Wilder, Billy, 324
Wilder, Thornton, 24
Williams, Charles, 275
Williams, Harold M., 45
Williams, John Henry, 114
Williams, William Carlos, 189
Wilson, Charles E., 96
Wilson, Joseph Ruggles, 271
Wilson, Sloan, 219
Wilson, Thomas, 74
Wilson, Woodrow, 18, 19, 91, 206, 295
Winpisinger, William, 118
Wittgenstein, Ludwig, 23, 275
Wodehouse, P. G., 209
Woollcott, Alexander, 64
Woolworth, F. W., 183
Wordsworth, William, 313
Wright, John David, 25
Wycherley, William, 9, 37

X

Xenophon, 200, 229
Xerxes, 289

Y

Yamasaki, Yoshiki, 256
Young, Andrew, 102
Young, Edward, 311
Young, James W., 161
Young, Owen D., 20, 137, 188, 321
Young, Robert R., 213

Z

Zanuck, Darryl F., 249, 277
Zolla, Elemire, 27